THE ELIZABETHAN
LOVE SONNET

The Elizabethan Love Sonnet

by

J. W. Lever

METHUEN & CO. LTD
11 New Fetter Lane, EC4

PR
539
.S7
L4
1966

First published in 1956
Second edition 1966
S.B.N. 416 57810 1
2.1

First published as a University Paperback 1966
Reprinted 1968
S.B.N. 416 69460 8
1.2

Printed in Great Britain
by Lowe & Brydone (Printers) Ltd., London

To ANITA

Distributed in the U.S.A.
by Barnes & Noble Inc.

PREFACE

THE Elizabethan sonnet, as a class of poetry expressing the lyrical outlook of an age, suffers from undeserved neglect. Individual poems receive attention, particularly, of course, the sonnets of Shakespeare. Investigations of sources, images, and conventions proceed. But since Lee's preface to his collection of sonnet sequences published in 1904, no one has attempted a wider critical estimate. Accordingly misconceptions prevail which in their application to other mediums have long since been dispelled. Appreciation still suffers from the late-romantic antipathy to form and convention, caused by the assumption that poetry should provide emotional self-revelation. An attitude which dissociated Shakespeare's plays from the conditions of his theatre, and isolated *Paradise Lost* from its epic tradition, necessarily found little virtue in the Elizabethan sonnet, with its thematic continuity, its principles of imitation, and its close patterning of form. In addition to the survival of discredited standards, a more recent distortion of perspective is linked with the present revolution of taste. Enthusiasm for metaphysical poetry has been carried to a point where this last manifestation of the Renaissance lyrical impulse is viewed as a kind of poetic spring. Autumn tints have their own splendour, but they foretoken the fall of leaf; and the very qualities for which metaphysical verse is most admired led on to the Augustan sundering of individuality and tradition.

The aim of this book is to direct interest back to the main period of the English Renaissance lyric, which commences with Wyatt and reaches its consummation in Shakespeare. During this time individuality and tradition were primarily integrated through the sonnet, with its characteristic verse forms and the thought processes to which they gave effect, and its concomitant use of imagery and diction. An assessment of the Elizabethan love sonnet does not require a comprehensive survey of all verse written in this form. Such a work would have its uses for scholars, but could not supply the literary perspective we need. It is in the creative development of the great Elizabethans that the sonnet displays its true functions and scope. Accordingly most attention has been given to the sequences of Sidney, Spenser, and Shakespeare, the work of lesser poets being treated more briefly and a good deal of sonnet writing being passed over with little mention or none. The surpassing importance of Shakespeare's sonnets justifies, in my view, a more detailed consideration than has been given to the verse of any one other writer.

Poetry must always be seen as the work of individual poets. Nevertheless, this book's underlying theme is the literary tradition which inspired even the greatest Elizabethan sonnets. The tradition reaches back to a European, especially an Italian past; but it was adapted and transformed by distinctively English attitudes, the resulting tension supplying the main dynamic of development. These complex effects should not be considered on too narrow a basis; all the same, their first crystallization will be found to lie in the verse form of the English sonnet. No scrutiny of its origin and significance can be too minute if the poetry of the age is to be fairly assessed.

Our starting point will therefore be the Petrarchan sonnet; both its formal characteristics and the vision it embodied. The verse-form is widely familiar, with its octave and sestet, each subdivided by syntax and linked back by rhyme-scheme. Calling it to mind we realize how misleading is the popular definition of sonnets, as poems factitiously restricted to fourteen lines ('why fourteen, no less and no more?'). The Petrarchan sonnet was a poem of two complementary verse units, governing two sequential processes of thought: it has been likened to the acorn, separable into 'unequal parts of a perfect organism'.[1] What then was its poetic significance? If so perfect, why did the English poets of the sixteenth century deviate from its principles? What distinctive character do the English variants show, especially that which has come to be known as the Shakespearian form? And in conjunction with what instruments of expression, what modifications of imagery and diction, do the English forms operate? Such questions will best be considered in the main body of this book: here it is enough to point out the issues that arise.

1. T. Hall Caine, *Sonnets of Three Centuries* (1882), p. xii.

One more general observation may be added. Figuratively, the chapters which follow might be described as a journey in stages, from Petrarch to Shakespeare, and from the Italian vision to the English. Not for nothing have the names of two poets been coupled each to the verse-form he adopted, though neither was its originator. Petrarch so impregnated the Italian sonnet with his genius that its essential qualities could never afterwards be dissociated from his work: which is equivalent to saying that his genius so expressed the outlook of his nation that no fundamental change was required while this outlook prevailed. In England, as we shall see, the staple sonnet-form of the Elizabethans was evolved at an early stage by the Tudor poets, who gave expression to their own national and contemporary attitudes, though confining these within a limited range. The greater poets who followed Wyatt and Surrey, not content with these limits, developed their medium on individual lines, which permitted them to explore particular regions of experience. For the later Elizabethans the staple form of the sonnet was to evince new potentialities; while in Shakespeare's vast transformation all potentialities became actual. Petrarch was the first great Italian humanist, and set the mould for his successors: Shakespeare, living towards the close of an epoch, consummated its lyrical development. Thus while Petrarch's sonnets typify the Italian Renaissance vision, the sonnets of Shakespeare extend to its utmost range the still integrated personal outlook of Elizabethan England.

In making my acknowledgements, my first thanks go to Professor H. B. Charlton, who twelve years ago suggested the subject of the Elizabethan sonnet for a Christmas vacation essay, encouraged me to choose it as the topic of a thesis, and benevolently watched this materialize. Much has been changed since then for which he need accept no responsibility; but the essential plan remains his. For reading and criticizing drafts of my book at various stages of its growth, I am very grateful to Professor Allardyce Nicoll, Professor J. Isaacs, and Mr E. Honigmann. I wish to thank Professor H. Peri for useful hints and corrections relating to my description of romance prosody; Mr F. W. Bateson for helpful suggestions regarding Wyatt's versification; Professor L. C. Knights for much

B

viii   THE ELIZABETHAN LOVE SONNET

detailed and sympathetic comment on my treatment of Shakespeare's sonnets; and Miss Mary M. Innes and Penguin Books for permission to quote from her translations of Ovid's *Metamorphoses*. Many friends and colleagues who have helped me in less definable ways deserve my gratitude; but none so much as my wife, the most cheerful, long-suffering victim of all.

J. W. L.

PREFACE TO THE SECOND EDITION

IN the ten years that have passed since this book was first published, several outstanding scholars referred to in it as living contemporaries have regrettably gone from us. So too has one unmentioned in these pages, though remembered with gratitude: J. B. Leishman, whose *Themes and Variations in Shakespeare's Sonnets* (1961) brought a lifetime of wide reading and humane understanding to bear on many topics raised in the later chapters.

Students today are far better placed to make a discerning approach to the Elizabethan sonnet than their predecessors of a decade ago. The true qualities of Petrarch's genius, and the positive side of Renaissance imitation, are now widely recognized. During recent years new, much-needed editions of the poems of Surrey (E. Jones, 1964) and Sidney (W. A. Ringler, 1962) have appeared, as well as at least three scholarly editions of Shakespeare's Sonnets. At the same time, critical assessments have penetrated far beyond the facile assumptions that used to be fashionable. Sergio Baldi's acute study of Wyatt's poetry is now available in English translation (*Sir Thomas Wyatt*, 1961), supplemented by Patricia Thomson's *Sir Thomas Wyatt and his Background* (1964). There is R. L. Montgomery's *Symmetry and Sense in the Poetry of Sir Philip Sidney* (Texas, 1961) and Murray Krieger's *A Window to Criticism: Shakespeare's Sonnets and Modern Poetics* (Princeton, 1962). Shorter essays are too numerous to be listed. F. T. Prince has contributed a brief but useful survey of the history of the Elizabethan sonnet in *Stratford-on-Avon Studies* 2 (1960). Among the most stimulating essays on Shakespeare's Sonnets are those of Edward Hubler and Northrop Frye in *The Riddle of Shakespeare's Sonnets* (1962), and of Joan Grundy and M. M. Mahood in *Shakespeare Survey* 15 (1962).

Apart from correcting a few slips of my own or the printer's, and adding one or two footnotes in square brackets, I have made no changes in this second edition. By and large, my views have not altered. Here and there I have felt, and resisted, the urge to argue back when some opinion has been challenged. I doubt if any such tinkering would really improve matters; as likely as not it would make them worse. There are just two remarks I feel obliged to make, both of a general character, both on the subject of Shakespeare's Sonnets. I do not think, nor have I ever thought, that my discussion of about half the sonnets in rough groups should preclude other arrangements or be taken, even within their limits, as a definitive order. I have found that the individual sonnets gain in depth and reson-ance when read in a wider context of images and themes; hence I have sought out what seemed to me the most likely groupings. Others are free and welcome to choose better arrangements. Secondly, I firmly believe that the experience imparted in the sonnets to the Friend is of a complex development, involving Shakespeare's whole inner life as a creative artist, through doubt, suspicion and mistrust, to a total affirmation of faith in the redemptive power of human love. Who the Friend was, and what his 'real' character may have been, I neither know nor care. As Northrop Frye has justly remarked: 'even Christianity, with all its theological apparatus, cannot clearly express the relation of whatever it is in us that is worth redeeming to what we actually are'. Accordingly I see these sonnets, not as what W. P. Blackmur has termed 'a poetics for infatuation', but as poetry for love; not as a record of disillusionment, but as a 'satire to decay'. My authority is Shakespeare himself:

> If this be error, and upon me proved,
> I never writ, nor no man ever loved.

December 1965.

CONTENTS

I	THE PETRARCHAN SONNET	I
II	WYATT	14
III	SURREY	37
IV	SIDNEY	51
V	SPENSER	92
VI	THE LATE ELIZABETHAN SONNET	139
VII	SHAKESPEARE	162

Series I: The Mistress 174

Series II: The Friend 183

(a) The Invitation to Marry 189

(b) The Poet in Absence 202

(c) The Friend's Fault 209

(d) The Poet and his Rivals 227

(e) The Poet's Error 236

(f) The Immortalization 246

CONCLUSION 273

INDEX 279

I

THE PETRARCHAN SONNET

THE sonnet tradition takes its descent from two strains of
poetry, one a native to the feudal courts of Provence,
the other to the city-states of thirteenth-century Italy.
Any reader of Provençal lyrics will recognize in them attitudes
and images which passed, through Petrarch's renderings, into
the literatures of western Europe. It is most unlikely that the
Elizabethan poets whose work we shall be considering presently ever read a line of Troubadour verse: yet as a man's voice
repeats the intonations of forgotten ancestors, so their sonnets
unconsciously echoed the expressions of Bernart de Ventadorn,
Peire Rogier, and their fellows. In prose translation some of
these lyrics look almost like paraphrases of familiar sonnets by
Sidney or Shakespeare:

> For love of her I live, and if I should die so that it should be said
> that I died loving, Love would have done me so great honour,
> that I know and believe she never did greater to any lover. . .
> From you I find all ills benefit, damage adventure, folly sense,
> wrongs justice and right.

> Those who think that I am here do not know how my spirit is
> private and at home in her, even if the body is distant: know the
> best message that I have from her is my thought, which recalls
> to me her beautiful appearance.[1]

The complexion of the sonnet heroine with its blending of rose
and lily; her glances like darts of the love-god; her cruel chastity; all these iterated eulogies and reproaches were commonplaces in medieval Provence, as were the experiences of the
lover, his sorrow in the midst of joy, his grief in absence, his
fears of rivalry and slander. But while the line of descent is
clear, it is also evident that the love sonnet could not have been
born from such lyrics without an accession of new blood. As
the Troubadour poets developed their art and found exalted

1. Peire Rogier, *Per s'amor viv*; Bernart de Ventadorn, *Sels qui cuion*.
Translations taken from L. F. Mott, *The System of Courtly Love* (Boston and
London 1896).

patrons, the ardour of their verses gradually cooled into set responses. The service of love became, like knight's service, a rigid feudal code; and the verse-forms through which it was expressed, growing ever more elaborate, became increasingly ends in themselves. In the thirteenth century, however, poetry of a different kind was being composed in northern Italy. Indirectly through allegorical romance, this had its kinship to the Provençal lyric; but its attitude to life was different, less prescribed and more sincerely idealistic. The Provençal lyric, despite its later refinements, remained at heart sensuous and erotic. Religious concepts appeared, but their function was to give added piquancy to physical desire; or—to put this differently—the real religion of Troubadour poetry was not Christian, but pagan and, in a literal sense, Aphrodisiac.

> Such is my desire and will
> That if Death shall come for me,
> I'll crave God less urgently
> In His paradise to rest
> Ever blessed,—
> Pleading mainly for the right
> To her bed for one whole night.[1]

But for the Tuscan poets of the late thirteenth century, Dante, Guinicelli, and others, the figure of the lady and the praises bestowed on her were mere 'objective correlatives', earthly symbols of transcendent beauty and ideal love. The full poetic expression of these concepts required, indeed, a wider scope and a more complex scheme of organization than the lyric could provide, and found its rightful place in the vast reaches of Dante's divine allegory. Yet writers of the *dolce stil nuovo* at least touched lyric verse with some qualities of this higher imagination, and the sonnet-form itself—hitherto not much more than a rudimentary rhyme-pattern brought through Sicily from the east—took shape from the contact.

1.
> *Que tan la desir e volh,*
> *Que, s'er' en coita de mort,*
> *No queri' a Deu tan fort*
> *Que lai el seu paradis*
> *   M'aculhis*
> *Com que ·m des lezer*
> *D'una noit ab leis jazer.*
>
> Raimon-Jordan (ed. Kjellman, p. 114)

Yet it was not the sonnets of these poets, but the love poetry of Petrarch, that shaped a new course for west European literature. Through Petrarch the elements of the Provençal lyric and the Tuscan sonnet meet and fuse; but no formula known to the literary historians, no 'combination of influences', will serve to describe the part played by individual imagination. 'Modern writers,' Petrarch observed in a letter to his friend Caloria, 'should emulate the bees, who do not merely return what they have taken from the flowers, but render this into marvellous compounds of wax and honey.'[1] Here was a man of rare sensibility and many-sided intellect, himself one of the first 'modern writers', who made personal experience the mainspring of poetic creation. Life shaped the course of his literary work, and the years he spent at Avignon fixed a permanent mark on his genius. Here, in the city where the new Italian humanism met the fading culture of medieval Provence, Petrarch first set eyes on the burgher's daughter Madonna Laura. For the rest of his life the roots of his imagination were to fasten themselves round an imperishable, for ever unattainable love. To such a man the prescribed attitudes of late Troubadour verse, the recurrent roses and nightingales, the ritual of devotion to the *châtelaine*, were meaningless until they could be regenerated in terms of his own vivid experience. Yet the idealisms of the *dolce stil nuovo* were too ethereal and bloodless; they must irradiate his vision of an earthly being. Laura was indeed the living manifestation of heavenly virtue; but she remained part of the natural world, not to be spirited away in concept and symbol. The literary medium of Petrarch's inspiration was a modified lyric, speaking with the simple lyric's immediacy and poignancy, yet so serious and premeditated that it would set forth a total attitude to life.

Poetry of this sort found its characteristic imagery in the metaphor, whose predominance in the literature of modern Europe was primarily due to Petrarch's example. Like much else that is familiar in lyric, its functions are easily sensed but infrequently described. Just as two strains of poetry meet in the Petrarchan sonnet, so in metaphor two kinds of imagery fuse. They may be described as similes and symbols, or even

1. *apes . . . imitandas, quae flores non quales acceperint, referunt, sed ceras ac mella mirifica quadam permixtione conficiunt.—Familiarium Rerum*, 1. 8.

more plainly, as free images and fixed. The free image, proper to the song or simple lyric, operates by flexible associations:

> O, my love's like a red, red rose
> That's newly sprung in June:
> O, my love's like the melody
> That's sweetly played in tune . . .

The subject of the image need have no rational bearing upon the theme of the poem beyond some special attribute that evokes a direct sensory response. Attention is held by this attribute just long enough to induce the required response, before the poem moves on to some other stimulus. There is no need to infer an essential similarity between the theme of human emotion and the image of impersonal nature, which returns to its proper sphere unaffected by the momentary connection. Thus when Burns declares that his love is like a red, red rose, he is merely suggesting properties of freshness, vitality, or sensuousness that love and roses may have in common. We are not intended to pursue the analogy on an intellectual plane. If the rose newly sprung in June resembles a love that will last till all the seas run dry, we should not infer that the rose itself will outlast December. Nor does the anomaly at all invalidate the poem as lyric, perpetuating the feelings of a moment. The fixed or symbolical image, which is proper to allegory and passes into the philosophical lyrics of Dante's contemporaries, functions quite otherwise. The subject of the image, once chosen, is abstracted from the world of nature and yoked to a conceptual scheme. Its natural properties are wholly subordinated to its place in the allegory, and are never regained. When therefore Guillaume de Lorris, moved initially, it may be, by a cognate impulse to that of Burns, makes his rose the *sanctum sanctorum* of courtly love, it gives up its being as a natural flower and becomes, like the Rosa Mundi, the lifeless and undying symbol of an idea. Henceforth it exists for ever in a garden where June is everlasting, where roses blossom, but, unlike real roses, never fade.

For Petrarch neither the 'free' image nor the 'fixed' could be entirely adequate. As the scholar and humanist, he found a merely sensuous response to natural beauty too limited; its essential being had to be united to his own spirit. Yet nature, like Laura herself, was too actual a presence to subserve a pattern of concepts. In a mood of exultation he was to cry:

> *Benedetto sia'l giorno e'l mese e l'anno*
> *E la stagione e'l tempo e l'ora e'l punto*
> *E 'l bel paese . . .*[1]

and alone in the mountains he would feel the companionship of unspeaking things:

> *Si ch'io mi credo omai, che monti, e piagge*
> *E fiumi, e selve sappian di che tempre*
> *Sia la mia vita, ch'è celata altrui.*[2]

Hence the major experiences of the sonnets found their channel in imagery where intellectual cognition and sensuous perception have fully combined. Thus in Petrarch's sonnet, *Rapido fiume, che d'alpestra vena*, it was the actual river Rhône, following its long course from the Alpine mountains to the sea, which the poet invoked, not a symbolical River of Love; yet the community between its aspiration to the calm airs and greener grass of the south, and Petrarch's aspiration to Laura, was no momentary association of ideas. River and man were driven by great elemental powers—

> *Amor me, te sol Natura mena,*[3]

and both were seeking the sun of life—

> *Ivi è quel nostro vivo e dolce sole*[4]

which was, again, not emotional hyperbole; since sunlight was to nature, as love was to man, the supreme regenerative force. Outer and inner worlds were made to interpenetrate at every point; spiritual states and natural phenomena became dual aspects of an integral, visionary truth.

Like its metaphorical imagery, the verse-form of the Petrarchan sonnet functioned to integrate experience. Two stages

---

1. Blessed be the day, and the month, and the year,
   And the season, the time, the hour and the moment,
   And the fair country . . .
2. Thus I believe that mountains and shores,
   And rivers, and forests, know of what temper
   Is my life, that is concealed from all others.
3. 'Love leads me: thee, Nature only'.
4. 'There is our living and sweet Sun'.

of a composite thought-process—the two parts of the acorn—
are embodied in the dual structure of octave and sestet. Each
verse unit operates with perfect economy: each requires to be
considered apart.

Two patterns of rhyme are co-present in the octave. One is
a progressive movement of alternations (*ab,ba*), suggesting the
logic of exposition or narration, as in meditative or allegorical
verse. The other is a static iteration of couplets (*aa,bb*) as in
the sensuous stresses of simple lyric. Each line of the octave,
between the first and the last, participates simultaneously
in these interlocked patterns, the relationship standing as
follows:

$$\overline{a\overline{b}\,\overline{b}\,a}\,,\,a\,\overline{b}\,\overline{b}\,a$$

The effect is of exposition or narration constantly being im-
pinged upon by lyric stress, which is itself absorbed back into
the expository process. Dante's *terza rima* provides the nearest
analogy, with its own kind of prosodic counterpoint which
stimulates emotion while at the same time maintaining interest in the flow of the narrative. The major difference is that the
constantly shifting pattern of rhymes in Dante ensures that
narrative or exposition will be the dominant factor and that
the intellectual process will, as is right in philosophical allegory, organize and direct the overriding movement of the
verse. In the sonnet octave, however, there is no such total
progression. The second sub-stanza of four lines is carried back
to the first by the integral rhyme-scheme; the progressive logic
of syntax is overborne by the emotional suggestions of rhyme;
and a stasis results wherein the imagination hovers over one
intense experience compounded equally of thought and feeling.

In the sestet, the act of correlation replaces the completed
act of intuition. More flexibility is permissible in the arrangement of rhymes, the main object being that syntax and rhyme
should now reinforce one another, the tercet sub-stanzas an-
swering back line against line in any appropriate symmetrical
fashion. There may be three sets of rhymes (*cde,cde* or *cde,edc*)
or sometimes only two (*ccd,ccd*). What is almost always desirable is that a rhyming couplet should not appear at the end,
which throws the structure out of balance by suggesting logical
deduction instead of rational correlation. The function of the

sestet is not to supersede the intuitive knowledge of the octave but to gather up its truth and apprehend it in the region of conscious thought. It supports the octave as the cup supports the acorn; and both processes are 'organic', whether intuitive or rational; not 'mechanical', as in logical analysis or deduction. Accordingly the significance of the octave is expounded in the six lines divided in complementary halves, and the integrated quality of the rhyme-scheme, which only progressively impresses itself upon the reader's consciousness, knits up the experience line by line into the poet's total interpretation of life.

Such, in so far as they may be abstractly described, would seem to be the main formal qualities of the Petrarchan sonnet. Its influence was to be carried throughout western Europe on the tide of humanism; variations on its themes were to be sounded by almost every poet in every country which had cultural ties with Italy. Each national literature was to take what it needed, to assimilate or discard the elements alien to it, and to adapt form and content to its special needs. Before turning to the fortunes of the sonnet in England, however, it is worth while considering briefly what is implied by the differences of background and tradition which were brought into play as soon as the Tudor poets applied themselves to the problem of using an Italian form for English lyrical expression.

However finely one may draw distinctions between the various literary forms whose influences coalesce in Petrarch's sonnets, the most impressive quality is their generic relationship, and the singleness of vision reflected in them all. The lyrics of Provence, the French allegorical romances, the sonnets and *canzoni* of thirteenth-century Florence and Bologna, even Dante's divine allegory, spring from the same primary conviction, however modified by place, time, levels of civilization, and the poet's individuality. Belief in a fundamental *rapport* between nature and the human spirit, and in woman as the mystic channel through which this passed, is at the core of the romance tradition. We should need to go beyond literature to the history of myth and religion to appreciate the vitality and persistence of this Mediterranean tenet. The ancient world, we know, hypostatized the magic of sex and fertility in woman's form. As queen of heaven she ruled a planet in the

sky; at Paphos she rose from the sea; the scarlet anemones of
April were the blood of her slaughtered lover. The conviction
was fixed in the subliminal mind, not to be dislodged by processes of reasoning. Even Socrates the moral philosopher, in
the course of a speech disparaging the senses, heard a sudden
call to halt and retract his words: *Is not Eros the son of Aphrodite,
and a god?* With the coming of the new religion the gods went
underground, but their mythologies still gripped the imagination in various disguises.[1] The Troubadour poets almost
avowedly defy the Church in their apotheosis of desire, the
quasi-divine attributes of their heroines, and the ritual of their
adoration. In that remarkable poem *Le Cour d'Amour*, the paradise of Venus and her worshippers on a hill of light, surrounded
by wild woods full of the song of birds, has taken the place of
the Christian heaven. Nor was this only the cult of a sophisticated few; its roots reached down into the anonymous verse of
the people. The May songs and *caroles* of the peasant girls of
Limousin and Poitou were half-obliterated memories of the
rites of Venus; the Tuscan *stornelli*, which Dante and Petrarch
must have heard in the streets of Florence, echoed the same
pagan sentiment.

> *Fiore di felce ...*
> *Dove passate voi, l'erba ci nasce*
> *E nel mese di maggio ci fiorisce.*[2]

In this rudimentary catch of three lines, Venus walked on
earth and restored the spring flowers as she had done a thousand years before.

For the intellectual, philosophically minded poet there was
of course no question of a return to pagan doctrines. But his
imaginative bias and his intuitions still functioned along the
lines of reciprocity between spirit and nature. Hence the correspondence between divine love and the experience of *amour
courtois*: hence the facility with which allegorical romance
employed images drawn from nature to represent conditions
of the soul—the briars of chastity, the guarded rose of heart's

1. See C. S. Lewis, *The Allegory of Love* (Oxford 1936), Chapter I, for an
excellent account of this transformation.
2.   Flower of the fern ...
      Where you walk you quicken the grass,
      That blossoms in May wherever you pass.

desire. Even on the most sublimated plane, Dante's Lady in the *Paradiso* preserved the identity of the Beatrice of *Vita Nuova*. When therefore Petrarch begins a sonnet to Laura by describing her as the joint handiwork of nature and heaven,[1] when he concludes another with the conviction that she will determine for him the course of all future springs,[2] he is voicing, in however philosophical or Christian a form, the primeval convictions of Mediterranean peoples.

But convictions such as these were essentially alien to the English mind. Needless to say, love and nature have always had their place in English literature, and the erotic mythologies of the south have from early times provided poets with decorative themes: but only in modern romanticism, in the writings of Lawrence or Shelley or Blake, are there serious attempts at the deification of woman or the procreative forces. This difference in the English tradition is sometimes attributed to Puritanism, or the Reformation; its origins, however, may reach into pre-history. In a stimulating essay, 'Beowulf: The Monsters and the Critics',[3] Professor Tolkien has drawn an effective contrast between the primitive mythologies of north and south. He has pointed out how the Anglo-Saxon genius, with that of other Germanic peoples, conceived of elemental nature in terms of permanent hostility both to man and the gods, fighting in the shape of sub-human monsters a perpetual war whose end would inevitably spell defeat for humanity and its allies. With Christianity came a new hope of redemption; but while memory of the somewhat ineffectual gods soon faded, the elemental foe persisted in the northern imagination, assuming moral and subjective disguises. The old war continued, with spirit arrayed against sense, and virtue, aided by heaven, embattled against natural desire. Up to a point Christian teaching could give countenance to this dualism; but it did not wholly justify the pessimism that prevailed in the traditional English lyric.

1.   *Chi vuol veder quantunque po natura*
          E 'l ciel tra noi, venga a mirar costei, (*Sonetto in Vita* ccx)
See *infra*, Chapter IV, pp. 58–62, for a discussion of this sonnet with reference to Sidney.
2.   *Ma come ch'ella gli governi o volga,*
          Primavera per me pur non è mai. (*Sonetto in Vita* IX)
3. *Proceedings of the British Academy* (1937), vol. XXII.

Professedly it is Christian poetry, but the colour of its sentiment is no essential part of the Christian attitude towards life. Perhaps we have to do with a matter of racial temperament rather than of creed, and it is the Anglo-Saxon melancholy that inspires so keen a sense of the transitoriness and uncertainty of all mortal things.[1]

Despite occasional touches of gaiety, the great majority of surviving lyrics view love as pitiable and frail, at the mercy of wind and weather:

> Mirie it is while sumer ilast
>   With fugheles song;
> Oc nu necheth windes blast
>   And weder strong.
> Ei, ei, what this nicht is long!
> And ich with wel michel wrong
> Soreghe and murne and fast.[2]

Here was a very different note from the Provençal poet's sadness at being alone in spring, when the nightingale sang by moonlight. The Troubadours were indeed well known at the courts of Angevin England, and lyrics were written in imitation of theirs;[3] but these were obviously derivative, and in marked contrast to the native strain. Even when no moralizing tone is heard, the true English love lyric shows none of the southern tendency to idealize or apotheosize the girl who is wooed. Courtship is simple, sincere, a pledge of quiet partnership through life. And most frequently of all, the conclusion is drawn that roses, romance, and the desires of summer are light things to set against the onslaught of winter and death:

> Nou skrinketh rose and lylie flour,
>   That whilen ber that suete savour
>   In somer, that suete tyde;
> Ne is no quene so stark ne stour,
> Ne no levedy so bryht in bour,
>   That ded ne shal by glyde.
>
> Whose wol fleyshlust forgon,
>   And hevene blis abyde,

1. E. K. Chambers and F. Sidgwick, *Early English Lyrics* (1907), p. 284.
2. *Ibid.*, p. 1.
3. See H. J. Chaytor, *The Troubadours and England* (Cambridge 1923).

> On Jesu be is thoht anon,
> That therled was ys side.[1]

The warning may owe something to monkish asceticism, but it descends straight from such Anglo-Saxon elegiacs as *The Wanderer* or *The Seafarer*, which ended with grave counsel to turn from the woes of the world and seek consolation in the Heavenly Father.

The English narrative poem, in treating the theme of physical love, rarely missed a chance to ponder its moral effects. *The Owl and the Nightingale*, by no means narrowly didactic, is a long debate between sense and spirit, with even the Nightingale conceding love to be ephemeral—

> for hit nis bute a lutel breþ,
> þat sone kumeþ, and sone geþ.[2]

Images of the countryside crowd thick and fast upon one another in this poem, but winter, cold, hunger, and death are never forgotten, for all that the setting is in summer-time: flowers and sunshine and bird-song—unlike those of the nearly contemporary *Cour d'Amour*—last only for a season and pass away into the dark. *Sir Gawain and the Grene Knight* is in its English form essentially the story of a testing and a temptation; the hero's repute depends as much on his chastity as on his valour. Chaucer, half French by blood, and culturally indebted to Italy and France, breathed no insular spirit; but at his most serious, in *Troilus and Criseyde*, he turned an impassioned romance of Boccaccio into an indictment of courtly love, shown as ending in dust and ashes, the corruption of a beautiful woman and the death of a brave man.

More typical of English medieval tradition was the poetry of Langland. *Piers Plowman* was preoccupied with social and moral issues, and gave very little attention to love; but the contrast between Langland's methods and those of De Lorris is not for that reason quite irrelevant. It is an unconscious pointer to the English distaste for a close identification of man and the impersonal that Langland's allegorical imagery should

1. Chambers and Sidgwick, p. 97.
2.   for it is but a little breath,
        that cometh fast, and fast goeth.
              (*The Owl and The Nightingale*, 1461–2)

be at its weakest (as that of De Lorris was at its strongest) when trying to symbolize moral conduct in natural forms.[1] On the other hand many of his personifications of human qualities, such as the Seven Deadly Sins, have a vitality unmatched by any of the corresponding figures in the *Roman de la Rose*. As for other English allegories, though certainly influenced by contemporary European fashions, they show few deep-rooted tendencies to share the southern attitude towards nature and physical love.

With such traditions at work in both lyrical and narrative verse, with such inherited modes of thought and feeling, the Tudor poets set out to make the Petrarchan sonnet their own. Even so, their problems were not confined to questions of subject-matter. They also suffered from a complete lack of formal tradition on which to pattern themselves, so that the mere rendering of Italian sonnet metre into an English verse-equivalent was a major task. A hundred and fifty years before, Chaucer had perfected the decasyllabic line in relation to the language of his time. But in the intervening period the language itself, both in speech and writing, was changing too fast for the Chaucerian metric to offer any real guidance. In particular the dropping of the final -*e*, and the uncertainty with regard to stress in words newly borrowed from Latin and French, threw narrative verse into chaos.[2] It is true that at the very worst time, lyrical poetry written for song or instrumental accompaniment developed new graces: for the musical revival associated with Dunstable offered structural supports, with metre and diction adapted to the melodies of the lute and the caden-

1. 'It is tedious to be told of a brook named "Be buxom of speech", and a croft called "Covet not men's cattle nor their wives", when nothing is made of the brook or croft by way of scenery.' (W. P. Ker, *Medieval English Literature* (1912), p. 195.)

2. 'Both orthography and orthoepy were, in the English of the time, at such a point of transition, and blending, and experiment, that they gave no solid base or standard at all . . . the materials crumbled under the hand of the verse-builder as he used them, and made matters still worse for the untempered mortar of his syntax and the treacherous line and trowel of his metre.' (G. Saintsbury, *A History of English Prosody* (1910), vol. I, p. 239.) While Saintsbury underestimates the importance of stress in English prosody, his account of the metrical chaos in the fifteenth century (pp. 218–45) remains valid. It should be supplemented by the article of C. S. Lewis, 'The Fifteenth Century Heroic Line', *Essays and Studies*, XXIV (1939), 28–41.

ces of the singing voice. But this was no help to the would-be sonnet-writer, whose compositions were for silent reading, and whose subject-matter reflected a different quality of mind from that which called forth the traditional lyric. The Tudor poets were indeed true pioneers both in form and content, breaking a virgin soil on which, in the fullness of days, the great Elizabethans were to raise their golden harvest.

II

WYATT

FTER centuries of neglect, Wyatt's reputation as a poet is now firmly established, and his lighter lyrics show up as a bright patch in any collection of sixteenth-century verse. Their attractive rhythms, their pure diction, above all, their blend of grace and forthrightness, make an immediate appeal to modern taste. But with his sonnets it is still quite another story. Literary historians commonly stress their importance as the first uncouth experiments in the English sonnet form, and point out that, from a purely technical viewpoint, Wyatt came near to inventing the standard Elizabethan model. But these frigid·praises hardly recommend the poems themselves to a reader's attention. Nor have the most influential critics encouraged a closer investigation. Even Dr Tillyard, who has done much to restore Wyatt to his rightful place, has felt the need to apologize for the sonnets:

> For the sake of his reputation, Wyatt had better not have imported the sonnet into England, for by so doing he purchased a text-book glory at the price of advertising the class of poems that does his poetical powers least credit.[1]

Recently, indeed, there have been signs of a more positive approach, and the claim has at last been made that Wyatt's sonnets deserve consideration as 'poems in their own right, and not merely as historically important bores'.[2] This is all to the good; but we shall perhaps see our way more clearly if at the start we avoid any assumption of a necessary polarity between historical importance and poetic merit. Had Wyatt's sonnets been mere exercises in rhyme-schemes and verse-forms, they would have had little formative influence upon other poets, and but small interest for the sixteenth-century public which

1. E. M. W. Tillyard, *The Poetry of Sir Thomas Wyatt* (1929), Preface, p. vi.

2. The phrase is quoted from Hallett Smith's valuable article, 'The Art of Sir Thomas Wyatt', *The Huntington Library Quarterly* (August 1946), IX (4), 323–55. This marks a turning-point in the appreciation of Wyatt's sonnets.

for generations read these poems in successive editions of Tottel's anthology. For us, on the other hand, a literary appreciation of the sonnets is bound up with a proper comprehension of their historical significance. Undeniably they present obstacles to the present-day reader; partly because of the awkward metres in which a number of them are written, partly because of the impression some give of being no more than rough translations. Just for this reason it is necessary to view Wyatt's sonnets in their right perspective and to judge them, not by our own unguided impressions, but by our understanding of what the poet was trying to achieve as a man of his age.

To reach this understanding, our point of departure must surely be that the sonnets are of quite another order than the Tudor lyric with its musical basis. For a gifted young writer like Wyatt, it was no great accomplishment to excel in such poems as 'Forget not yet', or 'And wilt thou leave me thus', whose style had deep roots in fifteenth-century lyric practice and its development in the song books of the Tudor court. But in his sonnets Wyatt was deliberately breaking new ground in a direction where he could expect no guidance from the literary past of his own country. It was a bold, worth-while enterprise, impelled by a stronger creative urge; for what the age needed most in poetry was a medium for self-expression more sophisticated, making more of an appeal to the trained mind, than the earlier type of lyric could afford. Wyatt's situation had, indeed, certain resemblances to that of the Imagist poets in the early years of the twentieth century, who, reacting against Georgian styles, looked to Europe for their inspiration.

If Wyatt's sonnets are to be considered as poems of a new kind, they must be scrutinized somewhat minutely. The relation must be seen between changes in conventional form and the exigences of a distinctive content; while the small but cumulatively important variants must be noted in what at first sight may appear to be mere copies of foreign models. Taken in the order of the Muir edition,[1] the sonnets fall into two groups. The first nineteen, which appear close together in the Egerton manuscript, written out carefully in Wyatt's own

1. *Sir Thomas Wyatt, The Collected Poems*, edited Kenneth Muir (1949). This edition, based on a re-examination of original texts, will be referred to for all quotations from Wyatt.

hand, are stylistically the earliest; while the remaining eleven, taken from later pages of the same manuscript and from other sources, show more mature characteristics. It is chiefly in the first group that we are conscious of the irregular metres and derivative subject-matter; and it is here that we must give our closest attention.

Nearly all the sonnets which make up this group are renderings from Petrarch and—occasionally—his Italian followers of the *Quattrocento*.[1] They are deliberate imitations, whose sources are well known; translations in the main, though, as will be seen, of an unusual kind. In rhyme-scheme and fourteen-line length they follow their originals; but there are subtle differences here too, and one difference which is obvious. Every sonnet has a couplet ending: a device which was rare, though not quite unprecedented, in the Italian sonnet, and which certainly did not appear in any of the models Wyatt chose. However he came by this, the consistent use of the couplet in all these sonnets indicates that it answered to some genuine and deep-seated need. Its special quality was to end a poem on a logical, critical note; and this change, altering the whole balance of the sestet, was bound, consciously or unconsciously, to affect the spirit of the sonnet in which it appeared. Furthermore, there are the peculiarities of metre. We shall do well to avoid reading into these sonnets any fixed or preconceived versification. There is very little to support the theory of a special Tudor metric with a set of rules so complex as to admit almost any exception.[2] Nor is the more recent suggestion that Wyatt's verse was based upon fifteenth-century 'pausing rhythm' really convincing, attractive as the idea may seem to readers who admire the 'sprung rhythm' of Hopkins.[3] The rough accentual prosody of late medieval plain-song, ballad, or alliterative verse was quite unsuited to the highly disciplined medium of the sonnet, and its sporadic appearance in these poems represents just the kind of anachronism Wyatt was progressively to overcome.

1. Exceptions seem to be sonnets x, xiii, xvi, and xxvii, for which no direct sources have been found. They are by no means superior poetically to the other sonnets of this group.

2. As in Agnes K. Foxwell, *A Study of Sir Thomas Wyatt's Poems* (1911).

3. D. W. Harding, 'The Rhythmical Intention in Wyatt's Poetry', *Scrutiny* (December 1946), xiv (2), pp. 90–102.

Actually, the sonnets of this group may be read in different
ways, and show a variety of metrical systems (with sometimes
no system at all). By way of example, the opening lines of
XXXIII may be considered:

> Like to these vnmesurable montayns
> Is my painfull lyff, the burden of Ire,
> For of great height be they, and high is my desire,
> And I of teres, and they be full of fontayns.

Here are two lines of ten syllables each, almost without any
stresses, and resembling in this the courtly kind of sixteenth-
century French verse; followed by a six-stress line that perhaps
imitates the French alexandrine; followed by a line of eleven
syllables based, it would seem, on the Italian pattern. Sometimes the lines, though we may count them on our fingers as
decasyllables, fall when read aloud into the old four-stress beat
of fifteenth-century verse—

> But reáson háth at my fóllie smýlèd,
> And párdond me sýns that Í me repént
> Of mý lost yéres and týme myspént;
> For yeúth did me léde and fálshode guýded. (XVI)

And again there are lines that seem to copy the Italian method
of combining a fixed number of syllables with a fairly free vari-
ation of stress:

> The longe love, that in my thought doeth harbar
> And in myn hert doeth kepe his residence,
> Into my face preseth with bolde pretence,
> And therin campeth, spreding his baner. (IV)

In so far as a common principle exists, it is the use, in the great
majority of lines, of the decasyllable, however free or irregular
the stress may be. (The Italian line-length of eleven syllables,
found in all Wyatt's models, appears only rarely and as it were
by accident.) This pattern comes out clearly when certain
licences are allowed for: the occasional sounding of a final -e,
-ed, or elision of the final -eth in verbs; the frequent pronunciation of words in the colloquial fashion of the time (*fire*, *higher*,
even, etc. as monosyllables; *every*, *passion*, etc. as two-syllable
words); and sometimes the running together, as in Italian, of
contiguous vowels. These freedoms do not amount to any-

thing like a regular 'system'; often the natural speech-stress ignores them, and they seem to have been quite mechanical devices. But they did provide Wyatt with a welcome degree of latitude in setting out to apply the yard-stick of the decasyllable to his unruly verse.

In these early sonnets, then, two new formal principles are at work: the final couplet and the ten-syllable line. With no English sonnet as a precedent, and without a model of versification ready to hand, Wyatt shows an interesting independence. At the very start he may, like Lydgate and other post-Chaucerians, have allowed decasyllables to appear side by side with other types of metre (as in XXVII and XXXIII); but soon they were imposed on whole sonnets (XXIX, XXXI, etc.). Beneath this artificial conformity the old English stress patterns with their turbulent beat fought hard to reassert themselves, like feudal barons under the yoke of Tudor despotism; and XXIX provides an entertaining example of this battle of the metres:

> Auysing the bright bemes of these fayer Iyes,
>> Where he is that myn oft moisteth and wassheth,
>> The werid mynde streght from the hert departeth
>> For to rest in his woroldly paradise,
> And fynde the swete bitter vnder this gyse.
>> What webbes he hath wrought well he perceveth,
>> Whereby with himself on love he playneth;
>> That spurreth with fyer, and bridilleth with Ise.
> Thus is it in suche extremitie brought:
>> In frossen thought nowe and nowe it stondeth in flame;
>> Twyst misery and welth, twist ernest and game;
> But few glad, and many a dyvers thought;
>> With sore repentaunce of his hardines:
>> Of suche a rote commeth ffruyte fruytles.

Here, after the first five tethered lines (containing three *-eth* slurs to preserve decasyllabic number and disregarding, incidentally, the mid-octave pause of the original), the traditional English rhythm breaks loose in a four-stress canter up to *bridilleth with Ise*. Bridled itself for two lines, it bolts again in lines 11 and 12, and is finally restrained in the couplet, which, significantly, falls into rough iambic pentameters.[1]

1. Here Wyatt in effect retraced Chaucer's line of development, as

True progress beyond such imposed uniformity was to call for more radical change. No mere compromise between essentially different conceptions of verse was possible: the old English moulds had to be broken up before anything new could be created. This came about through a deeper penetration into the rhythms, the verse-structure, and eventually the poetic nature of the Italian models. As usual the road to freedom lay through a willing acceptance of authority. The opening lines of III exemplify Wyatt's painstaking efforts to capture the flowing rhythms of Petrarch within the framework of the decasyllable. The Italian source of which they are almost an exact translation illustrates the peculiarities of the English rendering:

> *Cesare, poi che 'l traditor d'Egitto*
> *Li fece il don de l'onorata testa,*
> *Celando l'allegrezza manifesta,*
> *Pianse per gli occhi fuor, sì come è scritto . . .*[1]

> Caesar, when that the traytor of Egipt
> With th'onourable hed did him present,
> Covering his gladnes, did represent
> Playnt with his teres owteward, as it is writt . . .

Such careful patterning of the translation, word by word and stress by stress, upon the original, prevented the intrusion of traditional rhythms and in fact cleared the way for the emergence of a contemporary English style.

But gradually it became evident that a transfer of Italian versification to English was not really practicable. The texture of English weakened intolerably the delicate Italian rhythms, producing a switchback effect, with a kind of verse that lacked at once the vigour of the native tradition and the subtlety of the borrowed medium. With this realization the purely formal experiments passed over into problems of language and, necessarily, of content. Once the principles of sonnet versification

---

described by C. S. Lewis in 'The Fifteenth Century Heroic Line' (cf. p. 12 *supra*, note 2). 'On the one hand, he followed the French in having (usually) ten syllables in a line, and sometimes he had five full stresses, thus attaining the modern decasyllabic tune. But the other tune . . . was running in his head and he allowed it to intrude, he even welcomed it. . . I suspect that his verse was a precarious balance of different metrical forces.' (pp. 38–9.) What is said of Chaucer applies with even greater force to Wyatt.

1. *Sonetto in Vita* LXXXI.

had been grasped, Wyatt became increasingly concerned with an individual rendering. His verbal changes, at first very tentative, limited chiefly to variations of *nuance*, but steadily growing bolder, reacted progressively upon the Italian structure and versification. And at the same time the new devices of the decasyllable and the final couplet, which gave to the verse a logical or even epigrammatic quality, called for departures from the original phrasing, so that subject-matter too was gradually transformed. The two processes, in large measure interdependent, each prompting the other and finding its true complement in the other, were to set their joint stamp upon the English sonnet.

To see these processes actually at work, we have only to make a comparison between Wyatt's original models and his English renderings. I shall set down three examples, Italian and English side by side, which illustrate different phases in Wyatt's development. (It need not, of course, be assumed that the order of development in which these examples will be ranged is the same as their order of composition. Like other poets, Wyatt probably found his way to maturity by a winding route.)

(i) WYATT (Muir xxv)	PETRARCH (*Sonetto in Vita* XLI) [1]
Bicause I have the still kept fro lyes and blame	*Perch'io t'abbia guardato di menzogna*
And to my power alwaies have I the honoured,	*A mio podere et onorato assai,*
Vnkynd tong right ill hast thou me rendred	*Ingrata lingua, già però non m'hai*
For suche deserft to do me wrek and shame.	*Renduto onor, ma fatto ira e vergogna :*
In nede of succor moost when that I ame	*Ché, quando più 'l tuo aiuto mi bisogna*
To aske reward, then standest thou like oon aferd	*Per dimandar mercede, allor ti stai*
Alway moost cold, and if thou speke towerd,	*Sempre più fredda ; e, se parole fai,*
It is as in dreme vnperfaict and lame.	*Son imperfette e quasi d'uom che sogna.*

1. The text of Petrarch's sonnets follows the edition of Carducci and Ferrari.

And ye salt teres again my will eche nyght	*Lagrime triste, e voi tutte le notti*
That are with me when fayn I would be alone,	*M'accompagnate, ov'io vorrei star solo,*
Then are ye gone when I should make my mone;	*Poi fuggite di nanzi a la mia pace.*
And you so reddy sighes to make me shright,	*E voi, sì pronti a darmi angoscia e duolo,*
Then are ye slake when that ye should owtestert;	*Sospiri, allor traete lenti e rotti.*
And onely my loke declareth my hert.	*Sola la vista mia del cor non tace.*

The octave of the English sonnet is of chiefly formal interest. Subject to the licences in pronunciation already described, the lines are all decasyllables, with the exception of line 6, where 'thou' is probably out of deference to literary usage.[1] The verse is written in flowing rhythms, which may be read without any change from natural English stress; and although the switchback effect is still not quite overcome, it has been considerably smoothed. Furthermore, the influence of the decasyllable has produced a sharply defined line-ending and a more clear-cut quatrain unit, which leads to the elimination of Petrarch's characteristic run-over technique in lines 3–4 of the English, as well as to the full halt at the end of line 4 instead of Petrarch's half-pause. This is an important development, which divides the Italian unitary octave into two distinct quatrains.

While the English subject-matter does not differ greatly from the Italian, there are some minor variants to notice. *Ira e vergogna*—anger and shame—become *wrek and shame* in line 4, and *like oon aferd* in line 6 is a vivid original touch, consequent on Wyatt's own psychological perception.

The outstanding differences, however, appear in the sestet. Petrarch's rhetorical structure, with its repetitions and parallelisms, is accentuated by the introduction of the final couplet. There is no need for the slowing down of tempo and relaxation of tension which the Italian tercets impose. Hence the run-

1. Thus 'I have' in line 1 is colloquially elided into one syllable, and 'power' slurred to the same effect in line 2. There is also, I think, elision of 'the' with the first syllable of 'honoured' in this line. In line 6, 'standest thou' like would probably be pronounced as 'stand'st th'like'.

over of lines 12–13 in the original (bringing *sospiri* down into the penultimate line) is again broken away from in the translation, and the full force of repetition—*Then are ye gone . . . Then are ye slake*—is brought into play. Wyatt has simplified the rhyme-scheme of the Italian sestet to mark off his couplet, so that the first four lines make up a separate verse-unit *cddc*, analogous to the quatrains into which the octave has been divided. This modifies in turn his rendering of the content in line 11, and *when I should make my mone* is substituted for *di nanzi a la mia pace* ('in the presence of my peace'). The beautiful epithet for Laura, *la mia pace*, with its spiritual, Dantesque associations, is sacrificed, but a characteristic personal note is introduced. It is the self-absorbed Tudor amorist who calculates the occasions when he should 'make his moan', and the phrase goes with the realism of *salt teres* for *lagrime triste* and *owtestert* for *lenti e rotti* (again suggested by the need for a new rhyme) in lines 9 and 13 respectively. The final couplet has thus made its influence felt throughout the sestet, which shows a marked advance in metrical control. This appears not only in the smoothly managed five-foot lines where stress and number are brought into accord, but also in the well-planned alternation of stresses in the initial feet as between iamb and trochee. Perhaps too the four-stress character of the last line was deliberately introduced to lay special emphasis on the poet's final statement: the corresponding effect is brought about by the halt at the end of line 13 in Petrarch's sonnet.

(ii) WYATT (Muir XXIV)

PETRARCH (*Sonetto in Vita* XVII)

Som fowles there be that have so
  perfaict sight,
    Agayn the Sonne their Iyes for
    to defend,
    And som bicause the light
    doeth theim offend,
    Do never pere but in the darke
    or nyght.
Other reioyce that se the fyer
    bright
    And wene to play in it as they
    do pretend,

Sono animali al mondo di sí
  altera
    Vista che 'n contr' al sol pur si
    defende:
    Altri, però che 'l gran lume gli
    offende,
    Non escon fuor se non verso la
    sera:
Et altri, col desio folle che
    spera
    Gioir forse nel foco perché
    splende,

And fynde the contrary of it that they intend.	*Provan l'altra vertú, quella che 'ncende.*
Alas, of that sort I may be by right,	*Lasso! el mio loco è 'n quest'ultima schiera.*
For to withstond her loke I ame not able;	*Ch'i' non son forte ad aspettar la luce*
And yet can I not hide me in no darke place,	*Di questa donna, e non so fare schermi*
Remembraunce so foloweth me of that face,	*Di luoghi tenebrosi o d'ore tarde:*
So that with tery yen swolne and vnstable,	*Però con gli occhi lagrimosi e 'nfermi*
My destyne to behold her doeth me lede;	*Mio destino a vederla mi conduce:*
Yet do I knowe I runne into the glede.	*E so ben ch'i' vo' dietro a quel che m'arde.*

There is development here in every part of the sonnet. Petrarch's octave is unusual for him, with its balanced comparisons and contrasts built upon a purely logical thought-process. Wyatt may have discovered that in translating them his pen flowed with unusual smoothness. Here again he strengthened the parallelism by modifying in lines 1–2 and 5–6 the run-over structure of the Italian. The quatrains were also separated clearly by the full stop after line 4 followed by the strong opening stress of line 5. Moreover, the 'masculine' rhyme with its stress on the last syllable, better managed than in example (i), was a further aid in gaining the desired effect. Consequently Wyatt's first eight lines show a great advance in metrical control, the five-foot iambic principle almost superseding the earlier imitations of Italian rhythm. (Really what was happening, though it is doubtful whether Wyatt knew it, was that Chaucer's versification had in effect returned as an outcome of the emergent sonnet form. So much for the continuity of national literary traditions even in the course of the most sweeping changes.)

The sestet displays even more independence. Each of its halves, as well as the last line of all, which here carries special weight, is marked off by an emphatic opening stress. Thus while the five-foot iambic line is establishing itself as the norm of the English sonnet, some measure of traditional freedom is returning under the new discipline. The innovations in subject-matter come in the crucial lines where, owing to the final couplet, a new rhyme is required; and they have a more extreme character than in the last example. *Remembraunce so foloweth me of that face* in line 11 is a completely new phrase and an original touch of subjective detail; *I runne into the glede* in line 14 is far more vivid than Petrarch's *i' vo' dietro a quel che m'arde.*[1] More striking still is the subtle—and gratuitous—change of implication in line 9. Petrarch's *Ch'i' non son forte ad aspettar la luce Di questa Donna*[2] is in his characteristic transcendental strain, sublimating his lady into an almost divine being irradiated with heavenly glory. *For to withstond her loke I ame not able* carries no such suggestion, and refers merely to a woman whose physical appeal embarrasses her lover. The romance vision of apotheosized humanity is already challenged by this implied heresy. As Wyatt's technical self-assurance grows, he will return more boldly to the attack, and subject to open ridicule the whole cult of veneration for the sonnet mistress.

(iii) WYATT (Muir IX)	PETRARCH (*Sonetto in Vita* LXI)
Was I never yet of your love greved,	*Io non fu' d'amar voi lassato unqu'anco*
Nor never shall while that my liff doeth last;	*Madonna, né sarò, mentre ch'io viva;*
But of hating myself that date is past,	*Ma d'odiar me medesmo giunto a riva,*
And teeres continuell sore have me weried.	*E del continuo lagrimar so stanco;*
I will not yet in my grave be buried;	*E voglio anzi un sepolcro bello e bianco,*
Nor on my tombe your name yfixed fast,	*Che 'l vostro nome a mio danno si scriva*
As cruell cause that did the sperit son hast	*In alcun marmo, ove di spirto priva*
Ffrom th'unhappy bonys, by great sighes sterred.	*Sia la mia carne, che po star seco anco.*
Then, if an hert of amourous faith and will	*Però, s'un cor pien d'amorosa fede*
May content you, withoute doyng greiff,	*Può contentarvi senza farne strazio,*

1. 'I go into that which burns me'.
2. 'Since I am not strong enough to look upon the light of that lady'.

Please it you so to this to doo releiff:	*Piacciavi omai di questo aver mercede.*
Yf, othre wise, ye seke for to fulfill	*Se 'n altro modo cerca d'esser sazio*
Your disdain, ye erre, and shall not as ye wene;	*Vostro sdegno, erra; e non fia quel che crede;*
And ye yourself the cause therof hath bene.	*Di che Amor e me stesso assai ringrazio.*

In the octave of this remarkable sonnet Wyatt forcefully repudiates the central theme of his original model. The lover of Laura is exhausted with sighs and self-hatred: he looks forward to death as a relief from his long sufferings, and plans his sepulchre as a monument to his lady. It will be *bello e bianco*, fair and white, built of marble and graven with her name. But he still retains a last hope of survival, if she will instead content herself with his ever-faithful heart. Otherwise she must know that he can bear her disdain no longer. Wyatt's rendering strikes a deliberately contrasting note. He is cynical and rebellious. For Petrarch's idiomatic phrase *giunto a riva*—to the final limit—he substitutes in line 3 'that date is past': he has reacted against self-hatred, and is wearied of tears, in a different sense from that of the original—he is, in fact, 'tired' of weeping. Instead of planning a sepulchre, he informs his mistress that he will *not* yet in his grave be buried; nor will he have her name 'yfixed fast' upon his tomb. The meaning of the second quatrain is thus inverted, and there is no need to dwell on the beauty of the projected memorial: where Petrarch in line 7 speaks of *marmo*, marble, Wyatt substitutes another touch of invective. If there *were* a tomb—which will not yet happen!—the inscription would only commemorate his mistress as the *cruell cause that did the sperit son hast*. Accordingly she had better take what she can while it is yet to be had—the heart he still proffers, as it were at arm's length: *Please it you so to this to doo releiff.*—If she refuses, in hope of further sadistic entertainment, she will find out her mistake and have no one to blame but herself.

Content, rather than form, is the shaping factor in this sonnet. Heavy trochaic stresses fall on *never* and *hating* in the second foot of lines 1 and 3 respectively: not in imitation of the Italian rhythms, but for their declamatory force in Wyatt's own poem. The quatrain units are again marked off more distinctly than in the original, and lend themselves well to a detached, critical treatment of personal experience. In the sestet this independent approach is kept up, with Wyatt's characteristic interest in his own requirements rather than in service to his lady: *Please it you so to this to doo releiff*. In the couplet, with its two pauses in the last line but one, the rhythm breaks sharply away from that of the preceding four lines to convey the brusque anger of the speaking voice, and finally bangs the door on the whole argument with quite dramatic verve. Here the diction is remarkably vigorous, achieving its effects by a choice of simple, common monosyllables and a close approximation to speech rhythms. The basis of versification through the sonnet is now the flexible pentameter of the Elizabethan sonnets.

At the stage marked by this last sonnet, Wyatt passed the uncertain frontier that lies between translation and original composition. While infusing the Petrarchan medium with his own vigorous personality, he had laid the foundations of a new verse-form, built upon three quatrains of decasyllables and a final couplet, and of a revived English metric based, like Chaucer's, on five feet of iambics while allowing a modified freedom of stress. Form and content, as we have seen, interpenetrated closely, and the joint product was a sonnet reflecting a view of life almost directly antithetical to that of Petrarch. It was rational rather than imaginative, empirical rather than transcendental, and in matters of love it replaced romantic ardour by Tudor egotism.

To this stage of development belong 'Who so list to hount' (vii) and 'Farewell Love' (xiii), with their self-assurance and easy control of verse technique. 'Who so list to hount' was in fact a complete reconstruction of Petrarch's great sonnet *Una candida cerva*, where Laura was symbolized as a hind pursued by the wearied hunter, who, at the point of exhaustion, realized that she was sacred, belonging only to God. The allegorical, visionary spirit of the original was deliberately evaporated from the poem; its dream imagery superseded by simple hunting metaphors; and the hind-mistress represented, not as a mystically untouchable paraclete, but as a wild and wilful

beauty evading capture.[1] 'Farewell Love' was an original sonnet that owed nothing to an Italian model. Instead of the lore
of romance, Wyatt invoked the chief inspirers of Renaissance
humanism, Seneca and Plato. His repulse at the hands of his
mistress had taught him to value a free mind and to regret his
time wasted on 'trifles'. The follies of love were accordingly
spurned with rude invective—

> Me lusteth no lenger rotten boughes to clymbe.

This figure of 'getting to the top of the tree' was quite characteristic, and, like the invocation of Plato and Seneca, had little
to do with conscience or remorse. It reflected the sentiments of
an ambitious courtier of the Tudor monarchy, an enthusiast
for classical learning, and came the more easily from a poet
whose national literary tradition was by and large unaffected
by romance attitudes.

Besides the well-managed versification, the last two sonnets
show a further development of formal structure. There is a
marked pause after the twelfth line, which separates the couplet from the lines preceding it and adds to its epigrammatic
force. In 'Farewell Love' there are in effect three distinct quatrains, with a couplet to round off the sonnet, instead of the
Italian octave and sestet as major verse units. This change
completes the main process of differentiation from Petrarch's
form. Only the problem of finding a rhyme-scheme to suit the
new verse-structure still awaits a solution.

There is no sharp dividing line between 'Who so list to
hount', or 'Farewell Love', and the later sonnets; but as a
group these are more mature and have passed beyond the
apprentice phase. Wyatt is no longer preoccupied now with
the sheer technical difficulty of writing sonnets in English. He
adapts and improvises freely. 'The lyvely sperkes' (XLVII) is a
good example of the flexible new versification, with its smooth
opening quatrains and its skilful variations of stress at the
close. Regularity for its own sake was certainly not Wyatt's
aim, as may be seen in the deliberate roughness and vehemence

1. F. W. Bateson has made an apt comparison of these two sonnets in
English Poetry: A Critical Introduction (1950), pp. 141–2.

C

of the metre in the last lines, suggesting the reactions of a man dazed by lightning:

> Blynded with the stroke, erryng here and there,
> So call I for helpe, I not when ne where, . . .

The same vigour produces the word-play in the couplet, which gives edge to its epigrammatic effect:

> For after the blase, as is no wounder,
> Of dedly *nay* here I the ferefull thounder.

This independence of approach appears again in 'Such vayn thought' (LVI), where Wyatt characteristically gave the sonnet an introspective cast at the expense of romance idealizations. Petrarch's complaint that he was frustrated by 'armed sighs' induced by 'this fair enemy of Love and me'[1] became

> But armed sighes my way do stoppe anone,
> *Twixt hope and drede locking my libertie.*

Later in the same sonnet, however, he was so concerned to elaborate on these subjective aspects that he ran on into a six-stress line—

> Whiche comforteth the mynde that erst for fere shoke.

The result was a loss of balance and a general lapse into fif-teenth-century versification. It was a sign of over-confidence rather than of clumsiness.

Wyatt's growing impatience with his long apprenticeship to Petrarch came to a head in 'I abide and abide' (CLX), which is essentially an old-style Skeltonic verse masquerading as a sonnet. The holiday note is enjoyable in its way, but the way belongs to quite another kind of writing. In the same manu-script as 'I abide', however,[2] are three sonnets which are in many respects among the most successful that Wyatt wrote. They owe nothing directly to Italian models, and stand en-tirely without supports.

'Dyvers dothe vse' (CXLV) deserves to be quoted in full as an example of the new English sonnet.

> Dyvers dothe vse as I have hard and kno,
> When that to chaunge ther ladies do beginne,

1. *Questa bella d'Amor nemica e mia.*
2. 'Devonshire' MS., B.M. Add. 17492.

> To morne and waile, and neuer for to lynne,
> Hoping therbye to pease ther painefull woo.
> And some ther be, that when it chanseth soo
> That women change and hate where love hath bene,
> Thei call them fals, and think with woordes to wynne
> The hartes of them wich otherwhere dothe gro.
> But as for me, though that by chaunse indede
> Change hath outworne the favor that I had,
> I will not wayle, lament, nor yet be sad;
> Nor call her fals that falsley ded me fede:
> But let it passe and think it is of kinde,
> That often chaunge doth plese a womans minde.

Here is an explicit, clear-cut break with Petrarchan attitudes. In the first quatrain Wyatt sums up the traditional behaviour of slighted lovers; in the second, the alternative response permitted them according to the romance convention—a mixture of cajolery and abuse. The sestet declares Wyatt's own course of action: he 'will not wayle, lament, nor yet be sad'—

> But let it passe and think it is of kinde . . .

To the worshipper of the divine Laura, this conclusion is, of course, the most damnable of heresies. If the lady is susceptible to chance and change, what remains of the constancy and faith, the joys and martyrdoms of the lover's creed? Better the passionate blasphemies of the harassed believer, the imprecations of the scorned acolyte, than this cold, agnostic tolerance. Yet Wyatt's outlook is in the direct line of English tradition, with its deep-rooted conviction that love, like summer and all sensuous joys, is fickle and deceptive. The moral of *Sir Gawain and the Grene Knight* was that wise men should treat women precisely as Wyatt intended to do:

> For so watʒ Adam on erde with one bygyled
> And Salamon with fele sere, and Samson eftsoneʒ . . .
> Now þese were wrathed with her wyles, hit were a wynne huge
> To luf hom well, and leve hem not, a leude þat couþe.[1]
> (ed. Tolkien and Gordon, 2416 *passim*)

Moreover, since these frailties are 'of kind', since chance and change rule over all things, one should forget and forgive. In

1. For so was Adam on earth deceived of one,
   And Solomon with several, and Samson likewise . . .
   All were vexed with their wiles; what advantage it were
   To love them well and trust them not, if a man were able.

this light Chaucer judged his Criseyde and refused to condemn her:

> Gret was the sorwe and pleynt of Troilus,
> But forth hir cours fortune ay gan to holde.
> Criseyde loveth the sone of Tydeus,
> And Troilus mot wepe in cares colde.
> Swich is this world; who so it can biholde,
> In eche estat is litel hertes reste:
> God leve us for to take it for the beste![1]

Yet if the theme has behind it a tradition centuries old, Wyatt adds a touch of acid sarcasm that belongs to his own age and takes the place of his forefathers' philosophic calm. As for the form, it is quite new, a sonnet of entirely English stamp with its pure, monosyllabic diction, its masculine rhymes, its unobtrusive use of alliteration for knitting together the verse texture. All this, with the division into three balanced quatrains and a final couplet clinching the sense of the poem, bears the mark of Wyatt's vigorous, independent personality.

The other two sonnets of the Devonshire manuscript develop the same theme with almost equal proficiency. In 'Mye love toke skorne' (CLIII) Wyatt suddenly turns in the sestet to direct address, and shows an apt handling of speech rhythms and conversational idiom:

> But sins that thus ye list to ordre me,
>   That wolde have bene your seruaunte true and faste,
>   Displese the not, my doting dayes bee paste:
> And with my losse to leve I must agre;
>   For as there is a certeyne tyme to rage,
>   So ys there tyme suche madnes to asswage.

'To Rayle or geste' (CXXXIX) has a formal interest, in that it departs from the Petrarchan rule of separate rhyme-schemes for octave and sestet. In a sonnet of considerable poise, the repetition of the identical word 'not', ringing through all three quatrains, sets up a persistent note of truculence.[2] Sonnets

---

1. *Troilus and Criseyde*, v. 1744–50.
2.   Love yt who liste, in faithe I like yt not.
        And if ye ware to me as ye are not,
        I wolde be lothe to se you so unkinde;
        But sins your faithe muste nedes be so, be kinde:
        Tho I hate yt, I praye you love yt not.

such as these place Wyatt as first in the great 'line of wit' that
runs through from Sidney to Donne and the cavalier poets of
the seventeenth century.

Then, in the last sonnets,[1] comes a turning aside from erotic
themes (Wyatt's best love poetry was really out-of-love poetry)
to the expression of his predicaments in the yet more haphaz-
ard world of politics. They contain more or less explicit topical
allusions—to two spells of imprisonment suffered in May 1534
and May 1536 (xcii); to the fall of Thomas Cromwell, Wyatt's
chief benefactor, in the summer of 1540 (clxxiii); and (in the
double sonnet clxxv) to yet another period under arrest
in 1541. With this marked change of subject-matter the last
obligations to Petrarch's verse-form were ended, and a search
began for an entirely independent rhyme-scheme. Obviously
the device of verbal repetition, successful in an occasional sonnet like 'To Rayle or geste', would not do for standard use.
The new method came to hand, it would seem, by a somewhat
roundabout route, through experience of the short epigram or
strambotto, popular in fifteenth-century Italy. Its stress upon
wit and poise was congenial to Wyatt, and he frequently
adopted this form with its pattern of six alternating rhymes
followed by a couplet (*ababab,cc*). Twice he had tried, without
success, to adapt its subject-matter to his sonnets.[2] Then came
the discovery that his dissatisfaction with the Italian sonnet
rhyme-scheme and his interest in the epigram were really two
sides of the same problem. To extend the alternating rhyme-
scheme of the eight-line epigram through a fourteen-line sonnet made for formlessness,[3] but it might add pungency in the
sestet, which already ended with a couplet.

'You that in love finde lucke' (xcii) takes up a traditional

1. Muir, lxxix, xcii, and xcv (MS. Egerton), clxxiii and clxxv (MS.
Arundel).
2. In an early sonnet, 'My hert I gave the' (Muir xiv) Wyatt rather
clumsily converted two of Serafino's *strambotti* into English. Again, 'Vn-
stable dreme' (lxxix) expands a single *strambotto* of Filosseno into a very
prolix and confused English sonnet.
3. 'Such is the course' (clxxxiv) might have exemplified such an attempt, with its alternating rhyme *wrought : sought, stynges : thinges*, carried
on for twelve lines. But this sonnet appears only in Tottel's printed collection and its style is not very like Wyatt's. For its resemblance to two of
Surrey's sonnets, see *infra*, p. 42, note 1; p. 45, note.

theme: the sufferings of the solitary lover amid the universal gaiety of the May season. Scores of medieval lyrics had told the tale, but here the stress was laid rather on Wyatt's highly personal reflections. After contrasting the two aspects of the theme —May as a time of happiness for lovers, and of sorrow for the poet—he introduced some quite extraneous material in the sestet:

> In May my welth and eke my liff, I say,
> Have stonde so oft in such perplexitie:

The truth of the matter was that Wyatt had twice been imprisoned owing to the intrigues of the court, in May 1534 and in May 1536, and apparently ran the same risk again. Behind the conventional façade of a lover's lament—'oon whom love list litil to avaunce'—he was seeking to express his sterner anxieties as a Tudor politician. Here in the sestet for the first time the rhyme-scheme was patterned upon that of the epigram, with alternating rhymes followed by a couplet (*cdcd,ee*); and the innovation was repeated in the next two sonnets.

'If waker care' (xcv) ostensibly celebrated a change of mistresses, but its real theme was a veiled comment on the king's marriages as they affected Wyatt's position at court. A deleted version of line 8—

> Her that ded set our country in a rore—

no doubt referred to Anne Boleyn. Wyatt was of the Protestant party and enjoyed high favour while Anne's successor, Jane Seymour, was on the throne. Added to which there was a touch of grim humour in the last lines:

> My hert alone wel worthie she doth staye,
> Without whose helpe skant do I live a daye.

Wyatt's life very literally depended on the whims of Henry and his queens, and a good deal more was implied than a conventional compliment.

Unhappily for all concerned, Cromwell's venture in matchmaking after the death of Jane Seymour proved a failure. The subject of CLXXIII was the fall of the great minister as a consequence of Henry's recoil from Anne of Cleves, and expressed the poet's well-grounded fears of becoming himself involved in his patron's disgrace. A Petrarchan model was chosen, but the force of personal emotion was too strong to be kept within its bounds. In effect a completely new sonnet emerged. Petrarch, lamenting the double loss of his friend Colonna, and his beloved Laura,[1] had opened the sonnet with the symbolical cry:

> *Rotta è l'alta colonna e 'l verde lauro.*[2]

The 'laurel' had no significance for Wyatt, and the play on the name Colonna was irrelevant to his occasion: instead he rewrote the line as:

> The piller pearisht is whearto I lent

and altered the next line in keeping. Classical allusions likewise failed to interest the Englishman bewailing his political reverse: *Dal Borea a l'Austro* became simply 'Ffrom East to West'. The second quatrain was largely Wyatt's own. It was not so much Cromwell's execution that grieved him as the prospect of his own imminent downfall. So determined was he to be true to his feelings that he even changed *humidi gli occhi* in line 11 of the Italian to 'my penne in playnt'; for who could honestly say that he wept for Cromwell? Finally, the last lines, a meditation on the mutability of life,[3] were superseded by a crescendo of private grief:

> My mynde in woe, my bodye full of smart,
> And I my self, my self alwayes to hate,
> Till dreadfull death do ease my dolefull state.

The stimulus of acute feeling, and the artist's evident sincerity, make this sonnet one of Wyatt's best. He had indeed travelled far since his first crude efforts at translation some twenty years before.

'The flamyng sighes' (CLXXV) brings us to the end of Wyatt's development. This double sonnet was an impassioned protest against his imprisonment once again, with the confiscation of all his property, on trumped-up charges of treason made after the execution of Cromwell:

1. *Sonetto in Morte* 11.
2. 'Broken is the high column and the green laurel' (i.e., Colonna, Laura).
3.   *Oh nostra vita ch'è si bella in vista,*
        Com' perde agevolmente in un mattino
        Qual che 'n molti anni a gran pena s'acquista!

And whear as you in weightie matters great
    Of ffortune saw the shadow that you know,
    Ffor trifling thinges I now am stryken soo . . .

The emotion rings incomparably more true here than in the
early attempts to reproduce romance ardours. There is also a
further development in the sonnet form. Keeping throughout
to the Italian rhyme-pattern for quatrains, Wyatt introduced
an independent set of variants within each quatrain unit,
resulting in the arrangement *abba,cddc,effe,gg*. Again the result
was imperfect, and the burning sincerity of the poem cannot
make up for the awkwardness of some lines, due probably to
their conformity with an unsuitable rhyme-pattern in the
quatrains themselves.[1] In any case the vehemence of the
second part of this double sonnet, which broke down the inner
verse barriers, was out of keeping with so disciplined a
medium.

To complete his formal experiments, Wyatt had only to
combine the rhyme-scheme of his new sestet with the separate
rhyme-units of the quatrains in CLXXV. A form would then
have been evolved with all the desired qualities of flexibility
and lucidity. Had he lived, he would almost certainly have discovered this for himself in the course of his next sonnet or two.
But CLXXV was, by all indications, Wyatt's last. In the following year, at the early age of thirty-nine, he died, leaving
the final shape of the sonnet to be determined by his younger
contemporary Surrey.

Wyatt's outstanding characteristic, regarded from a formal
viewpoint, was his unceasing readiness to experiment, his
desire to explore all the possibilities of a chosen medium. We
may see his work in the sonnet as falling into three periods: the
early phase, when he was groping his way laboriously towards a suitable form; the middle period, to which belong his
mature and highly distinctive love sonnets; and the final
phase, when his interest in love had declined and the excite-
ments of public life took its place as a theme for personal
poetry. In the first period he succeeded in escaping from the

1. For instance, line 4: 'The payne thearof, the greef, and all the rest';
line 12: 'But for all this no force, it dothe no harme'.

morass of fifteenth-century narrative versification and laid the groundwork of Elizabethan lyrical technique. The admirable love sonnets which followed were, historically regarded, the first shoots of the new kind of poetry which attained its full stature in the last years of the sixteenth century. Wyatt's final phase of experimentation virtually established the standard sonnet-form employed by Surrey, which Shakespeare and his contemporaries were to adopt as an ideally suitable instrument.

But Wyatt was, it should now be clear, something more than a praiseworthy technician, a text-book paragon. He was, without any qualifications at all, a true poet. All these formal achievements sprang from the powerful initial impulse which drove him to seek original expression. A man of the new age, he was intensely responsive to the times in which he lived—the hectic, assertive, perilous times of the early Tudors. 'Chance' was one of Wyatt's favourite words; Chance was perhaps his presiding deity; but personal dignity also counted for much. It was the only stance that remained ultimately valid, whether one's mistress proved faithless or one's friends became estranged; whether one's benefactor fell from power or one's own head was in peril. Such was the conception that inspired Wyatt's sonnets; and it was a necessary consequence that in writing them the Petrarchan vision of life and of love should be rejected, together with the verse-form through which it was made manifest. If the stages by which the English sonnet replaced it make a pattern in retrospect, this does not mean that Wyatt himself followed any planned or foreseeable course. The aptest description of his methods of work remains that of Saintsbury:

> We seem to be looking from afar at a man walking or running over a course beset with all sorts of visible stumbling-blocks and invisible snares, into which and over which he is perpetually stumbling and tumbling, yet picking himself up and pressing on towards the goal.[1]

There were always fresh difficulties and fresh solutions. But at the end of his short life Wyatt had shown how a Renaissance form devised to express complex personal experience could be adapted to the traditions of his own nation and the outlook of

1. *Hist. Eng. Prosody*, vol. 1, p. 305.

c*

his age. Such an achievement sufficiently vindicates his right to rank as one of the pioneers of Elizabethan poetry, and supports the claim of these sonnets, not to a 'text-book glory', but to the sympathy of all who find pleasure in verse.

III

SURREY

BROUGHT up in childhood with the king's son, Henry Howard, Earl of Surrey, received an excellent grounding in classical and Renaissance literature, travelled on the Continent, and was for a time attached to the brilliant court of Francis I. But fortune soon turned against him, and his adult life was filled with anxiety and tumult. The greater part of his twenties was passed in fighting a series of military campaigns that were unsuccessful or inglorious through the faults of others. He suffered spells of imprisonment, once at Windsor, where he had known his happiest moments. Finally at the age of thirty-one, disappointed, embittered, and old for his years, he was executed on the scaffold under charges for which he might have been spared had Henry VIII died a few days sooner. Inevitably such a career left its mark upon his writing. Even in youth he tended towards a ruminative cast of mind, and the tendency must have been deepened by the experiences of later life. This outlook resulted in a distinctive approach to verse composition which, in the medium of the sonnet, was to have significance for all the poets of the Elizabethan age.

It is unlikely that Surrey will again be as highly rated as he was in the eighteenth century, when it was customary to praise his facility of versification to the detriment of Wyatt's more rugged style. This evaluation owed much to the habit, initiated by Tottel in his *Songes and Sonnettes*, of presenting Wyatt and Surrey as literary twins, without regard to Wyatt's seniority and his acknowledged position as Surrey's master in versecraft. More careful scholarship, together with a change in taste, has now reversed the balance of judgement. There is actually a danger today of Surrey's individual gifts being overlooked and of his being written off as a mere fashioner of smooth metres. This view over-simplifies the character of his poetry and fails to explain its far-reaching influence.

Wyatt has suffered much from the critical habit of setting up a contrast between his light lyrics, praised as genuine poetry, and the sonnets, generally dismissed as 'literary exercises'. No such contrast has been applied to the work of Surrey, whose lyrics are for the most part awkward and uninteresting. But it must be owned that amongst the sonnets themselves two incompatible approaches to writing may be distinguished. One is that of the industrious but uninspired craftsman, imitating the technical devices of Wyatt with certain improvements, and like him undergoing a phase of apprenticeship to the Italians. The other is the approach of a genuine poet whose verse, though without any temperamental brilliance, yet has an appeal of its own. In all the sonnets ostensibly concerned with love, Surrey is either experimenting quite cold-bloodedly with verse technique; or else he is using his Italian model as a mere spring-board for his own reflections, which really have nothing to do with the thought-patterns of the sonnet. It is only in another—and almost certainly later—group of his sonnet compositions, not relating to sexual love at all, that we find a true and satisfying interplay of form and subject-matter.

The first need is to come to grips with Surrey's individuality as a poet; otherwise his technical experiments will seem to be meaningless. The method of close comparison between particular poems and their models, applied to Wyatt's sonnets in the last chapter, will serve here likewise. By way of example we may take the first sonnet in Padelford's edition.[1] Whether or not it is chronologically Surrey's first, it shows very clearly his opening position when faced with the problem of making an English sonnet out of an Italian one. There is the further advantage that its original displays Petrarch in his most characteristic style.

SURREY (I)

PETRARCH (*Sonetto in Vita* CXIII(

Alas! so all thinges nowe doe
   holde their peace:
Heauen and earth disturbed in
   nothing;
The beastes, the ayer, the birdes
   their song doe cease;

Or, che 'l ciel, e la terra, e 'l vento
   tace,
E le fere, e gli augelli il sonno
   affrena,
Notte il carro stellato in giro
   mena,

1. *The Poems of Henry Howard, Earl of Surrey.* Edited F. M. Padelford (Washington 1928, revised edition). Quotations from Surrey and number references follow this text.

The nightes chare the starres
aboute dothe bring.
Calme is the sea, the waues worke
lesse and lesse;
So am not I, whom loue, alas!
doth wring,
Bringing before my face the
great encrease
Of my desires, whereat I wepe
and syng,
In ioye and wo, as in a doubtful
ease:
For my swete thoughtes some-
tyme doe pleasure bring,
But, by and by, the cause of my
disease
Geues me a pang that inwardly
dothe sting,
When that I thinke what griefe
it is againe
To liue and lacke the thing
should ridde my paine.

*E nel suo letto il mar senz'onda
giace;*
*Vegghio, penso, ardo, piango; e
chi mi sface,*
*Sempre m'è inanzi per mia
dolce pena:*
*Guerra è 'l mio stato, d'ira e di
duol piena;*
*E sol di lei pensando ho qualche
pace.*
*Così sol d'una chiara fonte
viva*
*Move 'l dolce e l'amaro, ond'io
mi pasco;*
*Una man sola mi risana e
punge.*
*E perché 'l mio martir non giunga
a riva,*
*Mille volte il dì moro, e mille
nasco;*
*Tanto da la salute mia son
lunge.*

The differences between the original and the English rendering become ever more pronounced as the two sonnets proceed, but they are seen in significant details from the beginning. Petrarch commences with various signs of the night's
oncoming: the silence of earth and air, the sleep of birds and
beasts, passing from these to a more sweeping vision of the
great chariot of stars and the expanse of tranquil sea. Surrey,
on the other hand, opens his poem with a general statement—
'So all thinges nowe doe holde their peace', and descends from
this to particulars. The effect is to convert a flow of apprehen-
sions imaginatively fused into a chain of observations logically
linked. The reasons for this change, which necessitated five
lines of natural description for the original four, appear when
the imagery is examined. Petrarch's second line, in mentioning
the wild creatures, speaks of them as being curbed by sleep; his
fourth, in referring to the sea, pictures it as lying motionless
upon its bed. Both images have human application and point
to an identity of experience for men and things; neither of them
arises from direct observation—since the beasts and birds

disappear from view at nightfall, and the sea-bed is at all times hidden. Here, almost unconsciously revealed, is the very essence of Petrarch's thought-process, his conviction of an inherent sympathy between man and nature; and here precisely Surrey makes his innovations. He substitutes the cessation of bird song for the advent of sleep because the impression comes from his sense of hearing, and in the description of a scene, things heard, seen, touched, and smelled—the knowledge derived from the senses—must predominate. By so doing he changes the construction of the line; for animals neither sing nor refrain from singing, and he is forced to employ a rather clumsy phrase to include them in the poem: 'The beastes, the ayer, the birdes their song doe cease'. Again in line 5, corresponding to line 4 in the Italian, he omits to mention the sea's bed, of which he has no sensory knowledge, and alters an instantly apprehended condition—*il mar senz'onda giace*—into a gradually observed process—'the waues worke lesse and lesse'.[1] Surrey's cast of mind has thus transformed the whole poetic treatment in the English version. His approach to impersonal nature does not lead to an imaginative identification. It is that of the detached onlooker, who delights to describe a scene without feeling personally involved therein. The observations are clear, precise, and sensitively chosen: but their merits belong to the class of descriptive poetry and not to the sonnet.

In the second part of Petrarch's octave the poet's subjective turmoil is contrasted with the calm of the outside world. The perplexing emotions directly evoked by his situation are set forth as they arise. *Vegghio, penso, ardo, piango* . . . he sees; thinks; burns; and weeps. No causative links are attached to what is actually an unbroken flow of intuitive response: sight provokes thought, thought changes into suffering, suffering finds vent in tears. Only after this condition has been set forth

1. Cf. E. M. W. Tillyard, *The English Renaissance: Fact or Fiction?* (Cambridge 1952): 'Surrey alters Petrarch with startling effect. First, he expands Petrarch's description by one line, and second he alters Petrarch's simple statement that the sea lies in its bed, waveless, to "calm is the sea, the waves work less and less". Now the last phrase is a wonderful rendering of a piece of sheer, detached, natural observation. . . And the touch is gratuitous; it does not correspond to any statement that, on the contrary, the passions in the lover's heart are beginning to increase in violence.' (p. 57.)

in words does its origin become explicit: *e chi mi sface Sempre m'è inanzi per mia dolce pena*.[1] The rest of the octave is a development of the personal theme. The poet's state is contradictory: his grief arises from love, yet it is only love that can dissipate his grief. From this realization springs a superb new metaphor in the sestet:

> *Così sol d'una chiara fonte viva*
> *move 'l dolce e l'amaro, ond'io mi pasco*[2]

where again Petrarch turns to the outer world for an expression of his inner condition; and the final correlation comes in the last three lines: *Mille volte il dì moro, e mille nasco*.[3]

Surrey throughout his rendering of this portion of the sonnet feels the need to supply logical comments binding statement to statement. The calm of the sea is directly contrasted with his own state of mind by the phrase 'So am not I', and in the account of his changing moods he proceeds from one stage to the next by reasoned exposition: '*whereat* I wepe and syng . . .' '*For* my sweete thoughtes' '*But*, by and by . . .' '*When that* I thinke. . .' Throughout the rest of the poem he expounds, explains, and rationally investigates his condition. *Chi mi sface* becomes 'the cause of my disease'; a diagnosis rather than a reproach. The affliction of love, as much physical as mental, which Petrarch expressed in one fierce word *punge*, is carefully redefined as 'a pang that inwardly dothe sting'. The Italian conclusion with its emotional hyperbole—*Mille volte il dì moro, e mille nasco*'—becomes in the English couplet a measured statement of the most important part of Surrey's findings—

> When that I thinke what griefe it is againe
> To liue and lacke the thing should ridde my paine.

Evidently while Petrarch finds peace *sol di lei pensando*, only by thinking of his lady, Surrey finds it by thinking of his own thoughts. His treatments of nature and of personality run on parallel lines; in both, his concern is to make exact observations and produce an objective report. Like parallel lines the

1. 'and that which is my undoing is ever within me through my sweet pain'.
2. 'Thus from a clear, fresh spring proceeds the sweet and the bitter upon which I feed'.
3. 'A thousand times a day I die, and a thousand times am born'.

two approaches never meet and are only bridged by logical constructions. Consequently there is no place in the English sonnet for the Petrarchan metaphor of the spring with sweet and bitter waters, and all reference to it is omitted.

Surrey's rhyme-scheme is probably taken from the epigram pattern of alternation. Wyatt had already adopted this in the sestet of some of his later sonnets, but here it is extended to apply to the whole poem.[1] It is true that the monotony and formlessness of a single alternating rhyme is modified by the introduction of half-rhymes, as *peace – cease, lesse – encrease, ease – disease*. But essentially the pattern is *abab* . . . for three quatrains. The effect is to weaken the quatrain units; and this exactly reflected Surrey's way of writing. His descriptive technique has expanded the first four lines in Petrarch to five lines of English, with the result that his second quatrain in turn overflows into the third. Moreover the discarding of the fountain metaphor eliminates a clear break between octave and sestet, and the flow of exposition is unimpeded to the very end of the sonnet. To Wyatt's versification Surrey owed the easy flow of his metre and the simplicity of his diction: his own contribution was to produce a form bordering on the descriptive or narrative verse paragraph, and far too shapeless for the sonnet.

This tendency, both in subject-matter and form, appears again in Surrey's well-known and much anthologized 'The soote season', an attractive piece of descriptive verse which was suggested by one of Petrarch's great sonnets, *Zefiro torna*, composed after the death of Laura. F. M. Padelford in his edition makes the following comparison:

> Petrarch's spring is typically Italian with its smiling plains and serene sky, and Zephyrus and Venus are introduced as in the beautiful spring pieces of Botticelli. Surrey's sonnet is as typically English with its green-clad hills and dales, its blossoming hedgerows and shady streams.[2]

However, the difference is not merely such as one might expect

1. It is possible that Wyatt completely anticipated Surrey's rhyme-scheme in the sonnet 'Such is the course' (Muir CLXXXIV). But for reasons already mentioned, I think it is unsafe to press this claim (*supra*, p. 31, note 3).
2. Padelford, p. 207.

to find in two passages of description, one concerned with a southern, the other with a northern spring. Petrarch's landscape was wholly visionary: it arose from an imaginative conception of life quite alien to Surrey. For the Italian poet, nature and spirit were alike rejuvenated in the new season. The western wind, personified as Zephyr, led out his family of herbs and flowers; the swallow and nightingale, as Procne and Philomela, were metamorphosed human beings eternally reliving their story of primitive desire; the meadows smiled, the sky took comfort; while Jove and his daughter, the ancient pagan deities, came forth rejoicing to preside over the year's rebirth. Mortals who were privileged to assist at this festival found themselves in an enchanted world where each element, every creature, shared their emotions and called upon them to enact the rites of love:

> L'aria e l'acqua e la terra è d'amor piena;
> Ogni animal d'amar si riconsiglia.[1]

Such was the happy land of Petrarch's vision; his grief arose from his inability to enter it. For Laura by dying had taken up to heaven the keys which unlocked its gates, and her lover was shut out for the rest of his life on earth. Hence another region of the spirit appeared before his eyes: the terrible desert inhabited by wild and savage beasts, where there was neither spring nor love nor joy.

Surrey's rendering grew from quite another mode of experience. For him the new season simply recurred as an agreeable natural phenomenon. He observed bud and bloom, watched the hills and valleys turn green, and heard the singing of birds. But he did not for a moment attribute to these sights and sounds anything but a strictly impersonal character. Spring for Petrarch appeared in the hues of a woman's complexion: it was *candida e vermiglia*, fresh and vermilion: Surrey chose the most obvious visual aspect of the season, its verdure, as the backcloth of the scene. In his stage setting the nightingale's part was not to speak with the accents of Philomela, but to display herself in new feathers; and although the turtle-dove, who took the place of Procne, was represented as talking to her

1. 'The air and the water and the land are full of love; every creature takes thought of loving.'

mate, the allusion was deprived of pagan associations by its echoes of the biblical Song of Solomon. Petrarch had unfolded, in the latter part of his octave, the amorous implications of spring for all creatures, under the patronage of the goddess of love. Not a word of this passed into Surrey's version, which instead went on to describe in detail the brisker, more business-like occupations of wild life in England:

> The hart hath hong his olde hed on the pale;
> The buck in brake his winter cote he flings;
> The fishes flote with newe repaired scale;
> The adder all her sloughe awaye she slinges;
> The swift swallow pursueth the flyes smale;
> The busy bee her honye now she minges.

Sympathy between mankind and the other creatures is limited to these healthy, extraverted activities; it does not extend to human love or animal mating, and no close identification between nature and spirit is implied. Accordingly no metaphor can come into being at any place in the sonnet, and it is not easy to find even a logical connection between the theme of the poem and a lover's mental state. The title in Tottel's edition— 'Description of Spring, wherein eche thing renewes, saue one-lie the louer'—assumes the conventional romance link; but in the sonnet itself, even in the final couplet where Surrey mentions his own reactions, it is not functionally present. The poet's sorrows amid 'these pleasant things' might proceed from any cause at all: he might have been laid up in bed by sickness, or kept at work in the City. No serious treatment of personal experience has thus developed out of Surrey's description of spring; it reaches as far as, and no further than, the active, observant man's response to the new season. This does not mean that the poem is unattractive or without beauty: it does signify that the poem shares the virtues and limitations of 'Alas, so all thinges nowe' in belonging essentially to a class of descriptive or near-narrative verse.

Had Surrey written verse of this kind only, he would have remained an estimable minor poet, belonging in spirit more to the eighteenth century than to his own day; but his influence upon the future Elizabethan sonnet would have been negligible. It is true that Wyatt also had tended to steer clear of the transcendental view of nature and passionate love that he found in Italian poetry: but he had instead designed a verse-form suited to his own impetuous ego. He had patterned his diction upon the modulations of the speaking voice; he had made rhyme and syntax express his scorn, eagerness, truculence, or whatever mood was called forth by the occasion. Surrey, however, lacked Wyatt's power, perhaps his inclination, to voice intimate experience. As a result the sonnet-form itself, in the two instances I have described, tended to lose shape and dissolve. The rhyme-scheme of 'The soote season' again adopted the epigram pattern of alternating rhymes,[1] but it was simplified so far that even the couplet introduced no variant, while the half-rhyme variants virtually disappeared. A fourteen-line stanza of alternating rhyme thus emerged, with practically no claim to rank as a specimen of sonnet versification.

'The soote season' and 'Alas, so all thinges nowe' are both, indeed, attractive poems, but unsatisfactory sonnets. A reader in our time may remark that he cares little for these formal distinctions, provided that the words on the page give him pleasure. But Surrey himself, by all the evidence, was not contented with this achievement. The sonnet-form itself fascinated him, as it did the late Elizabethans, for all that its thought-processes were baffling. Consciously if obscurely, he must have felt that this medium of self-expression needed to be mastered, so that one day it could be made to serve his purpose. And so, through a series of technical experiments, he worried at the adaptation of various Italian models or themes, caring little for the subject-matter of his sonnets provided that he could attain a formal proficiency.

This aspect of Surrey's writing has a minimal appeal as poetry, and need not be described in detail. But it should not be altogether ignored. There was, first, the problem of a suitable rhyme-scheme, that had not been quite solved by Wyatt. In 'I never saw you, madam, laye aparte', Surrey turned to Wyatt's last sonnet, 'The flamyng sighes', with its well-marked quatrains *abba,cddc*, etc. The rhyme-variations gave a new firmness to the structure, but a slight clumsiness yet re-

1. It may be noticed that this sonnet has the same recurrent rhyme, *brynges – singes*, etc. as Wyatt's sonnet (Muir CLXXXIV). Cf. p. 31, note 3.

mained, due to the use of a pattern in the quatrain which was originally designed for the integral octave. This deficiency was rectified in 'Love that doth raine' by Surrey's one and only significant innovation in rhyme-scheme. He employed the alternating rhymes of 'The soote season', but with a new variant now in each quatrain, concluding with yet another variant in the couplet, viz. *abab,cdcd,efef,gg*. The effect was to permit logical exposition, with its necessary contrasts and appositions, while strictly controlling its development within the limits of three balanced quatrains and ending with a summary in the last two lines. Surrey's model for this sonnet was Petrarch's *Amor, che nel penser mio vive*,[1] which had once served Wyatt's turn in his early work. His own rendering was far closer and more conscientious than in the examples previously described, though there were minor and characteristic changes. The suddenness of love's onset, represented on allegorical lines as the challenge of an armed foe,[2] was paraphrased as

> Clad in the armes wherein with me he fowght,
> Oft in my face he doth his banner rest.

—thus transforming it into a regular occurrence, to be objectively assessed. On the other hand, a certain martial quality was suggested by the abrupt opening stress in these lines; a device to be repeated in a more sincerely felt context. While Petrarch's figure was deprived of its immediacy, the compression induced by the new rhyme-scheme saved it from prolixity; the quatrain units were consistently maintained; and the diction became at once terse and precise.[3] This form, once tried out, showed itself to be exactly what Surrey most needed, and was applied consistently in all later sonnets. Nor, of course, were its virtues confined to Surrey's work only: it became the staple late-Elizabethan sonnet-form, which Shakespeare too was to adopt.

Perhaps the most successful of these technical experiments was 'Set me wheras the sonne dothe perche the grene', which shows marked poise and control. Petrarch's *Pommi ove 'l sole*

1. *Sonetto in Vita* CIX.
2.   *Tal or armato ne la fronte vène,*
                     Ivi si loca et ivi pon sua insegna.
3. Padelford, p. 49, has an acute assessment of this sonnet's formal merits.

occide i fiori[1] was unusually simple in its conception, the object
being merely to list a wide range of contrasted situations in
which the lover's affections would remain constant. The sonnet made up a series of balanced antitheses followed by a
direct and positive statement. Structurally these could easily
be grouped in three quatrains and a couplet, so that the task of
translation was particularly smooth. Surrey learned here to
express apposition and contrast in the simplest words and
shortest phrases. How much he benefited may be seen in the
flexible metre, the unobtrusive alliterative binding, and the
concision of the last quatrain:

> Set me in earthe, in heauen, or yet in hell;
> In hill, in dale, or in the fowming floode;
> Thrawle, or at large, aliue wheresoo I dwell,
> Sicke, or in healthe; in yll fame, or in good...

On the other hand, whenever Surrey attempted to write in the
romance convention without firm supports from his model, he
failed miserably. 'In Cipres' was an ill-advised rendering of
eight lines from Ariosto's *Orlando Furioso*.[2] The compact, fast-
flowing narrative stanza would not bear translation into the
fourteen lines of a sonnet, and Surrey strained to fill up space
with pretentious declamatory stuff:

> A welle so hote that who so tastes the same,
> Were he of stone, as thawed yse shuld melt,
> And kindled fynde his brest with secret flame;
> Whose moist poison dissolued hath my hate.
> This creeping fire ... etc.

With so little sense to support so many words, the scaffolding
of the new form broke down, and Ariosto's sharply defined
contrasts were smothered in a rubble of verbiage. Again, in
'The fansy which that I haue serued long', Surrey tried to express his homesickness whilst engaged in military operations

1. *Sonetto in Vita* xcv.
2.   *E questo hanno causato due fontane*
                       Che di diverso effetto hanno liquore,
                       Ambe in Ardenna, e non sono lontane:
                       D'amoroso disio l'una empie il cuore;
                       Chi bee dell'altra senza amor rimane,
                       E volge tutto in ghiaccio il primo ardore.
                       Rinaldo gustò d'una, e amor lo strugge;
                       Angelica dell'altra, e l'odia e fugge. (i, 78)

at Boulogne, but dressed up his feelings in the guise of a lover's lament. Writing without a direct model, his conceit was tenuous and ill-managed, and the poem soon turned into a diffuse account of thoughts and actions which broke through the quatrain divisions and was only brought to a halt in fourteen lines by the stringent brake of a triple rhyme.

How far Surrey was aware of the cause of these failures one cannot say; but in a late group of his sonnets he abandoned completely the subject of romantic love. These poems, which, strangely enough, have received very little attention, contain much of Surrey's best and most characteristic writing.[1] They are addressed to a noble lady; to Wyatt as tribute from a brother-poet whose admiration overcame his political and religious antipathies; to a comrade-in-arms who had been killed in a siege while saving the poet's life; and (under a historical fiction) to the monarch who was to bring about the disgrace of the Howards and, eventually, Surrey's own death. Such themes introduced a new type of sonnet content which derived its strength not from intensity of subjective feeling, nor from imaginative range, but from Surrey's capacity to set forth clearly and boldly the experiences of man in the social sphere. The relations between a poet and his colleague, a commander and his junior officer, a nobleman and his king, called forth a new order of perceptions and modes of expression. Public life with its daily contacts between man and man in political, military, and literary activity was Surrey's true field, where he applied exact observation and shrewd judgement.[2] Accordingly he fashioned the sonnet into a medium for pointed satire, apt eulogy, concise aphorism, and powerful invective.

In this group of sonnets the early trends of Surrey's experimental work reach their full development. His distrust of Petrarchan idealizations leads on to a positive and contemporary form of praise in 'From Tuscan cam my ladies worthi race'. Here Lady Geraldine's merits are seen as a product of her royal lineage and careful education:

1. Padelford xxix, xxx, xxxviii, xl, xliv, xlv, and xlvii belong to this group.
2. The expression of such interests in narrative form resulted in the translation of two books of the *Aeneid* into quite workmanlike blank verse.

Ffostred she was with mylke of Irishe brest;
Her syer an erle, hir dame of princes bloud;
From tender yeres in Britaine she doth rest,
With a kinges child, where she tastes gostly foode. (xxix)

For an English earl of the sixteenth century such advantages
no doubt carried more solid weight than all the transcendent
glory of Madonna Laura; but it required some boldness to
admit as much in sonnet form. As for Petrarch's vision of a
being who comprehended in her person both natural and celes-
tial perfection, this was shrunk to a neat aphorism that summed up all the right-minded sentiments of the poem:

Bewty of kind, her vertues from aboue,
Happy ys he that may obtaine her loue.

There is a similar continuity of development in the uses to
which Surrey put his knowledge of verse technique. In 'Set me
wheras the sonne dothe perche the grene' (vi) he had learned
how to balance antitheses in the smallest possible space:

Set me in base, or yet in highe degree;
In the long night, or in the shortyst day;
In clere weather, or whear mysts thickest be;
In lofte yowthe, or when my heares be grey . . .

The fierce, sustained invective of 'Th' Assyryans King' (xl),
directed covertly against Henry VIII, showed the practical
application of these lessons:

The dent of swordes from kysses semed straunge,
And harder then hys ladyes syde his targe;
From glotton feastes to sowldyer's fare a chaunge;
His helmet, far aboue a garlandes charge.

Again, the use of the strong opening stress in 'Love that doth
raine' was repeated with greater power and audacity in this
same sonnet:

Drenched in slouthe and womanishe delight,
Ffeble of sprete, vnpacyent of payne,
When he hadd lost his honour and hys right,—
Prowde, tyme of welthe, in stormes appawld with drede,—
Murdred hym self to shew some manfull dede.

By similar methods a clang of steel was brought into the opening lines of an epitaph to Surrey's soldier comrade:

Norfolk sprang thee, Lambeth holds thee dead,
Clare, of the County of Cleremont, though hight.   (XLVII)

Such writing anticipates not so much the major poetry of the
Elizabethans as that of the Augustans. Surrey's mental processes curiously resembled theirs, and if Wyatt initiates the
'line of wit', Surrey is the first to write 'polite' verse as the
eighteenth century understood the term. Yet it would be wrong
to dismiss his achievement as irrelevant to its age, or to narrow
it down to the mere formal invention of a staple rhyme-
scheme for the sonnet. Wyatt's experiments had so closely
approximated to this that Surrey's one innovation was in any
case almost inevitable. His own distinctive contribution was
to give the English sonnet a flexibility which made it serve the
needs of many poets in widely different circumstances.

Surrey's cast of mind had led him to deviate, not only from
Petrarchan romance attitudes, but also from the introspective, traditionally English, conception of love. Instead he had
learned to develop a medium whose chief merits were simplicity, elegance, concision, and all-pervading lucidity. It
could be put to a variety of uses, some quite unforeseen by its
inventor, for it gave point to the lightest of themes and clarity
to the most profound. For all who were capable of objectivity
in their response to personal experience, this medium, with its
logic of apposition, contrast, and final correlation, supplied a
perfect instrument. This is not to say, however, that the Surrey
sonnet-form immediately showed its potentialities. While
minor versifiers, whose emotions were never deeply involved
in their writing, copied it gladly, the major poets Sidney and
Spenser practised it only as a discipline in their early work.
Faced with complex subjective experience and wide moral
issues, these two writers developed their individual modifications of the sonnet. But it was in the last decade of the sixteenth
century, with a momentous shift in the intellectual outlook of
the age, that Surrey's sonnet pattern came truly into its own.
During these years it became, for reasons that we shall have to
consider in a later chapter, the indispensable medium of Drayton, Daniel, and Shakespeare; with the result that to this day
the character of the English sonnet bears Surrey's prototypal
stamp.

IV

SIDNEY

OVER thirty years elapsed between Surrey's execution in 1546 and the great Elizabethan revival of poetry. The times were unsettled and the two most talented Tudor poets had died in early manhood, leaving no worthy successors. Nevertheless the technical foundations which they had laid were to survive. Wyatt and Surrey's lyrical verse was made available to the reading public in Tottel's famous anthology, which went through five editions between 1557 and 1578 and exercised its influence upon English poetry to the end of the century. A few sonnets by other authors were included in the same anthology, eight of them following the rhyme-scheme characteristic of Surrey. In 1572 Gascoigne's *Sundrie Flowers* presented thirty-three sonnets, all but three adopting Surrey's form. So also did two of the three sonnets in a fresh anthology entitled *A Gorgious Gallery of Gallant Inventions* (1578). These compositions are listed rather as evidence of a continuity of technique between the early Tudors and the Elizabethans than for their literary merits. In all they made up a very slender store, and none had, to borrow Sidney's phrase, 'poetical sinews in them'. The true advance began only with the writers of the new generation, of whom Sidney was the first to bring the English sonnet to maturity.

The first poems we have of Sidney are interspersed in the prose text of his *Arcadia*, probably written in the early 1580s during a period of retirement from court. The leisurely narrative, modelled upon that of similar works by Sannazaro and Montemayor, offered ample scope for the insertion of new verse. Most of the poems were of the class known to the Elizabethans as 'songs and sonets'—that is, English variations on *rondeaux*, epigrams, and sonnets, of anything between six and eighteen lines in length; but nineteen may be described as sonnets proper.[1] For the most part they reproduce conventional

1. *Arcadia*, ed. Feuillerat, vol. I, pp. 21, 76, 147, 149, 253; vol. II, pp. 8 ('Since that the stormy rage', 'Harke plaintfull ghostes'), 9, 17, 24, 26, 32, 39, 42, 53, 55, 70, 91, 166.

treatments of conventional themes: they describe the conflict of eyes, heart, and reason, copy rather laboriously an Italian parody of Petrarchan similes,[1] and make some rather trite invocations to night, sleep, and time. Addressed to no particular person and written out of no depth of experience, such poems may be regarded primarily as experiments in metre and versification. Their main interest lies in the quick grasp they show of the rudiments of sonnet construction. Some freakish forms are tried out, such as quatorzains with rhyming couplets and hexameters,[2] or with a single rhyme throughout,[3] or identically rhyming quatrains;[4] but the Surrey pattern is the commonest and is generally put to good use. Once its virtues are thoroughly absorbed, Sidney enters upon mature composition. 'My true love hath my hart',[5] for its grace and finish, has rightly gained a place in most Elizabethan anthologies; and an equally good case could be made for the inclusion of 'Who doth desire that chaste his wife should be'.[6] Its sestet is an example of Sidney's early style at its best:

> As farre from want, as farre from vaine expence,
> (The one doth force, the later doth entise)
> Allow good company, but kepe from thence
> Al filthy mouth's that glory in their vice.
>   This done, thou hast no more, but leave the rest
>   To vertue, fortune, time and womans brest.

Here the possibilities of the new Surrey form are quite brilliantly exploited: there is wit, economy, simplicity, and balance. Noteworthy is the use of the couplet, whose epigrammatic qualities drive home a very English and un-Petrarchan conclusion. Its moral is almost a corollary to Wyatt's 'But let it passe and think it is of kinde, That often chaunge doeth plese a woman's minde'; and the underlying sentiment has a long poetic history.

The *Arcadia* sonnets show Sidney in his earlier work following in the steps of Wyatt and Surrey. Like them, he gradually learned to replace Petrarchan and *Quattrocento* attitudes by

1. Feuillerat, I. 21. Janet G. Scott in *Les Sonnets Elisabethains* (Paris 1929), traces the source of this poem to Berni's Sonnet II (*Sopra la bellezza della sua innamorata*) containing such phrases as *occhi di perle vaghi, luci torte, labbra di latte, bocca ampia celeste* (p. 17, note).
2. I, p. 21.   3. II, p. 9.   4. II, p. 39.   5. II, p. 17.   6. II, p. 70.

traditional English considerations; like them, too, he had
little regard for 'inkhorn terms' and imported phrases, but
chose rather the plainest English words in current use. Yet
there were symptoms in these poems of an incalculable future.
The very ease with which Tudor sonnet technique had been
mastered suggested the likelihood of a far more complex development. Moreover, Sidney had still not spoken in his proper
person. All his poems so far had been assigned to the tenuously
conceived inhabitants of Arcadia. It was only with some new
crystallization of experience, some further accretion of poetic
power, that he came to use the sonnet as an instrument of self-
expression.

Sidney's *Astrophel and Stella*, published without authority in
1591 and re-issued with many corrections in 1598, was universally acclaimed by readers of the time. Here at last was a
true English sonnet sequence, fit to rank with the most celebrated works from Italy and France. A sustained, well-knit
collection of 108 sonnets, accompanied by eleven lyrics, told
the story of a modern love affair in all its phases. Characterized
by a blend of wit and sensibility, of intellectual brilliance and
temperamental ardour, *Astrophel and Stella* was a literary
triumph of the new age. But more compelling than its intrinsic
literary appeal was the special fascination of Sidney's unique
personality. The poems, in their directness and spontaneity,
seemed to stand as the intimate record of a man known personally to hundreds and admired by the whole nation. From
beginning to end Sidney proclaimed the sincerity of his passion and the inspired originality of his verse.

> For me in sooth, no Muse but one I know:
> Phrases and Problemes from my reach do grow,
> And strange things cost too deare for my poore sprites. (III)[1]

> For nothing from my wit or will doth flow,
> Since all my words thy beauty doth endite,
> And love doth hold my hand, and makes me write. (XC)

He had long studied other writers in the hope of learning from

---

1. The text of quotations from *Astrophel and Stella* follows Mona Wilson's
edition (1931), based mainly upon the 1598 Folio. Departures from this
are specifically indicated.

them fit means to express his devotion; but all in vain. At last, when verging upon despair, he had found out the way:

> Biting my trewand pen, beating my selfe for spite,
> Foole, said my Muse to me, looke in thy heart and write. (1)

The vivid description of a mood familiar to every author seemed to ring with conviction. On the face of it, *Astrophel and Stella* was the most spontaneous and original creation of a poet in love that England had ever seen. Its appeal survived through generations of changing tastes and new fashions in verse until well on into the nineteenth century.

With the advent of 'historical' criticism, however, these assumptions, and with them Sidney's reputation as a poet, suffered a grave challenge. Literary historians and biographers pointed out that the impassioned Astrophel enjoyed, by all reports, a placid married life, while the chaste Stella of his poems, Lady Penelope Rich, was to figure in a divorce case, to marry twice, and to be viewed with some disapproval by her more strictly principled contemporaries. Meanwhile students of comparative literature found sources for the sonnets in French, Italian, and Neo-Classical poetry which seemed to destroy much of their 'inspired' character. Emil Koeppel in 1890[1] drew attention to the marked physical resemblance between Stella and Petrarch's Laura. The terms in which Sidney praised her features, her complexion, and her voice were borrowed from Petrarch and his numerous followers. Even circumstantial-sounding details of the romance had already been mentioned by poets long dead. If Astrophel remembered an excursion on the Thames when the breeze blew through Stella's hair, Petrarch had recalled Laura's voyage down the Rhône—and played upon the name of his beloved, which, as *l'aura*, signified breezes. Astrophel had been envious, on one occasion, of his mistress's lap-dog: oddly enough, Serafino a century before had expressed the same envy. Sidney's invocations to sleep, dreams, and to his bed could be matched in numerous French and Italian love-poems; his very turns of speech, his play on words, his rhetorical devices, were taken from the stock diction of the period. After Koeppel came Sid-

1. E. Koeppel, '*Studien zur Geschichte des englischen Petrarkismus im sechzehnten Jahrhundert*', *Romanische Forschungen* (1890), v. 65–98.

ney Lee,[1] with examples of the influence of *Pléiade* poets; and in our own day Janet G. Scott[2] and L. C. John[3] have supplied a greatly extended list of French, Italian, Neo-Latin, Latin, and Greek analogues.

These findings at first seriously shocked many scholars who had grown up, it would seem, with a literal faith in Sidney's repeated claims to originality and sincerity. Lee's righteous scorn at the 'thefts' he had uncovered is a curious illustration of critical methods half a century ago.

> Detachment from the realities of ordinary passion, which comes of much reading about love in order to write on the subject, is the central feature of Sidney's sonnets. His admirers dubbed him 'our English Petrarch' or 'the Petrarch of our time'. His habit was to paraphrase and adapt foreign writers rather than literally translate them. But hardly any of his poetic ideas, and few of his 'swelling phrases', are primarily of his own invention.[4]

Just so might a testy magistrate sum up the career of a notorious old lag. Other scholars were more temperate; there was qualified praise and cautious disparagement—but never glad, confident morning again. Moreover, the scandal had wide ramifications. It was not only Sidney who had been caught with his hands in the pockets of unsuspecting foreigners. On the same evidence a charge could be made out against Constable and Barnes, Drayton and Daniel, Spenser and Lodge—perhaps even the Immortal Bard himself, if the police records were made public. All the Elizabethan poets, high and low, might stand in the dock together...

Opinion in our time has veered a good way from such extremes. With a truer understanding of the Renaissance approach to composition, it is becoming recognized that imitation and convention were the prerequisites of all serious creative activity. They constituted, in fact, the answer of the age to a problem which, in one form or another, confronts the poet at all times, and very acutely at the present day. The late Theodore Spencer's fine essay on Sidney's poetry has made the point admirably:

1. *Elizabethan Sonnets* (1904) (2 vols.).   2. *Op. cit.*
3. L. C. John, *The Elizabethan Sonnet Sequences* (University of Columbia 1938).
4. *Elizabethan Sonnets*, 1, p. xliv.

To find his own voice, to discover his own poetic idiom and his own rhythm, is the main business of a poet. . . But there is one constant fact which is true of all poets and at all times; the discovery of oneself depends on an act of submission. For the poet, as for the human being, to lose one's life is to find it. . .

In the sixteenth century, this saving loss of personality, this discovery of self through submission to an 'other', could be accomplished to a considerable extent through convention. Convention is to the poet in an age of belief what the *persona* is to the poet in an age of bewilderment. By submission to either the poet acquires authority; he feels that he is speaking for, is representing, something more important than himself—or, in the case of the *persona*, he is at least representing something different from his own naked and relatively insignificant ego; in both cases he has taken the first step toward universality.[1]

For this reason the Renaissance sonnet, most personal of poetic forms, was also the most heavily indebted to convention. It is only with the advent of the Romantics that the individual artist has come to see himself as a misfit in society. Here we have to reckon with a culture in which he drew from society his main encouragement and inspiration. In the sixteenth century the poet who sought to express his own thoughts and feelings, who strove, above all, to voice the supremely personal experience of being in love, was doing exactly what the world required of him. Far from becoming a solitary exile, he found himself admitted to a most worshipful order, whose founder and lawgiver was a fourteenth-century Italian, writing in a modern language and famous throughout western Europe as the first to proclaim the humanist creed of personality. From Petrarch through the *Quattrocento* writers and the poets of the *Pléiade*, to Ronsard and Tasso and the Elizabethans, the stream of self-expression broadened down from precedent to precedent. For each poet of the Renaissance, the power to be himself had been delegated: each one imitated in order to be original.

Considered from the viewpoint of the Elizabethan reader, the same conception of imitation held good. It was the poet's duty to keep the channels of communication open. Mere plagiarism led, of course, to frigidity of response—

1. Theodore Spencer, 'The Poetry of Sir Philip Sidney', *E.L.H.* (December 1945), XII (4), pp. 266-7.

But truely many of such writings as come vnder the banner of vnresistable loue, if I were a Mistress, would neuer perswade mee they were in loue; so coldely they apply fiery speeches. . .[1]

Yet a neglect of vital convention cc.ild set up as formidable a barrier; for it was in the traditional patterns of thought and feeling that the distinctive personality of the poet became integrated with society's estimate of the individual. Without this constant process of integration, indeed, no culture can function healthily for long. It was the atrophy of positive convention during the nineteenth century, and the consequent splitting of the individual into a public and a private self, that explains why so much personal verse of the Victorians evokes a sense of embarrassment. The Elizabethans, with a prepared network of attitudes and responses maintained by implicit compact between poet and reader, were able to resolve the problem of communication more smoothly. In consequence the historical Sir Philip Sidney and Penelope Devereux, as Astrophel and Stella, found their places in the world of poetry with a minimum of artifice and—so long as the proper conventions were upheld—with no great strain upon the reader's credulity.

We must also remember to what extent life itself is patterned on literary modes: how men in one age tend to conduct their amours in all earnestness, like the heroes of Stendhal; in another, in all flippancy, like the heroes of Noël Coward. Literature will focus our attention on certain aspects of our own experience, certain possible reactions to life, making these appear more significant than we would have believed without being prompted. But it cannot influence us to remember what we never knew, or to actualize what was not at least potential. The ardour of the Petrarchan lover, the chastity of the Petrarchan mistress, no doubt had their correlatives in the relationship of Philip Sidney and Penelope Devereux while the poetry of the age lived within them. Stella's excursion on the Thames may only have become the theme of a sonnet because Laura's voyage down the Rhône invited Sidney's imagination to be kindled; but this does not mean that the excursion or the mood it induced were mere fictions. And as much may be said

1. Sidney, *Defence of Poetry*, in *Elizabethan Critical Essays*, ed. G. Gregory Smith, I, p. 201.

of the sleeplessness of Astrophel, his dreams, his journeys; even his irritation with the lap-dog, where Serafino's example may have led him to take notice of feelings that would otherwise have been passed over. 'Historical' critics are inclined to forget that literary influence and living experience are by no means mutually exclusive.

Nowadays, for good or ill, these conventions of Renaissance poetry have lost their appeal, and we must train our responses before we can read a sonnet sequence of the time with due sympathy. The danger is twofold; of naïvety, in accepting any sonnet as literal autobiography; or of false sophistication, in dismissing it off-hand as mere 'literary exercise'. The best remedy is to follow the advice of sixteenth-century teachers of literature, and start by considering 'the nature of the imitation'. This may be attempted by repeating the method adopted in previous chapters (and which will be followed wherever possible in this book) of examining representative sonnets in relation to their known models. Its object will be, not to supply a direct answer to questions about 'originality' or 'sincerity'—these questions will answer themselves in the process—but to understand the poet's own contribution to traditional themes; to note his shifts of tone and stress; to distinguish his modifications of imagery and verse-form: in short, as Ascham recommended to students of the classics, 'to busy ourselves with form of building'. In this way three of Sidney's sonnets, whose sources have been identified, may serve to guide our approach to the sequence as a whole.

(i) ASTROPHEL AND STELLA (LXXI)

PETRARCH (*Sonetto in Vita* CCX)

Who will in fairest book of
    Nature know,
      How Vertue may best lodg'd
      in beautie be,
      Let him but learne of *Loue* to
      reade in thee
Stella, those faire lines, which
    true goodnesse show.
There shall he find all vices
    ouerthrow,
      Not by rude force, but sweetest
      soueraigntie

Chi vuol veder quantunque po
    natura
      E 'l ciel tra noi, venga a mirar
      costei,
      Ch'è sola un sol, non pur a li
      occhi mei,
      Ma al mondo cieco che vertú
      non cura ;
E venga tosto, perché morte
    fura
      Prima i migliori e lascia star
      i rei :

Of reason, from whose light those night-birds flie;	*Questa, aspettata al regno de li dei*
That inward sunne in thine eyes shineth so.	*Cosa bella mortal, passa e non dura.*
And not content to be Perfections heire	*Vedrà, s'arriva a tempo, ogni vertute,*
Thy selfe, doest striue all minds that way to moue:	*Ogni bellezza, ogni real costume*
Who marke in thee what is in thee most faire.	*Giunti in un corpo con mirabil tempre;*
So while thy beautie drawes the heart to loue,	*Allor dirà che mie rime son mute,*
As fast thy Vertue bends that loue to good:	*L'ingegno offeso dal soverchio lume:*
But ah, Desire still cries, giue me some food.	*Ma se più tarda, avrà da pianger sempre.*

The resemblances between the two sonnets need only be summed up briefly. Sidney's opening lines were obviously inspired by those of Petrarch; his imagery in lines 7 and 8 echoed that of lines 3 and 13 in the Italian; his mention of Stella's beauty and virtue was matched by the description of Laura in the Italian sestet. But a closer examination brings out some striking contrasts.

The Italian sonnet opens with a call to come and behold what nature and heaven have together wrought for mankind: one who is herself a sun; and not for the poet only, but for the purblind world, that takes no heed of virtue. And let the would-be viewer hasten, for the marvel cannot last: death takes the best first, and this fair mortal is waited for in the kingdom of the gods. Should he arrive in time, he will behold all virtue, all beauty, all majesty, marvellously blended. He will declare that the poet's verse is made dumb, his intellect confounded by that sovereign light. But should he tarry long, he will have cause to weep evermore. In Sidney's poem the heightened tone, the transcendental vision, is lacking. His Stella is no miracle wrought by the combined powers of nature and heaven, to be seen once in a lifetime by the fortunate beholder. As the 'fairest book of Nature', she may at any time be read for edification—though not gazed at in wonder. Her 'lines', which are of course the lines of her countenance, show her true goodness: but she is still no more than a product of nature, and as such not distinguished in essence from other of earth's creatures. She is remarkable only in that she demonstrates better than any other person how two excellent qualities, beauty and virtue, may live together. While Laura is a revelation, Stella is merely a heroine. The eulogy of Laura constitutes a hymn of praise; that of Stella, a superlatively flattering characterization. The different approaches are reflected in a different use of imagery. Laura is likened to the sun, which, in the Ptolemaic system, has both natural and spiritual properties: it is matter, but matter in the purest form: it shines with heavenly light, but is accessible to the vision of every mortal. The metaphor irradiates Petrarch's whole sonnet; whereas Sidney's sun is but an incidental simile. Only its brightness counts in the poem, as a description of the light of reason in Stella's eyes. Having brought his theme down to the plane of ordinary perception, Sidney proceeds to its empirical significance. Stella would influence all mankind, her beauty moving the heart to love and her virtue shaping love to goodness: alas, in Astrophel's case, desire will not be stilled. All this has been drawn from Petrarch's secondary and derivative extension of his theme, unmentioned until the sestet. The English poet's major concern is with virtue and beauty as aspects of character; with their effects upon society; and lastly with his own subjective response.

In construction the two sonnets express these contrasts in theme. Petrarch's octave describes the apparition of Laura, miraculous (*quantunque po natura E 'l ciel tra noi*) but ephemeral (*perché morte fura Prima i migliori*). Lines 1 to 4 centre upon the first consideration; lines 5 to 8 upon the second. The two considerations are not bound by logical sequence: they are rather composite aspects of a single act of intuition. In consequence of each arises the original call (*Chi vuol veder ... venga*) in line 1, repeated in line 5 (*E venga tosto*), which binds together the octave. Plato's chariot, with its light and dark horses held in rein by an urgent charioteer, comes to mind as a figurative description of Petrarch's vision. In the sestet the implications are developed. The need for haste is reiterated with still greater urgency in the first line; the marvels of the apparition —the light horse of the myth—are dwelt upon in the next four; and in the last line we are left with the threat of death—the plunging black horse—and its consequences for the tardy charioteer: *avrà da pianger sempre*.

Sidney's sonnet is constructed upon entirely different lines. Its octave falls into two distinct quatrains. The first introduces Stella's 'true goodnesse' and the second elaborates upon it. The likelihood of her death is not thought of; and the person who, it is supposed, might wish to know 'how Vertue may best lodg'd in beautie be' plays a part of diminishing importance as the sonnet proceeds. Placed prominently at the beginning of the first quatrain, he serves as a mere curtain-raiser to the second, and is quite forgotten by line 8. The subjects of Petrarch's octave, constituting a single theme in the Italian sonnet, thus break up into their component parts. The appeal for a spectator, which was essential to the original structure, becomes here a merely decorative opening; the fear of the lady's death does not arise; only the description of her beauty and virtue remains. But this has itself undergone a change, and the account of the lady's merits, which Petrarch reached only in his sestet, becomes the primary concern of Sidney's octave. Thus a new theme has arisen, resulting from the elimination of all aspects of the original which proved uncongenial to the English poet. Its unity is felt in the rhyme-scheme of Sidney's octave, which, unlike the Surrey pattern, binds all eight lines together; but the syntactical divisions set up a full pause after line 4, marking the logical development from a general statement of the theme to an elaboration upon particulars.

The sestet has a more complex structure, for while there is a syntactical halt at the third line, suggesting a Petrarchan tercet arrangement, the rhyme-scheme sets up a quatrain and couplet division. These characteristics accompany the intricate logical relationships resulting from Sidney's treatment of his subject-matter. In Petrarch the dual aspects of a composite theme, implied from the start of the sonnet, were developed and balanced against one another in the sestet. In Sidney the sestet seems at first to proceed as a dual inference from the single theme of the octave. Stella's influence is universally beneficent: it operates by a kind of chain mechanism, her beauty moving men's hearts to love, her virtue 'as fast' directing the love into goodness. But in direct opposition to the smooth working of this mechanism comes the unforeseen irruption of Astrophel's desire, casting a well-aimed spanner into the works. Had it not been for this, the logical, and hence syntactical division of the sestet into a pair of balanced inferences might have been reinforced by a rhyme-scheme of similarly balanced tercets; as it is, a final couplet is required here to absorb the impact of the new theme. Hence the second half of the sestet participates in two distinct yet interlocking structures: one created by syntax, the other by rhyme-scheme. The resulting tension is brought to a climax in the last line, which, isolated by the pause at the end of line 13, stands out in antithesis to the thought-process of the entire sonnet. The effect is to establish a new pivot of interest, which may operate as a criticism of Astrophel as compared with the rest of mankind, or range back over the preceding panegyric to Stella; in either case it directs attention away from the ostensible theme to centre it upon the poet's subjective problems.

To sum up: Sidney's poem is indeed *similis materiei dissimilis tractatio*. Petrarch's sonnet has supplied the scaffolding upon which an entirely new work has arisen. The Italian poet's conception of love is transcendental, his preoccupations being with the mystery of beauty and virtue, the inevitability of death, and the attitude of the individual facing these great abstractions. Sidney—as his initial 'book' image suggests—is concerned with an empirical approach to love in terms of its psychological and moral effects. His interests lie not in the sphere of metaphysics but in observations of character and social conduct: the subjects of his sonnet are his lady, the world of men, and himself; its pivot, his own psyche. The difference of approach is matched by Sidney's distinctive verse-form, which, proceeding by logical deduction, at the same time applies an ingenious technique of prosodic counterpoint to express the subjective conflicts which are released by the poem.

(ii) Sonnet XVII, 'His mother deare *Cupid* offended late', is a fable in sonnet form whose rudimentary plot comes from a neo-Latin epigram of Pontano.

De Venere et Amore (or, *De Stella*)

Exhausit pharetram Veneris puer: at Venus ignes
Extinxit. Venus hinc, inde et inermis Amor.

> *Exhaustam hic pharetram, extinctas flet Cypria flammas.*
>   *Hic arcum lacrimis tingit; at illa faces.*
> *Neve puer, neu fle mater: dant spicula mille*
>   *Stellae oculi; puer his utere pro pharetra.*
> *Quin flammas mea corda vomant; his utere mater*
>   *Pro face; inexhausta tu face, et hic pharetra.*[1]

This slight poem may have appealed to Sidney the more in
that its heroine bore the name of Stella. According to Pontano,
Love has exhausted his quiver, and Venus has put out her
torch. Both are helpless and bewail their loss. But there is no
need to weep: Stella's eyes emit a thousand arrows which
Love may take for his quiver, and the poet's heart will provide
the flames to relight Venus's torch. The epigram, a typical
example of *Quattrocento* ingenuity, deftly handles its conceits,
and the result is a sort of witty hyperbole which makes no pretensions to explore any real depths of experience. Venus and
Amor are merely decorative figures; they symbolize nothing
but the obvious. The poet has introduced them partly to suit a
fashionable taste for classical allusion, partly as counters in his
display of mental agility. Just so might a performer in panto-
mime call out two fairies from the chorus to hold the properties
for his act and at the same time please the audience with a
show of spangles and femininity. As for the darts from Stella's
eyes, and the flames which consume her lover's heart, so coldly
are the fiery speeches applied that they remain mere courtly
gallantries, sweetened, perhaps, by a lingering aroma of
Petrarchan romance. It would be ponderous to inquire further into verse of this type.

Such were the foundations for the following sonnet of Sidney:

> His mother deare *Cupid* offended late,
>   Because that *Mars* growne slacker in her loue,
>   With pricking shot he did not throughly moue,
>   To keepe the pace of their first louing state.
> The boy refusde for feare of *Marses* hate,
>   Who threatned stripes, if he his wrath did proue:
>   But she in chafe him from her lap did shoue,
>   Brake bow, brake shafts, while *Cupid* weeping sate:

1. *Eridanorum* I. There are French variants upon the conceit by Jamyn,
Scève, and others. This source, with other sources or analogues cited in the
next example, was first identified by Janet G. Scott.

> Till that his grandame *Nature* pittying it,
>> Of *Stellas* browes made him two better bowes,
>> And in her eyes of arrowes infinit.
> O how for ioy he leapes, O how he crowes,
>> And straight therewith like wags new got to play,
>> Fals to shrewd turnes, and I was in his way. (xvii)

Sidney has taken from Pontano his two mythological figures, as well as the persons of the poet and his mistress. As in the epigram, Cupid (the name given here to *Amor*) loses his arrows and recovers them from Stella's eyes. The rest is of Sidney's own invention. He adds to the protagonists Mars the head of the family and Nature the mother of Venus. From this material a new poem is built. Love and Venus in the original poem were mere puppets, lacking both human personality and superhuman power. No reason was given why they should have exhausted their quiver or put out their torch, and their consequent tears were unbecoming for gods, foolish even for mortals. Sidney gives these vague shapes character and life. From his first line—'His mother deare *Cupid* offended late'— the immortals, in a familiar human relationship, become sympathetic and real. Line 2 introduces Mars, and with him a domestic entanglement. Cupid is expected to use his arrows on his mother's behalf to win back her inattentive consort. In the second half of the octave the tale turns into a lively domestic farce. A family brawl is going on, such as may break out in any peasant hut. Mars stands glowering and threatening to reach for the strap; Venus continues to urge Cupid on against his father. What should a small boy do? His mother pushes him off her knee and petulantly breaks his bow and arrows. No wonder Cupid sits on his stool and weeps. But soon, as often happens in the life of a child, Grandmother comes to the rescue. In the sestet she furnishes the boy with two new bows, and 'arrowes infinit'. Whence came these gifts? So interested has the reader grown in the development of the little drama that the mention of Stella takes him by surprise. Even the familiar conceits, the bows for her brows, the darts for her glances, become fresh and amusing in this unexpected setting. And now Nature's true function in the poem comes to light. She is not only the kind but meddlesome grandmother of folk tradition, but 'Kind', the symbol of mighty biological forces,

as in medieval allegory. In co-operation with Stella, her activities take on a menacing aspect for any mere man. But Cupid,
too, can no longer be watched with detachment. Armed with
his new weapons, turned loose upon the world, and in hilarious
mood, he 'fals to shrewd turnes': and, adds Sidney very
quietly, 'I was in his way.'

There is much to be learned of Sidney's outlook and
methods of composition by penetrating the surface of charm in
this attractive poem. The workings of love are considered seriously enough in terms of its symbols. Sidney's two human
characters, it will be noted, take only a passive or auxiliary
part in the action. Astrophel happens to be in the way of
Cupid's arrows: Stella supplies the weapons, but has no say in
the use to which they are put. The active protagonists are
Nature and the gods. These are virtually the same forces as
Petrarch's *Natura e 'l ciel* in the sonnet of our first example; but
the ironical treatment they undergo here shows the fundamental difference in Sidney's attitude. Instead of Petrarch's heaven
we are offered a mean domestic interior where pagan gods
brawl and wrangle with the rough manners of peasants. Of
them all, Cupid is the most likeable. As befits the Anacreontic tradition, he is the mischievous personification of desire—
the force which asserted itself at the end of 'Who will in fairest
book'. But, although impulsive and irresponsible, Cupid is
fundamentally guileless. Now so long as these stupid gods
are preoccupied with their domestic upsets, what they do is of
no concern to humanity. It is the interference of grandmother
Nature that brings the immortals into contact with men. She
is indeed a 'kind' old woman, or at least kind to her own; but
by giving Cupid access to Stella's charm she makes him a
potential source of danger; and Astrophel falls a victim.
Desire, Sidney concedes, may be a superhuman force; but it
does not therefore merit the worshipful treatment bestowed
upon it by the ancients. Even the goddess of love is petty,
vulgar, and of no account until Nature steps in—a truly formidable power, though scarcely venerable. But when Nature
gives Desire free play, and a beautiful woman lends her aid,
love becomes indeed irresistible. Even so, be it noted, neither
Stella, nor Nature, nor Desire, consciously aimed at Astrophel's mishap. The immediate cause was not blind Cupid but

blind chance—the accidental circumstance that the poet happened to be in Cupid's line of fire.

The verse-form of this sonnet closely resembles that of LXXI, and the same interlocking structure of syntax-formed tercets, and quatrain and couplet rhyme-scheme, is to be found in the last six lines. In the previous example logical inference dominated the structure: here the shape is given by the plot of the fable as it unfolds stage by stage. In the last three lines of the sonnet there is the same heightening of tension, evidenced by the change from past to present tense of narration; and here too the appearance of Astrophel in the last line changes the whole angle of approach, converting the fable from an impersonal narrative to an interpretation of subjective experience.

(iii) A long literary history underlies the conceit on which sonnet VIII of *Astrophel and Stella* is based. Janet G. Scott traced it back to Epigram CCLXVIII in the Greek Anthology, where the poet declares that he fears Love's arrows no longer; for the god has spent them all, and has now cast off his wings, leaving his body in the poet's heart. Propertius translated this into Latin, and both Chariteo and Serafino reshaped it in Italian.

PROPERTIUS

In me tela manent, manet et puerilis imago.
Sed certe pennas perdidit ille suas;
Evolat ei nostro quoniam de pectore nusquam.[1]

CHARITEO

La forma pueril, gli adunchi strali,
Provo di piombo, e quelli d'oro inseme,
Ma di cacciarti altrove nulla speme
Mi resta, ch'a l'intrar perdesti l'ali.[2]

SERAFINO

Tennemi un tempo Amor per suo ricetto,
finché fe una fornace del mio core:
ma come spesso per divin concetto
de la sua opra un fraudulento more,
volando un di dentro al mio ardente petto,
lui s'accese, e non mai più venne fore.[3]

1. II. xii, 13-15.   2. *Endimione*, VIII.   3. *Strambotto*, CXCIII.

Chariteo's addition had been that Love's form was made of lead, his arrows of gold; it was the leaden wings that were lodged in the poet's heart. Serafino discarded the lead–gold antithesis, and invented a story of how the wings came to be lost. Love, having taken up lodgings in the poet's heart, one day lit a furnace there; but, as a deceiver often falls into his own trap, so Love himself caught fire, and now was unable to get away. Here was a pretty anecdote for Sidney to work upon. Just as he took the theme of Pontano's epigram and elaborated it into a new shape in the sonnet we have just considered, so here he modelled that of Serafino to his own purposes. The material was promising, with a touch of irony in the phrase *de la sua opera un fraudulento more* which gave the little poem more genuine wit than Pontano's sterile classicisms. If in addition Sidney read *tenere ricetto* as 'to take refuge' as well as 'to take up lodgings', there was a hint that might have led him on to his conjectures about Love's previous history.

> *Loue* borne in *Greece*, of late fled from his natiue place,
>> Forc'd by a tedious proofe, that Turkish-hardned hart
>> Is not fit marke to pierce with his fine-pointed dart:
>> And pleasd with our soft peace, staid here his flying race:
> But finding these North clymes do coldly him embrace,
>> Not vsde to frozen clips, he straue to find some part,
>> Where with most ease & warmth he might employ his art:
>> At length he perch'd himself in *Stellas* ioyfull face,
> Whose faire skin, beamy eyes like morning sun on snow,
>> Deceiu'd the quaking boy, who thought from so pure light,
>> Effects of liuely heat, must needs in nature grow.
> But she most faire, most cold, made him thence take his flight
>> To my close heart, where while some firebrands he did lay,
>> He burnt unwares his wings, and cannot fly away. (VIII)

As in 'His mother deare', Sidney has invented a new story which takes up the whole of his octave, and has kept the original wing-burning in reserve, for the climax of the sonnet. He is thus able to spring the same pleasurable surprise upon the reader at finding a familiar subject in a novel setting. Love is once again presented in human guise, and a most interesting modern background is devised for his adventures. He is a Greek boy of the sixteenth century, whose country has been overrun by the Turks. These foreigners are Moslems and polygamists; romance does not appeal to them, and Love's occupation's lost. He becomes, like so many in Sidney's time, a refugee from Europe, and arrives in England. But the boy's troubles are not over. Love is a southerner who suffers from the cold; he thinks that Stella's beauty betokens a warmth of heart; but Stella only drives him away. He then takes refuge, or takes up lodgings, in the heart of Astrophel, which is 'close' and retentive of heat. Here he begins to make a fire, but—at last comes the ancient conceit—'He burnt unwares his wings, and cannot fly away.'

Once again a fable is told of two human beings and their relationship with an immortal. Stella again acts unwittingly as an auxiliary to Love, and Astrophel as an innocent victim plays the same passive part. But Love in this sonnet represents neither the deified force of procreation in nature, nor the elemental force of human desire. He signifies only 'romance'; a mode of behaviour, or a cast of mind, to be found in certain countries and amongst certain peoples. Thus Love has no necessary kinship to nature or the pagan gods. Since his activities are not authorized by any of these powers, they—and he —are entirely dependent on circumstance. Accordingly there is no need for any mention of the mythological beings who play their part—however satirically that part is treated—in sonnet xvii. Sidney's concern here is with the fate of Love in contemporary English society. Love, he declares, flourished once in the warm south, but fares otherwise in England, where temperaments, like the climate, are cold, and beauty is unaccompanied by passion. In the thematic development of the sonnet, the contrast between romantic love and harsh present-day reality is introduced at the start, and forms the subject-matter of the octave. In the sestet the concept of northern unresponsiveness becomes associated with the frigid behaviour of Stella, who now enters into the plot. But at the end yet another relationship is brought into being, when, through an unfortunate accident, Astrophel's heart is set ablaze. It is to be noted that Serafino's treatment has been modified in Love's favour. The boy is not *un fraudulento*, a deceiver, but is himself deceived in Stella; and instead of maliciously lighting a furnace in the poet's heart (as Cupid might have done) he merely lays some firebrands to warm his own shivering body. Astrophel does not blame him, but rather commiserates with him as a fellow-sufferer. Nevertheless, it is plain that contemporary England, Stella, and romantic love are all linked in the chain of negligence that has brought about the plight of Astrophel.

The verse-form of this sonnet is essentially the same as in the two previous examples. Rhyme-scheme and syntax-structure are played off against one another in the sestet for the same purpose of focusing attention on the last lines, where the personality of the poet appears; so that the whole sonnet is recast in a subjective mould. But the intricacies of four interacting themes—England, Stella, Love, and Astrophel—as compared with three in sonnets LXXI and XVII, required here a wider modification of form. Consciously or not (no one can say how far an artist is critically aware of what motivates his technique) Sidney had the alternatives of increasing the standard number of lines to make room for these complex relationships, or of following a French precedent and swelling out his five-foot lines into hexameters. The fourteen-line sonnet was a tried and approved form; any stretching of it would require cumbrous readjustments of rhyme-scheme. But hexameters expanded the framework of the sonnet without changing its structure, and provided scope for the balancing of four themes. The extraordinarily flexible use of caesuras, especially in the sestet where the most intricate relationships arose, avoided all clumsiness and gave further proof of Sidney's metrical skill. Thanks to the hexameters, the theme of Love in England could remain operative right through the sestet ('morning sun on snow', 'quaking boy', 'liuely heat', 'most faire, most cold') and take its place in the organization of the poem.

The three sonnets considered show very clearly how valuable the Renaissance doctrine of imitation could be for a poet of true originality. It should be noticed that, while Sidney has treated his source material with great freedom, his primary theme is expressed in and through the conventions of his medium. At the crux of attention in each sonnet, Sidney is at once most conventional and most himself. The fables of sonnets XVII and VIII gradually lead from an unusual situation to a traditional and familiar one; it is just when this point is reached, when Cupid shoots his arrow or Love lights his fire, that the poet's personality is disclosed and supplies the pivot from which the story is to be reviewed. The rationalistic and empirical treatment of Stella's virtues in sonnet LXXI reaches a conclusion where her chastity becomes a subject for lament on her lover's part. This is the traditional reaction of every romance poet; but the sudden juxtaposition of desire's cry is so personal that again it affords an individual comment on all that goes before. The fundamental irony that inspires all these poems lies in the fact that Sidney's complex, highly critical modern ego is involved in a pattern of experience for which the traditional themes of romance provide the only effective means of expression.

This interaction of conventionalized experience and an intensely personal response takes on added subtlety when we see the individual sonnets as units in a greater whole. Sonnets VIII, XVII, and LXXI are probably too far separated from one another in the sequence for direct correspondences to have been intended; yet there is certainly an implicit relationship between them. Both XVII and VIII show a comic treatment due not to any frivolity on Sidney's part, but chiefly to the need for a realistic approach to psychological issues. Love in the form of Cupid or Desire takes effect in much the same way as Shaw's Life Force. A childlike irresponsibility on the part of the sexual impulse, the acquiescence of a beautiful woman in placing her appeal at its disposal, and the chance proximity of those concerned, supply the formula. Desire is Nature's unruly grandchild, and Astrophel, like an Elizabethan John Tanner, directs his protest against the biological urge in his own psyche which interferes with his intellectual self-sufficiency. Yet Cupid is the most likeable of the immortals, and we cannot help but be sorry for him as he sits weeping over his broken bow. Romance, the other manifestation of Love, deserves even more pity, as the delicate, over-sensitive child who shrinks from the chilly common sense of English society, and whom Stella, as a representative of that society, drives away. Yet Romance and Desire, both companions of Astrophel, are brothers in adversity. While Romance shivers in the garret of the poet's heart, Desire is starved of food; and Stella, whose beauty and virtue are universally commended, is responsible for the sufferings of both these children. This is not to say that the praises to Stella in LXXI are deliberately ironical. The inconsistency springs from a genuine conflict of attitudes on Sidney's part. Rationally, he too should starve desire and shut the door on romance; but his imagination sympathizes with both impulses, for all their latent destructiveness. This contradiction underlies Sidney's treatment of his sources in general. His attitude to sexual love is centred in psychology rather than metaphysics, is more concerned with personal relationships than with impersonal forces, and expresses itself rather by logical inferences than by acts of intuition. But the conflict of attitudes is always present, mingling humour with introspection; adding undertones of irony to the rational exposition; and each time referring the experience back to the imponderables of the poet's own personality. The sonnets we have considered owe their subtle and intricate pattern of thought to this inner tension, and their intellectual pattern is reflected in their form.

To a great extent the entire sequence of *Astrophel and Stella* follows the same course. The exploration of Sidney's own personality is the subject of most of his serious sonnets. He views himself from many angles: as a literary artist, as a diplomat in the service of his country, as a soldier, as a cultured humanist, as a sincere practising Christian. His passion for Stella is, of course, the recurrent theme of every poem, and the problems to which it gives rise in relation to his activities, interests, and beliefs decide the character of his writing.

The sonnet tradition required that Stella should be endowed with all the womanly virtues. Accordingly she is chaste and fair; she exercises a beneficent influence upon those around her; above all, she inspires the poet to noble and unselfish conduct. Even in physical appearance she is a blood-relation to the Délies, the Dianes, and the Olives who populate the works of the *Pléiade*, and may trace her descent back to the incomparable Laura. But a closer inspection of Sidney's sonnets reveals a treatment of her character, and especially of the poet's reactions to it, which is markedly individual. Sonnet II is of special importance, tracing as it does the genesis of the love affair. Such a paragon as Stella must appear as a revelation to all mankind: a mere glimpse of her by her lover should be enough to change the whole course of his life. So it was at Petrarch's celebrated first encounter with Laura:

> Era il giorno, ch'al sol si scoloraro
> Per la pietà del suo Fattore i rai,
> Quand'i' fui preso, e non me ne guardai
> Che i be' vostri occhi, Donna, mi legaro.
>
> (Sonetto in Vita III)

The day itself, anniversary of the crucifixion, was set apart from all others in the year: Laura's advent was ever after associated in the poet's thoughts with the highest and holiest moment in Christian history. Yet Sidney could declare that the first sight of the lady he was to love made no startling impact upon his mind:

> Not at the first sight, nor with a dribbed shot
>   Loue gaue the wound, which while I breathe will bleed:
>   But knowne worth did in mine of time proceed,
>   Till by degrees it had full conquest got.
> I saw and liked, I liked, but loued not,
>   I loued, but straight did not what Loue decreed:
>   At length to Loue's decrees, I forc'd, agreed,
>   Yet with repining at so partiall lot. (II)

The account of approval gradually changing into love, and love with mental reservations passing over into love without question, was in itself a serious departure from tradition. It showed a determination to remain true to the facts of experience even at the cost of reducing Stella's pre-eminence. But even more is to be learned about Sidney's feelings by implication than by overt statement. The conventional figure of Love's arrows, which the sonnet had inherited from medieval allegory, is here carefully modernized. In the Roman de la Rose, the lover was struck by arrows from the bow of the love-god. He knelt, took an oath of allegiance, and became the god's sworn retainer. By Sidney's time more formidable weapons than arrows had been invented, and a more servile system than chivalric feudalism was known to exist in contemporary Russia. The slow maturing of the poet's love certainly lost none of its menace by being likened to the action of a mine; nor was the completeness of its final grip at all diminished by the comparison of Astrophel's state with that of the 'slaue-borne Mus-

couite' who 'call[s] it praise to suffer Tyrannie'. But on the
other hand something was added, discordant with the true
spirit of courtly love: an insistence upon the destructive and
degrading character of sexual passion. The same admission is
to be found in sonnet XVI. Astrophel had always been impres-
sionable, and had often fancied himself to be in love. At such
times the experience had been less painful than other men had
led him to expect, and he had come to despise those 'babes'
who 'of some pinnes hurt did whine'. Now he has met Stella,
and knows the meaning of love—'As who by being poysoned
doth poyson know'. The fierceness of the poison simile, and the
parenthetical question—'Mine eyes (shall I say curst or blest)
beheld *Stella*'—reveal a state of mind which reflects negatively
upon the lady's accredited powers for good. All romance
lovers, it is true, have reproached their ladies for coldness or
cruelty: but Astrophel seems inclined to regret ever having set
eyes upon his. Nor is such a recoil due to any specific rebuff: of
this there is no mention in either sonnet. It would seem that
some quality in the relationship itself has given rise to conflict.
In XXXIII there is a hint that Stella, even before her marriage,
had not been wooed by the poet with an entirely free mind;
that her much-abused husband was not, in fact, the only bar
to his happiness:

> No louely *Paris* made thy *Hellen* his:
> No force, no fraud, robd thee of thy delight,
> Nor Fortune of thy fortune author is:
> But to my selfe my selfe did giue the blow,
> While too much wit (forsooth) so troubled me,
> That I respects for both our sakes must show:

Why was he then so circumspect? Such extreme caution in a
young man is a doubtful augury for happiness in love. But the
reasons are made clear in XXI. Put into the mouth of a wise and
well-meaning friend, whose arguments are not rationally dis-
puted, is a declaration that the whole affair is improper for a
man of breeding, education, and high moral purpose:

> That *Plato* I read for nought, but if he tame
> Such coltish yeeres,[1] that to my birth I owe

---

1. Alternatively 'giers' (2nd Quarto), the version adopted by Miss
Wilson and printed by her as 'gires'.

> Nobler desires, least else that friendly foe,
> Great expectation, weare a traine of shame.

These hints and implications do not, and could not without
violating the tradition, make up a sustained attack upon
courtly love. Most often, Stella is described as in LXXI, as 'Perfections heire', the embodiment of virtue and beauty, who
strives 'all minds that way to moue'. As such she fulfils the part
of the beloved in Plato's Symposium, and should guide the
lover by ascending stages to the realm of pure ideas. Nevertheless in certain moods Astrophel is far from glad at having become involved with her at all: not because he meets with discouragement; not even because her marriage to another man
stands in his way; but because he finds that his preoccupation
with her distracts him from more serious concerns. The Platonic lover is, in effect, being driven to neglect his Plato. This
is made very clear in the confession that, to a trusted observer,
and even to himself in calmer moments, the affair appears dis-
ruptive and degrading, and that the experience may be resolved into nothing more than an overmastering infatuation
of the senses. The lucid self-examination in sonnet XVIII completes the picture. The school of Petrarch had seen the beloved
as the joint work of nature and heaven: Sidney finds that the
lover too is a beneficiary of these powers, while his very love
has robbed him of the means to repay his debt:

> And by iust counts my selfe a banckrout know
> Of all those goods, which heau'n to me hath lent:
> Vnable quite to pay euen Nature's rent,
> Whiche vnto it by birthright I do ow: (XVIII)

The sestet is a final bitter commentary on the moral confusion
induced by passionate love.

> My youth doth waste, my knowledge brings forth toyes,
> My wit doth striue those passions to defend,
> Which for reward spoile it with vaine annoyes.
> I see my course to loose my selfe doth bend:
> I see and yet no greater sorow take
> Then that I loose no more for *Stellas* sake.

The principal theme of *Astrophel and Stella* appears, then, as
a study of the inner conflicts that romance precipitates in the
personality of a contemporary man. Astrophel's character is

disclosed, in glimpse after glimpse, over the whole course of the sequence. He is a modern writer with decided views on poetry. Sonnets I, III, VI, XV, XXVIII, XXXIV, XL, L, LV, LXX, LXXIV, and XC all touch upon problems of composition. Much gentle fun is poked at the euphuists—'Pindare's apes'—who

> with strange similies enrich each line,
> Of herbes or beastes, which *Inde* or *Afrike* hold (III)

at the over-precious author who ransacks Parnassus for

> euerie floure not sweet perhaps, which growes
> Neare thereabout   (XV)

and at poor plodding hacks with even less invention:

> Ye that do Dictionaries methode bring
> Into your rimes, running in ratling rowes: (XV)

Even Spenser, Sidney's friend, does not entirely escape censure. His allegorical technique is described as a making of others' children into changelings (XXVIII), and Sidney declares with much emphasis that Stella is no cryptically-conceived Una or Britomart, but a character drawn from life. In all these sonnets her effect upon his own poetic powers is considered. She may claim credit for that spark of inspiration upon which he so persistently lays stress. At times he attributes to her his success as a poet:

> For let me but name her whom I do loue,
> So sweet sounds straight mine eare and heart do hit,
> That I well find no eloquence like it. (LV)

But on other occasions, he loses all confidence in his art: it becomes a mere escape from misery,

> As good to write as for to lie and grone, (XL)

and he will make a sonnet out of a debate with himself as to whether there is any point in making one:

> Thus write I while I doubt to write, and wreake
> My harmes in Inks poore losse, perhaps some find
> *Stellas* great powrs, that so confuse my mind. (XXXIV)

Poetry for Sidney, as for most Elizabethan authors, was one interest amongst many. He was also a skilful diplomat, a brilliant courtier, and a brave soldier. In several sonnets reference is made to his public life. He fights in a tournament against envoys from the French court, and is the hero of the day (XLI). The spectators of this match argue amongst themselves whether his victory should be attributed to his strength, his skill, his good fortune, or inherited talent. But the true cause is, '*Stella* lookt on'. Unfortunately, in another encounter, Stella's presence has quite the contrary effect:

> I look'd and Stella spide:
> Who hard by made a window send forth light,
> My heart then quak'd, then dazled were mine eyes,
> One hand forgat to rule, th' other to fight. (LIII)

Sonnet xxx lists the important foreign questions of the time. Will the Turks make another attack upon Christendom?— What chance have the Poles, with their miserable army, in a war against Russia?—Can the French achieve national unity? —What is the situation in Holland? in Ulster? in Scotland?— Astrophel is expected to know the answers, and, 'cumbred with good manners', does his best to express an opinion. But he marvels at himself in doing so, for his thoughts are all fixed upon Stella. He is silent and reserved with colleagues, and often lets his best friends pass by ignored (XXVII). No wonder then that curious rumours spread about him at court. It is said that he is deep in study, or meditating plans for political reform; more hostile observers insinuate that he is distracted with ambition. The true cause again is suspected by no one:

> O fooles, or ouer-wise, alas the race
> Of all my thoughts hath neither stop nor start,
> But only *Stellas* eyes and *Stellas* hart. (XXIII)

The conflicting claims of love and public duties are reflected in many of Sidney's characteristic similes and conceits. If Stella has a way of obtruding herself upon his thoughts in the course of a tournament or a discussion on foreign affairs, the rivals for his attention occasionally retaliate by giving a twist of their own to Sidney's love-imagery. We have already noticed the substitution of a mine for Cupid's arrow in II, and the identification of the love-god with a refugee from the Turks in VIII. There is likewise a startling word-play on 'touch' in IX. Stella's face is likened to the palace of 'Queen *Vertue*'—the ala-

baster front is her skin, the golden roof her hair, the red portals
her lips, and so forth. Her eyes are the climax of the description: they are like the black silica known as touchstone, used in
testing for precious metals. But 'touch' had another meaning
for the Elizabethan soldier. It signified the inflammable nitre
used for explosives.

> Of touch they are that without touch doth touch,
> Which *Cupids* selfe from Beauties mine did draw:
> Of touch they are, and poore I am their straw.

Having mentioned beauty's 'mine', Sidney was led on to this
second association, unconnected with the explicit theme of the
sonnet. The decorous accumulation of stock conceits lights
upon a single dangerous word, which itself blows up like a
mine and converts love into one of the disasters of war. Again,
in sonnet xx, the ancient myth of the lover struck by Cupid's
dart is given a new and arresting quality. The boy god is turned into a sniper: concealed in a bush, he fires at helpless
passers-by. The sonnet opens with the desperate cry of a
mortally-wounded soldier warning his friends to fly for their
lives. Only towards the end of the octave do we begin to recognize the familiar theme: the 'darke bush' becomes the 'sweete
blacke' of Stella's eyes: the 'bloudie bullet' is transformed—
but only in the final couplet—into Cupid's arrow. Here too,
the conceit gives immediacy to the experience described,
brings it into the contemporary world, and associates love
with one of the worst accidents that can befall a soldier. A few
years later, this conceit was re-enacted in grim reality when
Sidney met his death from a stray bullet on the field of
Zutphen.

But if love interfered with social obligation, its corrosive
effects left their deepest mark in the privacy of the soul. Sidney
was renowned for his courage and statesmanship: but perhaps
his greatest claim to distinction, in the eyes of the discerning,
was as a shining product of the new education. The Elizabethans were preoccupied with the training of their ruling
class, with what Spenser described as 'the fashioning of a
gentleman or noble person in vertuous and gentle discipline'.
Ascham's generation had evolved the formula of Protestant
Humanism—a blend of Greek philosophy, classical literature,

and the bible. Such was the training given at the new gram-
mar schools, and continued at the universities, where scholars
had, since the time of Grocyn and Linacre, taught a doctrine
which reconciled Platonism with the essentials of the reformed
creed. Sidney, perhaps more than any figure at court, was a
living vindication of these methods. He was patriotic, devout,
and yet culturally abreast of his age. There was nothing in him
of either 'monk' or 'libertine'. A good Protestant, he was
steeped in Platonic philosophy as interpreted by Englishmen
of the sixteenth century. He was virtuous, but not prudish:
courtly but not dissolute. Hence the violent infatuation recounted in *Astrophel and Stella* would be all the more shattering
in its effects upon his inward peace. Sonnets xviii and xxi have
revealed the profound anxieties of Sidney's Protestant, Platonist self when soberly facing this revolt of the senses. The clearest
exposition of all, however, is provided in v, where his fundamental tenets are set forth simply and concisely.

> It is most true, that eyes are form'd to serue
>   The inward light: and that the heauenly part
>   Ought to be king, from whose rules who doth swerue,
>   Rebels to Nature striue for their owne smart.
> It is most true, what we call *Cupids* dart,
>   An image is, which for ourselues we carue;
>   And, fooles, adore in temple of our hart,
>   Till that good God make Church and Churchman starue.
> True, that true Beautie Vertue is indeed,
>   Whereof this Beautie can be but a shade,
>   Which elements with mortall mixture breed:
> True, that on earth we are but pilgrims made,
>   And should in soule vp to our countrey moue:
>   True, and yet true that I must *Stella* loue.

Here are the Protestant teachings, that the godly life is also the
true 'life according to nature', and the cult of courtly love a
mere pagan heresy; while side by side with them marches the
Platonic doctrine that mortal beauty is no more than a weak
reflection of the heavenly or ideal virtue towards which man
on earth must aspire. In this context the flat assertion that
Stella must be loved has no more serious claim upon the intellect than Desire's cry for food in lxxi—and has clearly been
prompted by the same urge. Sidney's English training appears

most plainly, however, not in the moral principles to be
abstracted from the poem, but in their place as an integral
part of the poetic outlook of the sequence. Moral purity and
philosophic idealism were the watchwords of a European
movement which came to predominate in the sixteenth century, and the school of courtly Neoplatonism had among its
exponents such distinguished Italian poets as Bembo, Tasso,
and Della Casa. Bembo's diatribe against sensual love in *Gli
Asolani* was one of the representative documents of the age.
Yet in their love sonnets these poets were content to revive the
Petrarchan mode of adulatory eulogy which descended from
the old romance conventions. The ancient Mediterranean
view of life, with nature and spirit ever liable to be interfused
or metamorphosed into one another, prevailed creatively, and
as poets it was the myth-making, visionary sides of religion
and philosophy which inspired their greatest work. For Sidney, however, whose creed laid its main stress upon the individual conscience and practical morality, whose philosophical
grounding had lain chiefly in the moral and rationalistic
aspects of Platonism, and whose native tradition had no true
affinity with the romance outlook, creative expression op-
erated in more organic accord with intellectual principles,
and he incorporated these in the very texture of his sonnet
sequence.

Yet, despite all principles, desire persists: Stella must be
loved. Like any philosopher with the toothache, Astrophel perceives that no amount of reasoning will ease the pain.

> Vertue, awake, Beautie but beautie is,
>   I may, I must, I can, I will, I do
>   Leaue following that, which it is gaine to misse.
> Let her goe: soft, but here she comes, . . . (XLVII)

In recoil from the dilemma, he again allows himself to believe
that Stella, mortal woman as she is, can be virtue incarnate:

> Soules ioy, bend not those morning starres from me,
>   Where Vertue is made strong by Beauties might,
>   Where *Loue* is chastnesse, Paine doth learne delight,
>   And Humblenesse growes one with Maiestie.
> What euer may ensue, o let me be
>   Copartner of the riches of that sight:

> Let not mine eyes be hel-driu'n from that light:
> O looke, ô shine, ô let me die and see. (XLVIII)

But for all the profusion of idealistic epithets, it is undoubtedly baulked passion that breaks out in this delirious cry.

The affair continued. Stella began to relent: she begged him, like a true Platonist, to show his love by overcoming desire; she confessed to loving him in return, but urged him, in his own interests, to renounce her:

> . . . loue she did, but loued a Loue not blind,
> Which would not let me, whom she loued, decline
> From nobler course, fit for my birth and mind: (LXII)

Finally she accepted him as her lover, on condition that he 'take a vertuous course'. The history of the change in relationship occupies sonnets LXI–LXX. The result is a phase of jubilation, hectic and not without an undercurrent of fear:

> O ioy, too high for my low stile to show:
> O blisse, fit for a nobler state then me:
> Enuie, put out thine eyes, least thou do see
> What Oceans of delight in me do flow. . . (LXIX)

It is of short duration, for soon the clamours of Desire, the 'old companion', make themselves heard again. Stella grants further concessions, celebrated in sonnets LXXIX–LXXXIII; but at last, in LXXXVII, mention is made of a physical separation.

> When I was forst from *Stella* euer deere . . .
> By iron lawes of duty to depart:

Absence, and a resurgence of common male sexuality after the long period of frustrated ardour, eventually free him. Parted from Stella, he finds with some astonishment that other women can tempt him.

> When Sun is hid, can starres such beames display?
> Cannot heau'ns food once felt, keepe stomakes free
> From base desire on earthly cates to pray. (LXXXVIII).

Nevertheless, desire begins to drive out desire; and the process is perhaps even accelerated by Stella's dawning jealousy. Her power over him is evidently in decline; for the first time it becomes necessary for Astrophel to explain away, not very convincingly, his straying attentions.

They please I do confesse, they please mine eyes,
    But why? because of you they models be,
    Models such be wood-globes of glistring skies.
Deere, therefore be not iealous ouer me,
    If you heare that they seeme my hart to moue,
    Not them, ô no, but you in them I loue. (xci)

Gradually what is finest in his love for Stella takes on an impersonal, genuinely sublimated character. In the concluding sonnets of the sequence it is associated with the beauties of nature,
with the alternations of night and day, with rainfall and
flowers, with bird-song, winds, and flowing water. To this last
phase belong some memorable poems—'When far spent night
perswades each mortall eye' (xcix), 'O teares, no teares, but
raine from beauties skies' (c), 'O happie Tems, that didst my
Stella beare' (ciii). Passion has not yet left him, and frequently
its pain returns; but his thoughts are slowly passing to another
plane where the loveliness of the world of things impresses itself more and more upon his senses.

Who hath the crimson weeds stolne from my morning skies?
How doth the colour vade of those vermillion dies,
    Which Nature selfe did make, and selfe engraind the same?
                                 (cii)
    The bote for ioy could not to daunce forbeare,
        While wanton winds with beauties so deuine
        Rauisht, staid not, till in her golden haire
        They did themselues (ô sweetest prison) twine. (ciii)

The farewell of sonnet cvii shows renewed dignity and calm.
With the waning of passion, the demands of life in the world of
men are heard again and answered. It is the envoy of Elizabeth, not a tormented lover, who goes to his duty and the parting from Stella becomes identified in his thoughts with another,
more majestic leave-taking.

    Sweete for a while giue respite to my hart,
        Which pants as though it stil should leape to thee:
        And on my thoughts giue thy Lieftenancy
        To this great cause, which needes both vse and art.
    And as a Queene, who from her presence sends
        Whom she imployes, dismisse from thee my wit,
        Till it haue wrought what thy owne will attends. (cvii)

But although the Sidney of popular imagination has been restored, the secret wounds of the soul are not easily healed. The last sonnet of *Astrophel and Stella* is an inconclusive lament, and the haunted lyrics attached to the sequence proper add their poignant testimony to the emotional attrition that both lovers have undergone. Memory re-enacts the snatched, hopeless meetings of Astrophel and Stella—

> Him great harmes had taught much care,
> Her faire necke a foule yoke bare:
> But hir sight his cares did banish,
> In his sight hir yoke did vanish.

His pleadings and her whispered refusals become an eternal, inevitable refrain:

> Take me to thee, and thee to mee:
> *No no no no, my Deare let bee.*

Not formally connected with the sequence, and probably written after a considerable interval, are two sonnets declaring Sidney's final attitude to romance. Grosart, as a nineteenth-century editor, has been much derided for his 'sentimentality' in attaching them to *Astrophel and Stella*; yet it is surely natural to associate their themes with the central experience of the main body of love sonnets. One is a palinode written in furious castigation of desire and all its effects:

> Thou blind mans marke, thou fooles selfe chosen snare,
> Fond fancies scum, and dregs of scattred thought,
> Band of all euils, cradle of causelesse care,
> Thou web of will, whose end is neuer wrought.[1]

The other is an irrevocable farewell to the love that reaches but to dust, every word of which breathes resolution and spiritual integrity:

> O take fast hold, let that light be thy guide,
>   In this small course which birth drawes out to death,
>   And thinke how euill becommeth him to slide,
> Who seeketh heau'n, and comes of heau'nly breath.
>   Then farewell world, thy vttermost I see,
>   Eternall Loue maintaine thy life in me.[2]

Splendidis longum valedico nugis.

1. Feuillerat, vol. II, p. 322.   2. II. 322.

Such was the course of the love affair celebrated in *Astrophel and Stella*. An acute moral dilemma, expressed in fluctuating moods of desire and recoil, emotional transports and lucid self-probing, involves the many-sided personality of a great Eliza-bethan. It passes from phase to phase, reaching no solution until the romance experience itself is purged away by circum-stances, duty, and the poet's spiritual creed. The treatment of this complex theme is of necessity concerned mainly with an investigation of subjective states and inner conflicts, with re-sults apparent in every formal aspect of the sonnet. The wealth of ingenious and sensitive imagery, the flexible metres and lively diction, the exceptional variety of verse-forms, all draw their sanction and motivation from this primary need.

The device of personification is the outstanding feature in the imagery of *Astrophel and Stella*. It was a medieval habit of thought which continued to influence great poets well into the seventeenth century, when it was practised almost universally in sermons, pamphlets, novels, and even in chance, unstudied speech. Dr Janet Spens has aptly commented upon the impli-cations of its use:

> ... the Elizabethans tended to utter their own intense emotions through the imagery of human figures: the men of the nineteenth century had been trained to accept the expression of theirs through the imagery of inanimate nature. 'Strong imagination,' says Theseus, 'if it would apprehend some joy ... comprehends a bringer of that joy.' A vivid mental experience seemed to the Elizabethans like another personality affecting them from with-out. Personification was not a fully conscious mental acvitity, but an involuntary result of the combination of intense emotion with an inherited habit of mind.[1]

Practised thus as an almost unconscious descriptive habit, per-sonification crops up on every page of *Astrophel and Stella*.

> I sought fit words to paint the blackest face of woe (I)

> Honour is honour'd, that thou doest possesse
>   Him as thy slaue, and now long needy Fame
>   Doth euen grow rich, naming my *Stellas* name. (XXXV)

> And oft whole troupes of saddest words I staid,
>   Striuing abroad aforaging to go. (LV)

1. Janet Spens, *Spenser's Faerie Queene* (1934), p. 55.

But this device also performed a necessary function in Sidney's pursuit of self-knowledge, and in a number of well-worked-out conceits deliberate principles governed his choice. He was familiar with the Platonic psychology which divided the soul into three categories: the rational part which existed to serve truth; the spiritual part, promoting virtue (in its original connotation of courage and public spirit), and the sensual, appetitive part which represented physical desire. Whereas in the good man, reason was king and governed his lower faculties through virtue, in the weak or wicked, sense rebelled against the higher categories of the psyche and set up its own tyranny. This concept of the insurrection of sense against reason and virtue was in close accord with Sidney's own experience, and in seeking a poetic interpretation of his psychic conflicts the obvious course was to present them as quarrels between personified faculties. But Sidney was no doctrinaire moralist; he was more concerned with understanding himself than with edifying his readers. If his desire for Stella was irrational it was nevertheless very real. Intellectual honesty required that he preserve his sense of humour, and with it a capacity for accepting the most paradoxical situations. Accordingly the figures of Reason, Virtue, and Sense were given parts in miniature allegorical episodes, not unlike the comic scenes of contemporary Interludes. The more respectable protagonists were caught out in ridiculous postures, while the disreputable ones, like the Vice and his agents, were made to score over them by some quibble or trick. Desire or Sense, with Love as a close ally, played their parts in the symbolical drama, while Astrophel himself, the detached observer of his own psyche, and Stella, cause of all the troubles, completed the cast. Thus Reason was ordered to stop 'brabbling' with Sense and Love; if he refused, the aggrieved partners would join forces to strike him with Stella's glances, and he would be made to kneel and prove 'by reason good, good reason her to love' (x). Or Virtue and Love brought a law-suit, each claiming possession of Stella. Love argued that Stella's body belonged as a matter of course to him; Virtue answered that the true Stella was her soul. Astrophel, revealing in the last lines his own interest in Love's suit, gave Stella to Virtue . . . on condition that her body be handed over to Love, and that he himself be given a share in the spoil (LII).

Platonic psychology is overlaid in these conceits by direct observation, and as we have seen in sonnets VIII and XVII, realistic situations are contrived instead of the rather trite settings of the *Quattrocento* writers and later epigrammatists. While Petrarch's venerable *Amor*, invoked as *L'alto signor*, or even *Quell'antiquo mio dolce empio signore*, had long since become a merely decorative figure for these poets and their French imitators, Sidney gave the love god a new and positive rôle in dramatizing the erotic side of his nature. There are, indeed, two distinct personifications: the mischievous boy Cupid, who symbolizes the physical urge of desire, and the more sensitive, susceptible youth Love, who represents the imaginative condition of romance. Both are dramatically very much alive, in some respects calling to mind the child actors of the fifteen-eighties; and Astrophel is accompanied by one or other of these lads wherever he goes. Sometimes they mediate, sometimes interfere, between him and Stella, and in the course of their adventures enact the ups and downs of his shifting fortunes.

Most interesting of all, though it only appears sporadically, is a kind of personification which marks a new, highly significant trend in English poetry. It occurs notably in sonnets XXXI, XXXIX, LXXXIV, XCVIII, and CIII. Here, where Sidney invokes the moon, sleep, his bed, the highway, the river, the images confer personality not on a concept or a faculty of the mind, but on things inanimate. The poet's imagination is directed outwards to the world of impersonal nature, upon which he bestows his own moods and responses. It is a mode of perception with as yet few precedents in English verse tradition. Superficially a comparison might be made with the Italian mythopœic genius, best evinced, perhaps, in Petrarch's great nature metaphors, which penetrate to the inner life of rivers, mountains, and seas. But Sidney's penetration is far less complete. The objects he contemplates must be suffused with his own personality before they can arouse his poetic sympathy. Thus the Thames rejoices—not, like Petrarch's Rhône, in its own seaward course, but in bearing Stella, whose very boat dances for joy. Sleep is bribed with 'smooth pillows, sweetest bed': the moon's 'wan face' shows that it too has been in love: the highway, for its kindness to Astrophel, receives a blessing. These fancies, however, foreshadow a more complete integration of the destinies of nature and mankind in the poetry of the last years of the century. There will be, as it were, a stereoscopic focusing of the inner and outer panoramas within a single line of vision: yet the vision itself will be intrinsically different from that of the Italians, harking back in its essential character to a peculiarly English view of life.

Since the expression of a complex personality was the driving force of Sidney's sonnets, it is to be expected that metre and diction should display an extraordinary range and flexibility. The Tudor pioneers of the sonnet had been largely concerned with the primary need to evolve a standard poetic diction and standard verse-rhythms. For them the simplest epithets and the purest English terms were the best. Sidney had already grasped the rudiments of their technique in the sonnets of *Arcadia*: he was free now to strike out for himself and invent his personal idiom. In *Astrophel and Stella* he coined such compounds as 'rose-enameld skies', 'past-praise hue', 'long-with-loue-acquainted eyes'; employed technical and somewhat recondite words like 'quintessence', 'metamorphosed', 'demurre', 'flegmatike'; and indulged in elaborate word-play and burlesque alliteration—

> Of touch they are that without touch doth touch (IX)

> Into your rimes, running in ratling rowes (XV)

Even more striking was his use of colloquialisms and current speech-rhythms. To a certain extent Wyatt had practised these methods in his sonnets, but he was never so confident of his medium as to ring the changes we find in *Astrophel and Stella*:

> Guesse we the cause, what is it thus? fie, no:
> Or so? much lesse: how then? sure thus it is: (LXXIV)

> What, he? say they of me, now I dare sweare,
> He cannot loue: no, no, let him alone. (LIV)

Sidney's metres are in fact so closely associated with speech-rhythms that they can hardly be considered separately. The speaking voice determines the scansion of

Flie, fly, my friends, I haue my death wound; fly (xx)

Let her go: soft, but here she comes, go to, (xLVII)

I start, looke, hearke, but what in closde vp sence
      Was held, in opend sense it flies away (xxxVIII)

A comparison of such lines with the early experiments of
W. att makes it plain that Sidney's departures from the standard iambic pentameter were quite deliberate, the results not
of immaturity but of self-assurance. The octave of sonnet
LXVIII may be taken as an example of his remarkable subtlety
and flexibility.

> *Stella*, the onely Planet of my night,
>   Light of my life, and life of my desire,
>   Chiefe good, whereto my hope doth only aspire,
>   World of my wealth, and heau'n of my delight.
> Why doest thou spend the treasures of thy sprite,
>   With voice more fit to wed *Amphions* lyre,
>   Seeking to quench in me the noble fire,
>   Fed by thy worth, and blinded[1] by thy sight?

Astrophel's temperament informs the metre of every one of
these eight lines. The poet's epithets for Stella are impetuous
and hyperbolical. It is impossible to marshal them into the
steady pace of iambic pentameters: each of the first four lines
commences with a strongly marked trochee and has four main
speech stresses with only a light rest to make up the standard
five feet. In lines 5, 6, and 7 there is a return to metrical regularity, corresponding with the forced calm of a speaker trying
to use all the arts of persuasion, though the initial trochees in
lines 5 and 7 suggest the accumulated impatience which lies
below the surface. Then in line 8 the realization that Stella is
herself responsible for the fire she seeks to quench prompts a
return to the impetuous metre of the first quatrain.

Not always is Sidney concerned with articulating the moods
and passions of Astrophel. Sometimes the words and metres
seek to represent the personality of Stella, or of some unspeci-

1. I have preferred 'blinded' from the Folio of 1598 to the Q2 variant 'kindled' accepted by Mona Wilson (and previously by Grosart).
Its violence, and even the confusion of its transferred epithet, seems
more characteristic of Sidney's mood than the weaker, more consistent
word.

fied friend who gives advice and confers blame, or perhaps of
an allegorical figure: they talk, argue, jest, plead or remon-
strate, according to the requirements of the situation. But
whoever speaks, it is to the poet's own ego that we are eventually returned for self-analysis, self-pity, or self-congratula-
tion. Here lies the essential contrast to Shakespeare's approach
in the sonnets to the Friend. Both poets employ dramatic techniques, but Shakespeare's interests are far more genuinely extraverted, while for Sidney it is the inner, subjective drama
that chiefly matters. The outstanding exceptions appear in
that little group of sonnets already mentioned, where the
poet's imagination turns to consider the inanimate world.
Here diction and metre are subdued to what Sidney regards
as the intrinsic qualities of sleep, the moon, the highway, the
river.

> Come sleepe, ô sleepe, the certaine knot of peace,
>> The baiting place of wit, the balme of woe,
>> The poore mans wealth, the prisoners release,
>> Th' indifferent Judge betweene the high and low;
> With shield of proofe shield me from out the prease . . .

In these lines, Sidney's diction is full of hypnotic suggestion.
There is a flow of hushing sibilants through the first line,
echoed in the word 'place' of line 2. The b-labials, common to
both epithets describing the blessings of sleep in the second line,
are related in sound to the plosives in line 3, 'poore' and
'prisoner', where the accentuated words relate to human suffering. The s-assonance with its lulling effects appears yet
again in 'the prisoners release', followed by a quiet metrical
harmony which ends the quatrain. And in the fifth line the
hushing sounds return, with a sequence of sonorous long
vowels and an iteration of the word 'shield', as noun and again
as verb. It is a consummate piece of spell-binding, with its
powerful and sustained evocations of all that sleep signifies to
mankind, and here, where the impersonal outlook predomin-
ates, metrical regularity is scrupulously maintained.

Sidney's sonnet-form in *Astrophel and Stella* has sometimes
been termed a compromise between the 'Surrey' and 'Petrarchan' styles. It is a vague, unhelpful description which ignores the remarkable number of rhyme-variants to be found.
In the 108 sonnets of the sequence there are four types of

octave[1] and six types of sestet,[2] with fourteen different com-
binations of rhyme. On the other hand, the verse-structure
follows quite well-marked lines, and when taken in conjunction with the rhyme-patterns, there is no great difficulty in
stating the general principles of form.

Earlier in this chapter we saw that the three sonnets—
LXXI, XVII, and VIII—which were considered in relation to their
sources all showed a common structural basis. In these, the
octave followed the Petrarchan rhyme-scheme, but was subdivided by syntax into more clearly marked quatrain units
than the Italian form provided for. The sestet diverged considerably, being constructed on two distinct but interrelated
principles: a tercet division set up by the syntax, and a quatrain and couplet division established by rhyme. No less than
fifty-nine of the 108 sonnets in *Astrophel and Stella* follow the
same pattern, with its octave rhyme-scheme (*abba,abba*) and
its interlocking technique in the sestet (*cdc,dee*). In other sonnets the octave variants show no serious departure in basic
structure. They stress the quatrain subdivision with greater or
less emphasis; but, with the exception of only one minor sonnet (XXVI), they preserve the integral rhyme-scheme of the
octave. With regard to the sestet structure, twenty-two of these
remaining sonnets repeat the pattern of the majority group,
and four (XIII, XXII, XXXV, and LVI) show only the insignificant
variant *cdd,cee*. The basic form of our first three examples is
thus maintained through eighty-five of the sonnets. Finally,
the main sestet variants, *ccd,ccd* and *ccd,eed*, prove on examination to be carrying out much the same function as the staple
form. Unlike the Petrarchan sestet, whose purpose is to corre-
late the perceptions expressed in the octave, and the Surrey
form, which adds a third verse unit and a final summing up in
the couplet, these balance opposite considerations and induce
a kind of surprise conclusion in the last lines. Sonnet XCI is a
typical example:

> Now since her chaste mind hates this loue in me
>> With chasten'd mind I straight must show that she
>> Shall quickly me from what she hates remoue.
> O Doctor Cupid, thou for me reply;

1. *abba abba : abab abab : abab baba : abab cbcb.*
2. *cdcdee : ccdeed : cddcee : ccdccd : cdcdcd : cddece.*

> Driuen else to graunt, by angels sophistry
> That I loue not without I leaue to loue.

This rhyme-pattern in the sestet is generally reserved for the lighter poems of the sequence. With its two sets of rhyming couplets, it produces a somewhat jaunty impression, and has not the subtlety of the staple interlocking technique. It may be said of Sidney's verse-forms that, despite their seeming variety, they nearly always serve one function, which is to give effect to the poet's sense of unresolved subjective tensions: usually through a tripartite syllogism which is wrought up, through the interplay of syntax and rhyme-scheme, or the balancing of separate rhyme-units as above, to a conclusion of succinct paradox.

The staple sonnet-form of *Astrophel and Stella* is not really a modification of Surrey's 'English', or of Petrarch's 'Italian' models, and certainly not a 'compromise' between the two. In all probability it was suggested by the maturer sonnets of Wyatt, to which there was easy access in Tottel's anthology. Wyatt it was who first set forth the arrangement of quatrain and couplet in the sestet, following an integral rhyme-pattern in the octave. The steps he took have been described earlier in this book: it will be remembered that three of his sonnets, numbered XCII, XCV, and CLXXIII in the Muir edition, have the rhyme-scheme *cdc,dee* in their sestet, the others showing the variant *cdd,cee*. Moreover, the interlocking of rhyme and syntax, which Sidney exploited so brilliantly, appears in Wyatt's sonnets LVI, XCII, and CLXXV. The structure of the following sestet is a prototype of Sidney's form:

> Sephame saide true that my nativitie
>   Mischaunced was with the ruler of the May:
>   He gest, I prove, of that the veritie.
> In May my welth and eke my liff, I say,
>   Have stonde so oft in such perplexitie:
>   Reioyse! let me dreme of your felicitie. (XCII)[1]

For the most part Wyatt's sonnets are built upon clear-cut emotional contrasts, between his mistress's behaviour and his own, between his misery and the joys of others, etc. In this poem, a subsequent train of thought, relating to the unlucky

1. Muir, p. 75.

character of the month for him, introduces a subsidiary theme running over into the final couplet. But the last line breaks away, dismisses the subject, and returns to the original theme of the octave. Sidney would have found means to bring out the paradox with all possible force. For him, emotional states were also intellectual and spiritual dilemmas requiring analysis and definition. He built upon the technical foundations that Wyatt had laid, but exploited their potentialities more fully than the earlier poet had either envisaged or required.

Finally, in the separate sonnet 'Leaue me ô Loue', there was a return to the verse-form of Surrey which had characterized the best work of the *Arcadia* period. The storm and stress of the infatuation was over; singleness of purpose and a resolved state of mind had emerged from the inner conflicts of the *Astrophel and Stella* sequence, and taken the shape of a bitter scorn for earthly love and an ardent longing to 'aspire to higher things'. Released from its perplexities, his genius leapt forward and made this sonnet perhaps his greatest poetic triumph. Surrey's form lent itself to simple logical constructions, and set forth aphorism and wit with much economy and grace; it could give a mature appearance to the work of a juvenile composer, if he was sufficiently dexterous; but in the hands of a great poet it was a means to the simplicity which accompanies the sublime. Sidney had used this form skilfully enough in his younger days; he had discarded it when experience grew more complex; and now he turned to it again when his problems were resolved. The wheel had come full circle, and the facility of his early work was transformed into power under perfect control.

V

SPENSER

DURING the four years that followed the appearance of *Astrophel and Stella* in 1591, more sonnets saw the light than in all the decades since Wyatt made his first renderings from Petrarch. A wave of literary fashion carried the sonnet on its crest, and most of the younger writers were quick to seize the chance of winning early celebrity. Certain generic qualities belong to the work of this period, which will be described in the next chapter; but Spenser's *Amoretti* sequence has a marked independence which calls for separate attention. Unlike most of the poets who were caught up in the sonnet vogue, Spenser was fully mature. Over forty years old in 1595 when *Amoretti* was published, he had completed six books of *The Faerie Queene*, besides a great many shorter works. A complex poetic development lay behind his sonnets, and while it is plain that they were influenced by the techniques of the young generation, we shall only understand their true character by relating them to Spenser's own literary past.

In 1569, as a youngster of seventeen, Spenser had contributed some crude 'sonets' and 'epigrams' to Van der Noodt's tract, *Theatre for Worldlings*. Translations of verse by Marot and Du Bellay, they set forth a number of fables and symbolistic 'visions', and were accompanied by a set of emblematic woodcuts, according to a common sixteenth-century fashion. The so-called 'sonets' were rhymeless stanzas, all but one of them fourteen lines in length; two of the 'epigrams' adopted Surrey's sonnet rhyme-scheme; none of the verses showed the slightest grasp of the principles of sonnet construction. Ordinarily, such juvenilia would be charitably forgotten; but Spenser himself showed a surprising desire to keep the world in mind of what he had once written. Twenty-two years later, in 1591, he republished the verses from the old tract in his new volume of *Complaints*, under the titles *Visions of Bellay* and *Visions of Petrarch*. There was a certain amount of polishing: some 'sonets' were fitted with the Surrey rhyme-scheme, and the twelve-line 'epigrams' were expanded by couplets stating an explicit moral; while in place of the original *envoi* to the *Petrarch* a new sonnet was written, using an original scheme of interlacing rhymes.[1] But the subject-matter was still in the creaking didactic strain of the earlier work, and there was still no apparent interest in the customary themes of the sonnet medium. Finally, in *Visions of the Worlds Vanitie*, which formed part of the same volume, a general system of interlacing rhymes was established on which the characteristic 'Spenserian' form was based.

Here was indeed a strange development. It is certain that Spenser, as the friend of Sidney and the admirer of Tasso's works, must have been familiar at an early stage with the forms and functions of the Renaissance love sonnet. Yet for close on twenty-five years he was content to use this form for little more than pious exhortations and homiletic laments on the mutability of worldly things. During this time he developed a form which, beginning as a crude rhymeless stanza, proceeded to a mechanical imitation of the Surrey sonnet—whose quatrain units with their clear-cut logic were never purposefully applied—and thence to a kind of expository verse paragraph which had no real affinity to the sonnet medium. Spenser was a master of verse-craft: there can be no question of mere technical incapacity. Evidently some deep-rooted aversion to the sonnet as a mode of self-expression, and to the forms which reflected its processes of thought, underlay this negative approach.

No reader of Spenser's major poems should be in any doubt as to the real cause of such antipathies. They lay in a cast of mind, and a conscious view of life, that required all sensuous experience to be interpreted on a conceptual plane as a preliminary to its expression in verse. This requirement governed Spenser's treatment of his own personality as well as of the men and women he knew. Thus in *The Shepheardes Calender*, his first serious work, the poet himself, his friends, and his lady appear only as the stock figures in a pastoral setting. Of all

1. The following developments in rhyme-linked quatrains may be noted. Linking of the first and second quatrains: *Visions of Bellay* 7, 8, 11, and *Ruines of Rome*, st. 30; of the first and third quatrains: *Bellay* 3 and *Rome* 3, 29; and of the second and third, *Rome* 6 and *envoi*.

literary forms, the pastoral is probably the least suited to an intensive exploration of character. In essence it is a mode of simplification, a deliberate quest for general principles of human conduct. Love is indeed one of its main themes; but only as a universal experience, like birth and death, spring and winter. In treating the effects of love upon the individual, the pastoral is a primitive instrument that strikes only two notes: love scorned, and love requited; all finer modulations lie outside its range. By presenting himself through the figure of Colin Clout the shepherd, Spenser chose to confine self-expression within the narrowest bounds. All that went to make up the courtier, scholar, and poet was excluded: there remained only those qualities which he shared with undifferentiated mankind.

But *The Shepheardes Calender* was merely a preliminary to *The Faerie Queene*, where Spenser's wide range of interests found their positive expression. In allegory, actuality is projected into myth, and personified concepts take the place of individuals. Characteristically, Sidney had shown little interest in its methods. 'When I say Stella, I do mean the same', he had declared. Symbols and personifications were only devices to forward the primary task of self-analysis: personal expression was a necessity of his genius, so that his more serious love poetry was inevitably voiced through the sonnet. But for Spenser love was a cosmic force, not to be apprehended within the limits of one man's experience, nor analysed according to the promptings of the fallible ego. Hence individual perception became part of a more widely integrated vision. The rudimentary self-portrait of Colin Clout was followed by a sustained exploration of all the complex modes of love known to the romance tradition, in a medium that transcended the distinction between personal and impersonal forms of expression. Thus the episode of Amoret and Scudamour was neither an account of Spenser's own courtship, nor a tale about some other man and woman, real or fictitious, but a treatment of the *idea* of betrothal. So too with the negative or harmful aspects of romance as they had been known to Sidney. In the Masque of Cupid the mental sufferings of an Astrophel were taken into the annals of erotic torment down the ages; Desire's cry for food was heard again in the House of Busyrane, not solely from one man's lips; the temptations of the eye, which Sidney found so hard to resist, became a universal seduction in the Bower of Bliss.

For Sidney, as for all the poets of courtly love, romance was bound to have an end in dust and ashes. Sooner or later must come a time for renouncing the vanities of sense; and for an English Protestant the end was foreseen from the beginning. But Spenser, sharing the same religion and outlook, proposed a new and lasting resolution of the ancient dilemma. Instead of writing palinodes to the love of the senses, he terminated his allegorical episodes with marriage. The nuptials of *The Faerie Queene* were, of course, symbolical unions, not matches between actual men and women. Yet in terms of the allegory they performed a special function. Marriage for the Elizabethan was not merely a social convention, still less a 'private affair': primarily it was a sacrament, the outward and visible sign of an inward and spiritual grace. It bridged the gulf between the ideal and the actual; it reunited spirit to sense, and was at once symbol and reality. As the figurative knights and ladies passed to their nuptials, the allegorical shapes of romance dissolved before the greater allegory of life itself; and love, purged and consecrated in marriage, was left as the indestructible residue of truth. Consequently a stage was reached in Spenser's poetry where symbolism achieved its proper consummation, and sublimated reality took its place. This becomes apparent in the final cantos of Book VI of *The Faerie Queene*, which restore the pastoral setting of *The Shepheardes Calender*. On the high plateau of Mount Acidale, rising above the bewildering forests and enchanted castles of allegory, the shepherd folk reappear, amongst them the poet himself in the person of Colin Clout. A great spiral of experience has been traced—the distance between the two pastoral extremes of love scorned and love requited. Colin Clout is now betrothed to his shepherdess, while a hundred graces, naked and unashamed, surround her radiant form.

With the completion of Book VI of *The Faerie Queene*, the process of purging love from romance illusions was complete. Henceforth in the poems that Spenser wrote up to the time of his death, personal experience, subject always to the necessary moral qualifications, was directly voiced. To this final period

belong the great marriage hymn *Epithalamion*, the *Hymnes*, and
the principal sonnets of courtship and betrothal in *Amoretti*.

   Amoretti first appeared in 1595, in a small octavo volume
published by William Ponsonby, which also contained *Epithalamion* and four untitled epigrams inserted between the
longer poems. Eighty-eight sonnets make up a sequence describing the poet's courtship.[1] A few details are lightly sketched
in: there is mention of the lady gazing in her mirror (XLV);
wearing a golden hair-net (XXXVII); or busying herself with
embroidery (LXXI). An evening when the poet leaves her
house to make his way home in the storm is commemorated
(XLVI), and also a time when she burnt his letter (XLVIII). But
none of this has the vividness of Sidney's descriptions, and in
general the sonnets are more concerned with the state of mind
of the poet and his lady than with the circumstances of their
love affair. From references to the seasons it appears that the
sequence covers a span of rather more than a year. After re-
jecting the poet's suit for some twelve months, the lady's attitude changes. She begins to show him favour, and they are betrothed. The courtship proceeds harmoniously for a while;
then in LXXXVI there is a bitter complaint that the poet has
been slandered. The last three sonnets are a lament at the
separation of the lovers, and the reader is left in some doubt as
to the final outcome.
   According to the traditional view, *Amoretti* and *Epithalamion*
were to be taken together as a single, composite work in cele-
bration of Spenser's courtship and marriage. In consequence
a tendency appeared to approach the sonnets rather as frag-
ments of autobiography than as poems. Guesses were made as
to when the love affair began, how long the betrothal lasted,
and what was the exact date of the wedding. Critical estimates
frequently depended on the particular reader's liking or dislike for Spenser in the part of a lover. If the reader sympathized most with passion, wit, and gallantry, he would usually find
Sidney's sonnets more appealing; if he drew greater satisfaction from a calmer, more domestically approved brand of
love-making, he would incline towards *Amoretti*. The question

   1. Eighty-nine sonnets are printed in the text, but XXXV and LXXXIII are
virtually identical. See p. 101.

of literary achievement was largely overlooked in the more or less conscious reaction to what was thought to be a kind of confessional verse.

About half a century ago, however, such interpretations became a target for much the same attacks as were directed against traditional estimates of *Astrophel and Stella*. Spenser's 'originality' and 'sincerity' were both called into question. Research into foreign sources, vigorously pursued by Lee— and followed later by L. E. Kastner, Janet G. Scott, and others —showed that many of the sonnets, besides their generic relation to the Petrarchan tradition, were undoubtedly imitated from poems by French and Italian writers of the sixteenth century. Moreover, it came to be questioned whether the sequence could, after all, be closely linked with *Epithalamion*; whether it was addressed to the poet's intended wife or to some imaginary person; whether the sequence was indeed a sequence, or 'merely an agglomeration of two, or even three, earlier-composed sets of sonnets'.[1] Now from the viewpoint adopted in this book, a great deal of such speculation is irrelevant or misleading. A Renaissance poet need not lack originality because he writes within a tradition and bases his work on earlier models. Nor need his poetic sincerity be impugned because he fails to keep to biographical fact. It is a matter of indifference to criticism whether Spenser 'addressed sonnets' to his actual fiancée or to a fictitious heroine; whether he took just twelve months to write the sonnets relating to a year of courtship, or whether, for that matter, he sat up industriously through his wedding night composing the last stanzas of *Epithalamion*. But when all this has been discounted, certain problems remain which are of true critical relevance.

It is evident that the number of sonnets bearing upon events after the mention in LX of a complete year of courtship is disproportionate to the whole; that the ending of the sequence is oddly indecisive; and that there is a clash in spirit between what one writer has termed the 'conventional' and the 'loverlike' elements. These defects, whatever their causes, pertain to the literary value of the sequence, its structure and integrity. More remarkable still, perhaps, are the inconsistencies in the

1. See the controversy between Percy W. Long and J. C. Smith in *Modern Language Review*, III (1908), pp. 257–67 and V (1910), pp. 273–81.

characterization of the heroine. The Petrarchan beloved certainly underwent a transformation in the Elizabethan sonnet. Her attributes of virtue as well as of beauty often proved skindeep, and while alluding to them in set terms, the English poet usually managed to reveal his more individual interests. The result was a crop of minor descriptive anomalies which should not be considered too solemnly. But Spenser's characterization went far beyond this. We need only pick a run of seven sonnets early in the sequence to find contradictions which even the most liberal allowance for convention must fail to reconcile. Sonnets VII–X take for their theme the lady's eyes: in VII the poet speaks of their miraculous influence upon his soul:

> For when ye mildly looke with louely hew,
>   then is my soule with life and loue inspired
>   but when ye lowre, or looke on me askew,
>   then doe I die, as one with lightning fyred.

This is followed in VIII by a far-reaching discovery:

> Thrugh your bright beames doth not the blinded guest
>   shoot out his darts to base affections wound:
>   but Angels come to lead fraile mindes to rest
>   in chast desires on heauenly beauty bound.

The age-old comparison of the lady's glances to the mischievous darts of Cupid has been abandoned; they have become an angelic ministration, spiritual and Christian, with no taint of pagan eroticism. And in IX, after this has been dwelt on for three sonnets, the climax comes in the last two lines:

> Then to the Maker selfe they likest be,
>   whose light doth lighten all that here we see.

All this promises interesting developments in the treatment of love: yet in the very next sonnet the little blind god returns to his ancient seat:

> See how the Tyrannesse doth ioy to see
>   the huge massacres which her eyes do make:
>   and humbled harts brings captiues vnto thee,
>   that thou of them mayst mightie vengeance take.

XI is in the same tone: the lady is the 'cruell warriour', not to be moved with reason or with ruth; and XII speaks of

> a wicked ambush which lay hidden long
> in the close couert of her guilefull eyen.

Yet xiii reverts to the lofty conception of sonnets vii–ix as though nothing had intervened.

> In that proud port, which her so goodly graceth,
>> whiles her faire face she reares vp to the skie:
>> and to the ground her eie lids low embaseth,
>> most goodly temperature ye may descry,
> Myld humblesse mixt with awfull maiesty.

Similar inconsistencies recur frequently in the first sixty sonnets; and there are, besides, two distinct anachronisms. xxxvii alludes to the golden hair-net the lady wears. The poet warns his eyes to take heed lest they become trapped in 'that guilefull net', and concludes:

> Fondnesse it were for any being free,
> To couet fetters, though they golden bee.

The implication is that the poet still regards himself as a 'free man' with hopes of escaping from love's entanglements. Yet the sonnet occurs at quite an advanced place in the sequence, after he has protested many times against his intolerable thraldom. Secondly, there is a break in the explicit time-span. Sonnet iv refers to new year, when 'lusty spring . . . is ready to come forth'; xxii mentions Lent, the 'holy season fit to fast and pray'. lx describes the completion of twelve months of courtship; and lxx alludes again to spring. But xxiii, placed straight after the first Lent sonnet, refers to about the same date as lx:

> for with one looke she spils that long I sponne,
> and with one word my whole yeares work doth rend.

From such discrepancies it is clear that we have to face not merely unevenness in quality, or hesitation between a 'conventional' and a 'lover-like' approach, but an attempted blending of two collections of sonnets, differing in subject-matter, characterization, and general conception. As a *poetic* creation—leaving aside all biographical questions—the lady of sonnets vii, viii, ix, and xiii is not the lady of sonnets x, xi, and xii; the author's attitude is not the same; and the ana-

chronistic time-references also heighten the sense of incongruity. When Spenser's methods of composition are kept in
mind, this will not seem very strange. He was in the habit of
tinkering with his works up to the last minute before publication, and there were frequent changes of plan, requiring insertions or omissions not always very skilfully carried out. *The
Faerie Queene* shows many traces of drastic and hasty revision,
and even in the relatively short poem *Colin Clouts Come Home
Againe* there was a sudden shift from panegyric to satire, almost
certainly as the result of a late insertion after the poem had
already been dedicated.[1] What probably happened with
Amoretti was that round about 1594 Spenser felt the urge to
make his own contribution in the sonnet medium. He had by
him a fair number of individual sonnets, some dating back a
few years, others written in recent months during the pause
following the completion of Part II of *The Faerie Queene* which
is mentioned in sonnet LXXX. To make up a sequence, convention required him to recount the story of his courtship from
its inception onwards, providing an adequate record of the
lovers' moods and encounters. At this stage of his literary
development, however—and perhaps at this point in his private life—he was no longer imaginatively concerned with the
wide range of erotic experience that had already been explored on the level of allegory. His interest lay in a single,
resolved state of love: the condition of assured courtship awaiting its consecration in marriage. A large number of the recent
sonnets would tend to celebrate betrothal, and relatively few
would probe its antecedent anxieties. To redress the balance,
the simplest expedient would be to take up some earlier sonnets on the vicissitudes of *amour courtois*, written experimentally
as off-shoots of the main allegorical work, and attach as many
as were needed to the opening and middle portions of *Amoretti*.
It was not uncommon for Elizabethan poets to adapt old verse
to new purposes—Spenser's own treatment of the verse in der
Noodt's tract is an obvious example—and this would explain,
though not artistically condone, the presence of sonnets that
jarred with the dominant tone of the sequence.

Whatever Spenser's intentions were, there are unmistakable

1. This was noted by Emile Legouis, *Spenser* (1931), p. 13 (English
edition).

signs of haste and botching in the little 1595 volume containing *Amoretti* and *Epithalamion*. Spenser was in Ireland at the time, and Ponsonby was given far too much of a free hand. The edition abounded in printer's errors, both of spelling and punctuation. There was a prose dedication to a minor figure whose sole connection with the poems seems to lie in the not so striking coincidence that they had travelled with him in the same boat from Ireland (Spenser never failed to dedicate his works to some eminent, carefully chosen personage). Tacked on to the end of the sequence was a set of so-called epigrams, unlike any poem from Spenser's pen, unmentioned on the title-page and printed, it might seem, for no other purpose than to fill up gatherings in the little volume. Looked at in detail, the blunders in arrangement are such as a sharp-witted but unimaginative member of the book trade would commit when the author was out of reach. The anachronisms of XXIII and XXXVII, for instance, were either implied or occurred at the end of a long conceit: a quick glance over the poems would pass them by. The sonnets now numbered VII, VIII, IX, and XIII were 'about eyes', and so too were those now numbered X and XII; while the conceit on 'weary war' in XI matched that on 'massacres' in X: the easiest arrangement was to lump them together. Most striking of all was the printing of two versions of the same sonnet, differing in only one word, as nos. XXXV and LXXXIII. Perhaps the 'hasty accidents' mentioned at the end of *Epithalamion* had something to do with this muddle; perhaps the manuscripts were disarranged in transit. Certainly we are not obliged to treat the printed edition as definitive or immutable.

There would seem to be only one way of doing justice to Spenser's sequence, and that is by setting apart those sonnets which evidently belong to an earlier phase and run counter to the general stream of thought and feeling. The sonnets numbered X, XI, XII, XXIII, and XXXVII are, as we have seen, out of place and out of accord. XX, XXXI, XLVII, LIII, and LVI resemble these so much in style, and conflict so manifestly with the dominant tone, that they may reasonably be taken as belonging to the same class. A further eight sonnets—XVIII, XXV, XXXII, XXXVIII, XLI, XLVIII, XLIX, and LIV—are less marked in character, but certainly add nothing to the merits of the sequence and show few traces of Spenser's mature style. In all, there are at least some eighteen sonnets best considered apart from the main group.[1]

All these relate to the experience of the scorned lover. The lady is represented not only as proud and disdainful—familiar attributes of the Petrarchan heroine—but also as sly, licentious, savage, and guileful. Her influence upon her lover is wholly and designedly evil: she takes pleasure in enticing him by every feminine wile, and once he is in her clutches she torments him and mocks at his plight. She is a 'Tyrannesse' whose eyes have wrought 'huge massacres' (x); a 'cruell warriour' who 'greedily her fell intent poursewth' (xi); a beast 'more cruell and more saluage wylde Then either Lyon or the Lyonesse' (xx). These perfervid epithets, and many others, are far from playful. Precedents may be found for one or another in French or Italian sonnets of the time, but their cumulative effect is quite distinctive. Yet the verse shows no trace of personal excitement, let alone hysteria. Not once is the smooth sweep of iambics halted or given a jolt; nowhere does the thread of logic snap; and the carefully interlaced rhymes ensure throughout an unperturbed, harmonious flow of exposition. To understand these sonnets we must again look to Spenser's general poetic development. For many years he had been engaged upon an allegorical treatment of the sinful or negative aspects of love. In allegory, as in dreams, experiences were most effectively suggested by a heightening of qualities. Thus the woman who in real life exploited her sexual attraction became figuratively an enchantress murdering her victims. The lover's 'bleeding heart' underwent a literal vivisection with its attendant tortures. As with the pictures in the House of Busyrane,

> A thousand monstrous forms therein were made
> Such as false loue doth oft vpon him weare,
> For loue in thousand monstrous formes doth oft appeare.

But while this dream-technique served a useful function, there was no need for it to imitate the stresses of real life. For Spenser and his readers alike, the episodes were enacted on

1. In the traditional order: x, xi, xii, xviii, xx, xxiii, xxv, xxxi, xxxii, xxxvii, xxxviii, xli, xlvii, xlviii, xlix, liii, liv, and lvi.

a purely conceptual plane. All the allegorical monsters were made of pasteboard, however brightly painted. There was no reason why the most ghastly encounters and horrific spectacles should not be recounted in a style that remained polished, sonorous, and even.

But allegorical romance was one medium, and the sonnet another. The sonnet, indeed, came into being because a new, personal attitude to experience demanded expression. Why then did Spenser confound two distinct ways of writing? The answer seems to be that his outlook, grounded upon philosophical idealism, tended to a blurring of the distinction. In his view, perception and sensory experience were not intrinsically valid; the emotions of unhallowed or sensual love belonged at best to the category of half-truths, and could only be presented as fallacies, to be reviewed in the light of total, spiritual reality; could only be treated poetically, that is, in figurative terms. Hence whatever medium was chosen, a mistress who aroused sensual love would take on the semblance of an allegorical figure. If stern, she would be likened to a lioness; if pitiless, to a female tyrant whose hands dripped blood. Just as in allegory the descriptive hyperbole found no reflection in the form, so in these sonnets, too, there was no interruption of the alliterative euphony and the smooth flow of metre.

The remaining seventy-one sonnets make up the solid core of the *Amoretti* sequence. In considering Renaissance poetry, the first step must always be to determine 'the nature of the imitation'—in other words, to ascertain the distinctive qualities of a work by comparison with its models. While Spenser's sonnets were products of a lifetime's development and drew their ideas and inspiration from many sources, it is easy to distinguish certain immediate influences. For the general conception of the sequence we may look to the famous discourse of Bembo on *amor razionale* which ends the fourth book of Castiglione's *Il Cortegiano*. Widely known to English readers through Hoby's translation *The Courtier*, this popular work was certainly not the only channel through which a poet of Spenser's learning might discover the attitude of sixteenth-century Neoplatonism towards sexual love. But its mode of presentation made it especially suitable as a model. Instead of a formal disquisition, Castiglione set forth his opinions through a dialogue between a number of distinguished Italian ladies and gentlemen on the subject of courtship. The view is expressed that love is all very well for the young, but rather absurd and undignified for older people. Amidst laughter from the company, Bembo undertakes to show 'that olde men may love not onely without slaunder, but otherwhile more happily than yong men'. He proceeds to deliver an exposition of the nature of reasonable love, inspired by the attraction of soul, not sense, though without altogether excluding physical manifestations. For Spenser, himself approaching the age of forty, the discourse had a direct personal bearing, especially since the term 'old' was later defined as to be taken 'not for the age at the pits brinke, nor when the cannelles of the bodie be so feeble, that the soule can not through them worke her feates, but when knowledge in us is in his right strength'. Here was a serviceable bridge between philosophical theory and the personal medium of the sonnet-sequence, and it is easy to understand why in *Amoretti* Spenser patterned many phrases, images, and turns of thought upon the speech of Castiglione's 'not yong' courtier. However, his adaptation was by no means subservient. Castiglione's exposition was in fact a rather awkward attempt to combine the intellectual sublimation of courtly love with loftier flights of purely Platonic idealism. The approach in *Amoretti* was more subtle and integrated; it followed the lines of Spenser's own intellectual and spiritual development, shaped by Protestantism, by traditional English attitudes, and indeed by a first-hand knowledge of Neoplatonist teaching.

Besides this general influence, two sixteenth-century poets supplied models for particular sonnets. At least seven numbers of *Amoretti* were suggested by the verse of Desportes and twelve more by that of Tasso.[1] The resemblances vary considerably, some of Spenser's sonnets showing only minor variations, others diverging in important respects from their originals. The influence of Desportes counts chiefly in the earlier part of the sequence; that of Tasso is to be seen throughout, but predominantly in the later numbers. Spenser's indebted-

1. The combined investigations of Lee, Kastner, and Scott associate *Amoretti* XV, XXII, XXX, XLII, L, LX, and LXIX with Desportes, and IV, V, XIII, XXI, XLIII, LXVII, LXXII, LXXIII, LXXVI, LXXVII, LXXIX, and LXXXIV with Tasso. Detailed imitation is not generally implied.

ness to the French poet was occasioned by the same motives as
affected most of his contemporaries. Ingenious but second-rate,
Desportes was popular amongst the Elizabethans generally,
because his works made up in effect an omnibus collection of
the most celebrated themes of the age, rendered into a graceful, non-idiomatic French which could be read easily by most
educated Englishmen. Poets in search of a witty conceit or a
well-turned phrase consulted his volumes much as some
people do a dictionary of quotations. Tasso's influence was
more vital and individual. During the sixteenth century a new
school of poetry had arisen in Italy which rejected the super-
ficialities of the *concettisti*. Serious speculation took the place of
mere cleverness; Platonic or Neoplatonic teachings shaped the
treatment of themes; and chastity, both of style and sentiment,
was restored as a criterion of good verse. With this change of
outlook, the sonnet was preferred to the epigram and celebrated again, as in Petrarch's time, the divine qualities and
spiritual affinities of beauty. It was natural for Spenser to feel
a close sympathy with the new school, and especially with
Tasso, its leading figure. Some of his finest and most characteristic verse was directly inspired by the work of his Italian
contemporary.

Our initial approach to *Amoretti* will accordingly be made
through a comparison of some of his characteristic sonnets
with their models or analogues in Desportes and Tasso. One
comparison with the French poet will serve to distinguish
Spenser's own treatment of the same theme.

Diane 1, XLIII[1]

Solitaire et pensif, dans un bois écarté,
Bien loin du populaire et de la tourbe espesse,
Je veux bastir un temple à ma seule déesse,
Pour appendre mes vœux à sa divinité.

Là, de jour et de nuit, par moy sera chanté
Le pouvoir de ses yeux, sa gloire et sa hautesse;
Et devôt, son beau nom j'invoqueray sans cesse,
Quand je seray pressé de quelque adversité.

Mon œil sera la lampe et la flamme immortelle,

1. There are several versions of this sonnet, the above appearing in
editions from 1573 to 1581. Kastner's text (*Mod. Lang. Rev.* IV (1909),
p. 67) derives indirectly from a Rouen edition of 1611.

Qui me va consumant, servira de chandelle :
Mon corps sera l'autel, et mes souspirs les vœux.
   Par mille et mille vers je chanteray l'office,
Puis, espanchant mes pleurs et coupant mes cheveux,
J'y feray tous les jours de mon cœur sacrifice.

Amoretti XXII

This holy season fit to fast and pray,
   Men to deuotion ought to be inclynd:
   therefore, I lykewise on so holy day,
   for my sweet Saynt some seruice fit will find.
Her temple fayre is built within my mind,
   in which her glorious ymage placed is,
   on which my thoughts doo day and night attend
   lyke sacred priests that neuer thinke amisse.
There I to her as th'author of my blisse,
   will builde an altar to appease her yre:
   and on the same my hart will sacrifise,
   burning in flames of pure and chast desyre:
The which vouchsafe O goddesse to accept,
   amongst thy deerest relicks to be kept.

The broad similarities between the two sonnets are plain. Both poets attribute to their heroines semi-divine properties, and both employ a conceit whereby the services of love are likened to religious rites. In structure, the English poem resembles its French model. Spenser introduces no fresh material, and, like Desportes, makes the sacrifice of his heart the climax of the sonnet. But the details show some important contrasts. Desportes, wishing to build a temple to his 'only goddess', seeks escape from the crowd in the depths of some remote wood. He thinks of love as flourishing best in solitude and the wild, where the cult of Diana will not be desecrated by the humdrum life of the community. The temple is of course figurative, and the ritual, as the sestet reveals, is a piece of physical symbolism. The poet's eye will be the perpetual lamp before his lady's image, his body will be her altar, and his heart the daily sacrifice. The heathen worship of a goddess is thus transformed into the rites of *amour courtois,* to be enacted with a conscious air of defiance. Spenser immediately departs from this in his opening reference to Lent, 'this holy season fit to fast and pray'. Since he venerates his lady, he seeks likewise to perform 'some service fit'. This purely Christian sentiment completely disavows any suggestion of participation in a secret, half-pagan cult. Courtship for Spenser requires no escape from the community; on the contrary, at this season 'men to devotion ought to be inclynd', and the poet 'likewise' has his duties. By serving his beloved he is, in effect, taking part in a universal act of Christian worship. In keeping with this attitude, 'my sweet Saynt' is substituted for *ma seule déesse*, and the temple, with its heathen associations, is explained as a temple of the mind, already built and attended by thoughts like sacred priests.

The sestet develops these implications. Since love is in essence not a physical passion but a mental state, the conceit of Desportes, likening the service of love to a temple ritual, cannot be elaborated to include the body and its appurtenances. Only one image is kept, and so transformed as to be entirely in keeping with Spenser's attitude. The seat of affection is the heart: if the poet's love is to be made acceptable to his lady, its carnal defects must be atoned for. Therefore the heart is to be led, like a sacrificial victim, into the temple of the mind, and burned there 'in flames of pure and chast desyre'. So purged, it will take its place amongst the 'deerest relicks' of the sanctuary, and the virtue of the poet's love will have been reaffirmed. The genius which went to the making of *The Faerie Queene* is apparent in this fine conceit. After it, the careless use of the word 'goddesse' in line 13 strikes a false note, but still cannot obliterate the cumulative effect of what has gone before.

The second example of 'imitation' is not so much the modified version of Tasso's original as a parallel approach to the same theme.

TASSO (II. 316)[1]

> *Quell' alma ch'immortal, donna, traesti*
> > *Non dal girar de le superne roti*
> > *Ma dal grembo d'Iddio, macchiar non puote*
> > *Chi l'ammantò de le caduche vesti;*
> *E sono i suoi bei nodi in te contesti*
> > *Sì sottilmente, ch'ella indi si scuote*
> > *E vole verso il sole e forme ignote*

1. Ed. Solerti.

Vede a' mortai, bellezze alte e celesti.
Vede se stessa nel cristallo eterno
  Quasi 'n ispecchio, e vede a sé sembianti
  Mille che già peregrinaro al mondo.
Poi riede, e 'l limo suo purgato e mondo
  Rende così che col sembiante esterno
  Prende ed alletta i più cortesi amanti.

Amoretti (XIII)

In that proud port, which her so goodly graceth,
  whiles her faire face she reares vp to the skie;
  and to the ground her eie lids low embaseth,
  most goodly temperature ye may descry,
Myld humblesse mixt with awfull maiesty.
  For looking on the earth whence she was borne,
  her mind remembreth her mortalitie,
  what so is fayrest shall to earth returne.
But that same lofty countenance seemes to scorne
  base thing, and thinke how she to heauen may clime:
  treading downe earth as lothsome and forlorne,
  that hinders heauenly thoughts with drossy slime.
Yet lowly still vouchsafe to looke on me,
  such lowlinesse shall make you lofty be.

Tasso's sonnet restores, and indeed refines upon, the transcendental vision of Petrarch. His lady's soul—the true object
of love's desire—is no product of circumstance or the revolutions of the spheres, but emanates directly from the lap of God.
It cannot be soiled by the body's mean vesture, which it
shakes off at will to make its ascent heavenwards. On the way
it beholds unknown shapes, high and heavenly beauties. In
the eternal crystal of the sky it sees, as in a mirror, its own reflection, and views thousands of others making their pilgrimage on earth. Pitying them, the soul returns and, availing itself of its now purified clay, draws to it by means of its outward
garb those whose love is most deserving.—According to this
lofty conception, the nature and purpose of beauty, the relationship between body and spirit, are interpreted in the light
of Platonic idealism. Detailed representation of character is
not attempted, nor are the circumstances of courtship revealed. The theme emerges, not from empirical observations
of the lady's virtues, but wholly from an intuitive conviction.

Indeed the poet does not even speak of himself and his individual reactions—he is only included by implication amongst *i più cortesi amanti*, and seeks no more than his just deserts.

Like Tasso, Spenser professed himself a follower of Plato, and accepted the same doctrines as to the origin of beauty and the nature of love. Yet his treatment differs here profoundly. The main theme of the English sonnet is the lady's character as exhibited in her conduct, not the mystic essence of her soul. She is described as she might be encountered in life, and from her outward bearing her inner virtue may be deduced. She reveals a 'most goodly temperature', or balance of humours, defined as 'myld humblesse mixt with awful maiesty'. (The deliberate running over of the sentence into a fifth line lays grave emphasis upon this definition, which contrasts markedly with Sidney's use of the same phrase in the perfervid context of *Astrophel and Stella* XLVIII.)[1] She remembers at once earth to which her body must return, and heaven on which she must set her thoughts. Spenser's heroine is neither goddess nor saint, but a woman of natural piety, proud in her scorn for base and worldly things, humble in the knowledge of her defects. Her soul cannot soar to heaven in rapid flight; she is privileged with no special revelation of divine mysteries. Faced like other mortals with the heavy task of winning redemption by her own deserts, she thinks 'how she to heauen may clime'. Moreover, in these considerations her lover has an active part to play. He is, for the present, her humble suitor, but by stooping to look upon him she will make herself the loftier. It is the creed of the practising Protestant, rather than Platonic theory, which gives rise to this thought. For love is not only a means to the apprehension of true ideas; it is also the road leading through betrothal to sacramental marriage; and marriage, with its concomitant blessings and its fulfilment of the divine behest, is more exalted than the single state. Therefore the coming together of virtuous lovers is a happy event for which they are mutually beholden; and provided that mental esteem, not physical desire, is the primary impulse which unites them, both parties thereby enhance their spiritual condition.

In the second example from Tasso, Spenser found a model which required expression in a double sonnet.

1. See pp. 79–80 *supra*.

TASSO (III. 133)

Non son sì belli i fiori onde natura
  Nel dolce april de' vaghi anni sereno
  Sparge un bel volto, come in real seno
  È bel quel ch'a l'autunno Amor matura.
Maraviglioso grembo, orto e cultura
  D'Amore e paradiso mio terreno!
  Il mio audace pensier chi tiene a freno
  Se quello onde si nutre a te sol fura?
Quel che i passi fugaci d'Atalanta
  Volser dal corso, o che guardò il dragone,
  Son vili al mio desir ch'in te si pasce:
Né coglie Amor da peregrina pianta
  Pomo ch'in pregio di beltà ti done
  Ché nel tuo sen sol di te degno ei nasce.

Amoretti (LXXVI, LXXVII)

Fayre bosome fraught with vertues richest tresure,
  The neast of love, the lodging of delight:
  the bowre of blisse, the paradice of pleasure,
  the sacred harbour of that hevenly spright.
How was I ravisht with your lovely sight,
  and my frayle thoughts too rashly led astray?
  whiles diving deepe through amorous insight
  on the sweet spoyle of beautie they did pray.
And twixt her paps like early fruit in May,
  whose harvest seemd to hasten now apace:
  they loosely did theyr wanton winges display,
  and there to rest themselves did boldly place.
Sweet thoughts I envy your so happy rest,
  which oft I wisht, yet never was so blest.

Was it a dreame, or did I see it playne,
  a goodly table of pure yvory:
  all spred with iuncats, fit to entertayne
  the greatest Prince with pompous roialty.
Mongst which there in a silver dish did ly
  twoo golden apples of unvalewd price:
  far passing those which Hercules came by,
  or those which Atalanta did entice.
Exceeding sweet, yet voyd of sinfull vice,
  That many sought yet none could ever taste,
  sweet fruit of pleasure brought from paradice

by love himselfe and in his garden plaste.
Her brest that table was so richly spredd,
my thoughts the guests, which would thereon have fedd.

So far we have been concerned with various idealizing treatments of love: but here are sonnets which—ostensibly, at least—engage in frank, whole-hearted praise of the body. Sonnets LXXVI and LXXVII of *Amoretti* are frequently pointed to as evidence of Spenser's failure to reconcile his natural sensuousness with his moral creed. But the charge is based on a dangerously over-simplified estimate both of Spenser's religion and of his philosophy. For the true Protestant and the true Neoplatonist, the ladder leading from sense to spirit was a two-way thoroughfare, on which ascending and descending angels crossed; not, as some critics have implied, part of a game of snakes and ladders, where poets who step on the wrong square slip down abruptly to starting point.

Tasso opens with one of those highly evocative metaphors which so surely establish his place in the great Italian tradition. So characteristic is it of the Italian outlook that its meaning can only with difficulty be paraphrased in English.—The flowers of April, which Nature scatters upon earth, are not so fair as that bosom-fruit which Love is ripening for the Autumn. —As in Petrarch's sonnets, human life and inanimate growth are generically akin. *Amor* and *Natura* preside respectively over the maturing of the lady's physical beauty and the advent of the spring. The metaphor is expanded through the octave. How marvellous is this bosom, the garden and nursery of love, the poet's earthly paradise! Who can curb his thoughts when they break forth to steal their food from this sole source? In the sestet the loveliest and most far-ranging of classical myths illustrate the main image. That which turned from their course the fleeing footsteps of Atalanta, that which the dragon guarded, was mean in comparison with such fruit. For Love has never plucked from foreign plantation an apple so fair and precious as that which has its birth in the lady's bosom and alone is worthy of her. The whole sonnet is permeated with the atmosphere of pagan myth, an atmosphere directly diffused by that imaginative apprehension of life which views all physical beauty, all sensuous desire, as manifestations of the unseen divinity in nature.

By cumulative modifications of language, changes of stress, and significant insertions, Spenser produces a very different rendering of Tasso's theme. Sonnet LXXVI begins by discarding the metaphor of seasonal fruition with its accompanying personifications, the first four lines being devoted to direct eulogy, with two notable substitutions for the original imagery. The lady's bosom is 'fraught with vertues richest tresure', and is 'the sacred harbour of that heuenly spright'.[1] Physical beauty may and should be admired, so long as it is understood to be no end in itself. The rest of the sonnet centres upon the poet's state of mind. Whereas Tasso spoke with defiance of his 'bold thoughts' and in line 11 identified them openly with desire, Spenser is at first slightly embarrassed. There has been a sudden act of truancy. His 'frail thoughts' have 'too rashly' strayed away from their usual course: it is hoped they will come to no mischief. Like a parent who sees his young children scamper off down the street, he gazes after them with a mixture of pride and anxiety. The third quatrain takes up Tasso's first image, but it is emptied now of all mythological content. *Amor* and *Natura* have disappeared, and the metaphor is reduced to the incidental simile 'like early fruit in May', with but a subsidiary relationship to the main conception. Finally, in the last two lines, a decision is reached as to the propriety of the lover's thoughts. These have calmed down after their initial frolic and are safely asleep in the lady's bosom. Indulgently the poet envies them their happy rest: they have entered Love's paradise and recovered their first innocence.

> There with thy daughter *Pleasure* they doe play
> Their hurtlesse sports, without rebuke or blame,
> And in her snowy bosome boldly lay
> Their quiet heads, deuoyd of guilty shame,
> After full ioyance of their gentle game . . .
> *Hymne of Love*, 287–91

Sonnet LXXVII continues the theme of LXXVI. After the qualifications already set forth, the lady's physical person now be-

1. This image is paralleled in Annibale Romei's treatise, translated in 1598 as *The Courtier's Academy*, cited by Theodore Spencer, *Shakespeare and The Nature of Man* (1943), p. 4: 'This heavenly creature whom we call man, was compounded of soul and body, the which body, having to be the harbour of a most fair and immortal soul, was created . . . most exquisite.'

comes the poet's main concern. But her naked presence is still partly hidden behind a veil of imagining, and the first lines prepare a visionary setting for what is to come. 'Was it a dreame, or did I see it playne?' the poet asks himself; and at once it is clear that the table spread with junkets, the silver dish, and the golden apples, are dream-symbols that transpose physical phenomena into the ambience of psychic truth. Hence arises the fundamental dissimilarity between Spenser's imagery and that of the original. When Tasso mentions fruit, he means products of natural growth, entirely comparable with the bosom as it matures under the patronage of love. The metaphor permits both the image and its subject to co-exist as autonomous entities. In Spenser's sonnet, however, the imagery is of the emblematic type—it abstracts as in allegory from the natural world. How did these golden apples grow? In what season did they ripen? We first become aware of them in a silver dish, on a 'goodly table' with other prepared delicacies. Their figurative character is borne out in line 9: no natural fruit can be intelligibly described as 'free from sinful vice'. Only late in the sonnet, in lines 11 and 12, are we told of their origin. Unlike Tasso's apples, ripened by Love in his most favoured plantation, these were brought from Paradise and set, already perfect, in love's garden, which is the lady's bosom. The beauty of woman is thus a metaphysical attribute projected into the world of sense; and love, with its 'sweet fruit of pleasure', becomes, not a natural force operative in all animate beings, but the agent of a supernal, and by inference divine, will. It was more correct, declared Plotinus, to say that body was in soul than that soul was in body. Here the body is indicated by denaturalized symbols, and physical love described in terms of mental states. Accordingly in the final couplet, where the symbols are interpreted, it is again impressed upon the reader that the vision subsists entirely in the realm of thought. The theme of the poem is in fact a development of that of the previous sonnet, and both are descriptions of psychic experience.

Thus in four representative sonnets, Spenser not only maintained an independent attitude towards his originals, but evinced a unity of thought for which he has rarely been given due credit. The supposed oscillation between idealism in philosophy and sensuousness in poetic practice is absent in sonnets where the author had every inducement to follow his models to either extreme. Neither excessive sublimation of the beloved nor unprincipled eroticism was in any way countenanced. The lady was not apotheosized as a pagan goddess, nor translated into a pure spirit privileged to take mystic flights in regions beyond human ken. With Shakespeare, Spenser could say, 'My mistress, when she walks, treads on the ground'. But he would have hastened to add that, while she so trod, her thoughts remained fixed upon her heavenly home; for it was her moral qualities that called forth his highest praise. Love for him was neither a demiurge immanent in nature nor a spiritual revelation (in the romance vision, the two concepts were nearly interchangeable), but a vastly comprehensive relationship between two human beings, equally subject to the divine law, equally mindful of their moral obligations. The proper response on the woman's part was a balance of modesty and pride; on the man's, a subordination of physical desire to mental esteem. Yet, as human beings, the lovers were not exempt from the divinely ordained law of life. Beauty, emanating from on high, served a necessary function in the phenomenal world; and sexual attraction, when properly exercised, answered to the Creator's plan:

> For beautie is the bayt which with delight
> Doth man allure, for to enlarge his kynd;
> Beautie the burning lamp of heauens light,
> Darting her beames into each feeble mynd:[1]

True love thus postulated a conscious effort of the mind to integrate body and spirit, and this was indeed the proper function of courtship. In its beginnings an ideal attachment, love was to be tested and tempered over a period of time. After suitable proofs of loyalty and sincerity, betrothal might ensue. At that stage more psychic latitude would be permitted to the lover, whose thoughts might range over his lady's physical beauty and add this appreciation to his estimate of her moral worth. The consummation of the whole process was to be

---

1. *Colin Clouts Come Home Againe*, 871–4. A fuller exposition of the same idea is given in the *Hymne of Loue*.

effected in holy matrimony, bringing body and spirit into a blessed union. Throughout the probationary period, the active, integrative principle lay in the operation of the mind, a faculty which penetrated into the field of sense-perception, yet apprehended the realm of the spirit.

How close this highly flexible conception was to Neoplatonist doctrine is well illustrated in the following passage from a standard work on Plotinus:

> The Soul . . . stands midway between the phenomenal world, of which it is the principle, and the world of Spirit, which is its principle. But the Soul is not only an intermediary between appearance and reality. It is the point where all converging and diverging lines meet; 'it binds extremes together', and it is in vital correspondence with every region to which these lines lead. Within the Soul all metaphysical qualities are represented. It touches every grade in the hierarchies of value and of existence, from the super-essential Absolute to the infra-essential Matter. It has its own centre, a life proper to itself; but it can expand indefinitely in every direction without ceasing to be itself.[1]

If we equate the term *soul* (or psyche) with the word 'mind' as used in *Amoretti*, we have here a precise elucidation of Spenser's approach to experience generally, and to human love in particular.

In the sequence taken as a whole, Spenser's main concern is with the reciprocal influence of his psyche and that of his beloved. Ordinary characterization is negligible: we learn next to nothing about the poet or his lady as everyday persons. There are only sketchy indications of what company they kept, what their social activities were, or how they spent their time. Certainly there is nothing so memorable as the tournament when Stella looked on, or the river excursion when the wind ruffled her hair. All such details, which went to make up the excellence of earlier sonnets, are missing from *Amoretti*—and designedly so. To Spenser's way of thinking, social personality belonged to the deceptive world of appearance; the accidents of circumstance and daily life, commonly called experience, did not shape the outcome of true love.

The first three sonnets are introductory. Sonnet 1 sets the

1. W. R. Inge, *Plotinus* (1920), I, p. 202.

tone with its echo of the *ter felix* benediction: happy the leaves of the book, happy the lines of verse, happy the rhymes they contain, all dedicated to the lady. Her 'lamping eyes' will read these with 'starry light', and the rhymes themselves will behold 'that Angels blessed looke'. The courtship is thus announced on a level of extraordinary sublimation, with cosmic images drawn from the outer spheres of stars and angels rather than from earthly aspects of beauty. In sonnet II the poet addresses his own 'unquiet thought', bidding it break forth from his body and seek its own sustenance until it finds the beloved. When it comes into her presence it must 'fall lowly at her feet', begging pardon for itself and grace for him. Characteristically, Spenser makes his thought the principal agent in the drama of courtship, and it is in terms of the mind's abstractions that the lady herself first appears in III. Alluding to 'the souerayne beauty' of his admiration, Spenser signifies at the outset not a person, but the pure idea of beauty—

> the light wherof hath kindled heauenly fyre,
> in my fraile spirit by her from basenesse raysed.

This conception seems to echo the final passages of Bembo's discourse in *The Courtier*, where, following Plato's Symposium, he described the emancipation of the soul from the world of sense:

> Thus the soule kindled in the most holy fire of true heavenly love, fleeth to couple her selfe with the nature of Angels, . . . and enjoyeth the soveraigne happinesse, that can not be comprehended of the senses.[1]

It is one step down from this pinnacle of idealization when, in the following lines of the sonnet, beauty begins to attach itself to a human form. The beloved is now neither wholly an idea, nor wholly a person. She affects the poet as a dazzling light which blinds him to all earthly objects:

> That being now with her huge brightnesse dazed,
> base thing I can no more endure to view:
> but looking still on her I stand amazed,
> at wondrous sight of so celestiall hew.

Here too the image is suggested by Castiglione, in his inter-

1. *The Courtier* (*Everyman* edition), p. 319.

pretation of the beauty manifested in human beings that stirs
men to love:

> we will call it an influence of the heavenly bountifulnesse, the
> which for all it stretcheth over all things that be created (like the
> light of the sunne) yet when it findeth out a face well propor-
> tioned . . . thereinto it distilleth it selfe . . . and decketh out and
> lightneth the subject where it shineth with a marvellous grace
> and glistering (like the sunne beames that strike against beauti-
> full plate of fine golde wrought and set with precious jewels.)[1]

Only in the last lines of the sonnet is the lady fully envisaged as
a person to be humanly praised; and this is still only a conception of the heart; for his tongue is yet stopped with 'thought's
astonishment', and his pen 'ravisht' with 'fancies wonder-
ment'.

Instead of the usual mention of the lovers' first encounter,
or praise of the mistress's physical beauty, this sonnet sequence
opens on the highest spiritual plane, where considerations of
time, place, and personality have no relevance. Nevertheless
it will be seen that there is a gradual movement towards a
materialization of the concept in terms of human experience,
in notable contrast to the progressive sublimation which Castiglione adopted from Plato.

Sonnet IV, celebrating the advent of a new year, is anomalous with its conventional references to the 'wanton wings and
darts' of love and its comparison of the lady to a spring flower
(perhaps this new year follows the traditional calendar, com-
mencing in March). It bears the marks of an insertion taken
from earlier work for the purpose of introducing a time-
scheme. On the other hand this very purpose indicates a descent to the temporal world after the idealizations of the first
three sonnets; and when, in the sonnets which immediately
follow, the lady is considered as an ordinary mortal, the intervening time-references will have served to protect the reader
from a sense of abrupt transition.

During the year of courtship described in sonnets V–LX,
attention is concentrated upon the psychic relationship of the
poet and the lady. We have already noted the description of
her in XIII, at once mild and majestic, humble to God and

1. *Ibid.*, p. 304.

haughty to man. In v her proud bearing is considered. The
world's estimate is based upon the treatment she accords it,
and she is sometimes censured for what is thought to be arro-
gance. In reply the poet declares that her pride is a spiritual
quality. The 'lofty lookes' imply 'scorn for base things' and are
therefore to be admired, not censured:

> Such pride is praise, such portlinesse is honor,
>   that boldned innocence beares in hir eies:

Here, as often in these sonnets, Spenser's *Hymne of Love* supplies the best commentary:

> So hard those heauenly beauties be enfyred,
> As things diuine, least passions doe impresse,
> The more of stedfast mynds to be admyred,
> The more they stayed be on stedfastnesse:
> But baseborne mynds such lamps regard the lesse,
> Which at first blowing take on hastie fyre,
> Such fancies feele no loue, but loose desyre.
>
>   (169–75)

Even when her pride is exercised to his own discomfiture, he
resolves not to be dismayed:

> such loue not lyke to lusts of baser kynd,
>   the harder wonne, the firmer will abide. (vi)

Expecting therefore no easy or early victory, he disciplines
himself to a long trial of all his powers of resolution and
endurance.

> Then thinke not long in taking litle paine,
>   to knit the knot, that euer shall remaine.

And meanwhile the influence of the beloved remains with him
as an elevating and tranquillizing force:

> You frame my thoughts and fashion me within,
>   you stop my toung, and teach my hart to speake,
>   you calme the storme that passion did begin,
>   strong thrugh your cause, but by your vertue weak.
>
>   (viii)

Here, in what is perhaps the most lucid passage of detached

self-examination in the sequence,[1] lies at once the reason for
his persistence in the face of discouragement and the promise
of a happy outcome.

Writing within the sonnet tradition, it was necessary for
Spenser to dwell upon the superlative beauty of his lady. But
on almost every occasion he took pains to represent her physical beauty as the outer manifestation of an inner perfection of
the soul. Thus in xv, following Desportes, he likens her features
to precious jewels, her hair and hands to gold and silver, yet
departs from his model to add:

> But that which fairest is, but few behold,
> her mind adornd with vertues manifold.

In xvii his praise of her 'angels face' is bestowed not so much
upon her complexion, features, or hair, as on her expression
when it is, in the true sense, animated—when it manifests her
soul. All else, he avows, may be depicted by a skilful painter;
but not her glances, her smiles, 'the lovely pleasance and the
lofty pride': these belong to 'the life of things indeed'. It is to
such manifestations that most of his eulogies are devoted. Her
eyes are not, as poets feign, the armoury for Cupid's darts,
which goad the courtly lover into frenzy, but rather the abode
of angels, and best comparable to the 'Maker selfe' (ix). In
similar fashion sonnets xxxix and xl celebrate her smile. The
first commences with an apparent evocation of classical myth:

> Sweet smile, the daughter of the Queene of loue . . .

Yet according to the ancients, Venus had no daughter. The
reference, properly considered, is not to the classics, but to
Spenser's own allegory. It is Amoret who is in his thoughts, the
type of the chaste beloved, described as the adopted child of
Venus who was reared by Psyche.[2] In sonnet xl there is a
further echo of *The Faerie Queene*:

> Mark when she smiles with amiable cheare,
> and tell me where to can ye liken it:
> when on each eyelid sweetly doe appeare
> an hundred Graces as in shade to sit.

1. It is no accident that this sonnet should be the only one in *Amoretti* to
be composed in the 'Surrey' sonnet-form.
2. III. vi. 51.

This recalls the scene on Mount Acidale where Sir Calidore espies Colin Clout and his sweetheart:

> There he did see, that pleased much his sight,
> That euen he him selfe his eyes enuyde,
> An hundred naked maidens lilly white,
> All raunged in a ring, and dauncing in delight. (VI. X. 11)

Here the sonnet helps us to interpret the episode, for the maidens evidently represent the hundred graces in the lady's eyes while she gazed at her lover, disappearing as she became aware of the stranger's glance.[1] Such analogies between the last book of *The Faerie Queene* and the present sequence are a further indication of the unity of all Spenser's love poetry. The personification of virtuous love called Amoret in Book III is transformed into the central figure of a sublimated pastoral in Book VI and finally appears as the actual heroine of *Amoretti*.

A lady endowed with such virtues cannot degrade her lover or drive him to despair. Her chaste and sweet demeanour are themselves an assurance that his devotion will not be in vain, and service becomes a discipline of the soul. Yet the trials to be faced are rigorous enough; perhaps the more so because no concessions whatever are made. Again and again during the long year of courtship the poet gives expression to his sufferings. Sometimes he even begins to wonder whether this oft-celebrated pride might not be at bottom, as the world thinks, mere self-conceit. He reminds his lady that 'all worlds glorie is but drosse vncleane', and that the only lasting relic of her charms will be 'this verse that neuer shall expyre' (XXVII). Even the qualities which inspire his love may be corrupted through excess of pride, the sin for which angels fell:

> . . . then all her natures goodly guifts are lost.
>   And that same glorious beauties ydle boast,
>   is but a bayt such wretches to beguile:
>   as being long in her loues tempest tost,
>   she meanes at last to make her piteous spoyle.
>   O fayrest fayre, let neuer it be named,
>   that so fayre beauty was so fowly shamed. (XLI)

Less frequently now can he console himself with the thought

1. Greene uses 'amorets' to signify 'loving glances' in *Friar Bacon,* scenes 8 and 11.

that each of his woes will one day be translated into a reward; but the conviction is not wholly lost, and in LI, as the year draws towards a close, it is voiced in a comparison between the inflexibility of his lady and the hardness of the marble from which the most lasting monuments are hewn. But perhaps the finest expression of the struggle between sheer human impatience and Spenser's underlying faith in the psychic discipline of courtship is to be found in XXXIV and LIX. From Petrarch's famous 'galley' sonnet, or from one of its numerous imitations, he borrowed the metaphor of the storm-tossed ship of love. But while the original poem built up a cumulative impression of ruin and despair—the sails of the ship torn away, the stars hidden from sight—Spenser introduced a new and more cheerful note:

> Yet hope I well, that when this storme is past
>   my *Helice* the lodestar of my lyfe
>   will shine again, and looke on me at last,
>   with louely light to cleare my cloudy grief. (XXXIV)

Now, in order to answer doubt with faith, he asks in LVIII whether the lady's self-assurance be not a mere worldly thing, and in the next sonnet replies that its qualities are wholly spiritual. Here the metaphor of XXXIV is beautifully adapted from his own case to that of his beloved, who

> ... like a steddy ship doth strongly part
>   the raging waues and keepes her course aright:
>   ne ought for tempest doth from it depart,
>   ne ought for fayrer weathers false delight. (LIX)

And he concludes:

> Most happy she that most assured doth rest,
>   but he most happy who such one loues best.

Indeed, they are both like ships that keep resolutely to their course; and the time is at hand when they will make harbour together. In LXII the second new year is commemorated. It opens mildly, with promise of fair weather 'betokening peace and plenty to ensew'. In sober but hopeful mood the poet reviews the past, makes resolve to amend his life, and calls upon his love to 'chaunge old yeares annoy to new delight'. This time the appeal is answered. A perceptible change has come over the lady's mind, and at last the prospect of an end to the long period of trial shows on the horizon. Again he returns to the Petrarchan metaphor of the ship in distress:

> After long stormes and tempests sad assay,
>   Which hardly I endured heretofore:
>   in dread of death and daungerous dismay,
>   with which my silly barke was tossed sore:
> I doe at length descry the happy shore, . . .   (LXIII)

At the sight of land his confidence fully returns, and he concludes the sonnet by brushing aside, as if in retrospect they are of no account, all the tribulations he has had to face.

> All paines are nothing in respect of this,
>   all sorrowes short that gaine eternall blisse.

Sooner, perhaps, than he expects, the rewards of patient courtship are forthcoming, for the next sonnet celebrates the first kiss. The imagery of LXIV shows a sensuousness which takes the modern reader aback in this setting of idealized love. Again he is inclined to feel that Spenser has inadvertently slipped into the reactions of the 'common sensual man'. As a corrective to this view, Bembo's speech in *The Courtier* is illuminating.

And because you may moreover the better understand, that reasonable love is more happy than sensuall, I say unto you that selfe same thinges in sensuall ought to be denyed otherwhile, and in reasonable, graunted: because in the one, they bee honest, and in the other dishonest. Therefore the woman to please her good lover, beside the graunting him mery countenances, familiar and secret talke, jeasting, dalying, hand in hand, may also lawfully and without blame come to kissing: which in sensual love according to the Lord Julians rules, is not lawfull. For . . . the reasonable lover woteth well, that although the mouth be a parcell of the bodie, yet is it an issue for the wordes, that be the interpreters of the soule, and for the inwarde breath, which is also called the soule. And therefore hath a delite to joyne his mouth with the womans beloved with a kisse: not to stirre him to any dishonest desire, but because hee feeleth that that bonde is the opening of an entrie to the soules, which drawne with a coveting the one of the other, poure them selves by turne the one into the others bodie, and bee so mingled together, that each of them hath two soules. . . For this doe all chaste lovers covet a kisse, as a coupling of soules together.[1]

Spenser's own contribution was to carry this theoretical doctrine to an ultimate degree of sensuous practice in his verse, 'binding extremes together', yet without losing sight of the primary distinction between rational and sensual love. In terms of traditional sonnet imagery this was almost impossible; but a further hint from *The Courtier* suggested an approach that was well suited to his own genius. After the passage just quoted on the spiritual virtue of the lover's kiss, Castiglione went on to adduce authority from scripture.

And because the separating of the soule from the matters of the sense, and the through coupling her with matters of understanding may be betokened by a kisse, Salomon saith in his heavenly booke of Balates, O that he would kisse me with a kisse of his mouth, to expresse the desire he had, that his soule might be ravished through heavenly love to the beholding of heavenly beautie . . .[2]

Accordingly Spenser took as his guide two celebrated passages from the Song of Solomon, borrowing from the first its aromatic suggestions, from the second its sequence of images.

A garden inclosed is my sister, my spouse; a spring shut up, a fountain sealed.
Thy plants are an orchard of pomegranates, with pleasant fruits; camphire, with spikenard,
Spikenard and saffron; calamus and cinnamon, with all trees of frankincense; myrrh and aloes, with all the chief spices:

My beloved is white and ruddy, the chiefest among ten thousand. . .
His eyes are as the eyes of doves by the rivers of waters, washed with milk, and fitly set.
His cheeks are as a bed of spices, as sweet flowers: his lips like lilies, dropping sweet smelling myrrh.

(iv, 12–14; v, 10, 12–13)

His own version was remarkable in its originality:

Her lips did smell lyke vnto Gillyflowers,
her ruddy cheekes lyke vnto Roses red:
her snowy browes lyke budded Bellamoures,

1. p. 315.   2. pp. 315–16.

F

> her louely eyes lyke Pincks but newly spred.
> Her goodly bosome lyke a Strawberry bed,
> her neck lyke to a bounch of Cullambynes:
> her brest lyke lillyes, ere theyr leaues be shed,
> her nipples lyke yong blossomd Iessemynes.

For Spenser and Castiglione alike, the Song of Solomon was a poem of mystic symbolism. In catching its echoes, yet at the same time replacing its exotic similes by familiar English garden allusions, Spenser borrowed a sensuousness that had obtained full religious sanction, yet kept his sonnet true to its function of describing earthly courtship, and free from pretensions to the higher flights of spiritual allegory.

A new quality begins to reveal itself in the ensuing sonnets. Hitherto the poet has been the humble suitor, watching every transient expression on the face of his beloved for some hint of favour. But once she has given him her consent, his status rapidly changes. Henceforth he appears as the superior partner, and is accepted as such by the lady, who has voluntarily committed herself to his keeping. Gently yet firmly he assures her that her loss of personal freedom will be amply recompensed by the comfort and kindly treatment that she will receive.

> Sweet be the bands, the which true loue doth tye,
> without constraynt or dread of any ill:
> the gentle birde feeles no captiuity
> within her cage, but singes and feeds her fill.
> There pride dare not approch, nor discord spill
> the league twixt them, that loyal loue hath bound:
> but simple truth and mutuall good will,
> seekes with sweet peace to salue each others wound:
>   (LXV)

In the next sonnet it is his turn for self-examination. He wonders, now that he is the victor, whether he is indeed worthy of the prize. But the question is, at this stage, purely theoretical, and the reply he makes to himself, that his inferiority will serve the better to offset her excellence, is hardly more than a light conceit. More serious is sonnet LXVII, with its remarkable metaphor of willing subordination. The figurative deer-hunt had first appeared in Petrarch's *Una candida cerva*, on which Wyatt had modelled his early piece 'Who so list to hount'.

Petrarch's quarry had eluded the huntsman: on its neck was
written *Noli me tangere*. In Tasso's sonnet on this theme the
metaphor was given a new turn, according to which the deer
voluntarily came and submitted itself to capture. The varia-
tion had a comprehensible appeal for Spenser; and applying
it to his own experience, he infused a characteristic delicacy
into his treatment of the sestet. Tasso had concerned himself
mainly with the joys that the mistress's change of attitude
afforded to her lover:

> *Vedete, omai come 'l celeste riso*
> > *Benigna v'apre, e come dolcemente*
> > *I rai de' suoi begli occhi in voi raggira.*
> *Pavesi, s'or tal gioia al cor v'inspira,*
> > *Che sarà poi quando più volte il viso*
> > *D'amor vi baci e di pietate ardente?*[1]

Spenser, on the other hand, devoted the last six lines of his so-
net to a study of the lady's state of mind at the moment when
she consented to throw in her lot with her husband to be:

> There she beholding me with mylder looke,
> > sought not to fly, but fearlesse still did bide:
> > till I in hand her yet halfe trembling tooke,
> > and with her owne goodwill her fyrmely tyde.
> Strange thing me seemd to see a beast so wyld,
> > so goodly wonne with her owne will beguyld. (LXVII)

The whole rendering is a triumph of that intense concentra-
tion upon the psychical aspect of love which characterizes
Amoretti.

Sonnets LXVIII–LXXXV celebrate the happy conclusion of
long endeavour. Easter comes round again, and for the first
time the poet is able to offer his prayers on behalf of both himself and his betrothed. Now, when all Christendom rejoices at
its redemption through the divine love, the festival has a
special import for the two earthly lovers. Their mutual devotion is in accord with the lesson the day teaches to all human
beings, and is in fulfilment of the holy will.

> So let vs loue, dear loue, lyke as we ought,
> > loue is the lesson which the Lord vs taught. (LXVIII)

1. II. 429 (Solerti): *Questa fera gentil.*

In LXIX the poet again commemorates his victory, this time with ringing self-confidence. His verse will be its 'immortall moniment', and 'tell her prayse to all posterity'. The full reward has come,

> The happy purchase of my glorious spoile,
> gotten at last with labour and long toyle.

There follows a spring sonnet, calling upon the betrothed to awake and do observance to the new season, written in a style with marked resemblances to the *réveil* in *Epithalamion*.

> Goe to my loue, where she is carelesse layd,
> yet in her winters bowre not well awake:
> tell her the ioyous time wil not be staid
> vnlesse she doe him by the forelock take. (LXX)

The lady's self-subordination is again referred to in LXXI. Clearly it is no longer a serious issue between the lovers, and the spider and bee conceit treats it with easy pleasantry. At the present stage of courtship all the old problems have been resolved and the lovers face the future with serenity. They have entered a spiritual haven in which, it would seem, nothing further is to be desired.

> Hart need not with none other happinesse,
> but here on earth to haue such heuens blisse. (LXXII)

Even now, when the early restraints are forgotten and false modesty has no place in the relationship, the betrothal remains in essence a union of souls. In paying his debt of gratitude to the 'three Elizabeths'—his mother, his queen, and his future wife—Spenser thanks his lady for the gifts of mind she has conferred upon him (LXXIV); and in LXXIX he insists once more upon the psychic aspect of her beauty. The 'trew fayre' is her 'gentle wit and vertuous mind'. All other fairness is transient: this alone, being derived from God the source of true beauty, is for ever enduring. Even physical attraction is praised as a manifestation of the soul. Thus of all features it is her lips that he most admires, since they are the gate

> throgh which her words so wise do make their way
> to beare the message of her gentle spright. (LXXXI)

(Again, Spenser is remembering Castiglione in the passage already quoted—

> but the reasonable lover woteth well, that although the mouth be a parcell of the bodie, yet is it an issue for the wordes, that be the interpreters of the soule . . .)

Spenser's response to the lady's beauty is admittedly sensuous now to a degree which he would never have permitted himself in the earlier phases of courtship; but, as we have seen in sonnets LXXVI and LXXVII, it is still subject to the qualifications of a prior moral esteem. It may even be described, according to Neoplatonist metaphysics, as an extended activity of soul.

> In the Enneads the sensible world is the creation of the Universal Soul, through the medium of Nature which is its moving power. Nature is the active faculty of the World-Soul, its outer life, the expansion of its energy, that without which it would be shut up in itself, mute and inactive.[1]

There are, indeed, isolated moments when these considerations are half-forgotten; but the asperity with which the poet castigates himself for such lapses bears witness enough to the habitual rigour of his standards.

> Let not one spark of filthy lustfull fyre
>> breake out, that may her sacred peace molest:
> ne one light glance of sensuall desyre
>> Attempt to work her gentle mindes vnrest. (LXXXIV)

His happiness, he well knows, is already in full proportion to his deserts, and gratitude should be his one actuating thought. The last sonnet of this group vigorously defends his praise of the lady against all accusations of flattery, and concludes with a proud and defiant proclamation of her virtue.

> Deepe in the closet of my parts entyre,
>> her worth is written with a golden quill:
>> that me with heauenly fury doth inspire,

---

1. Inge, I. 155. Compare Donne in *The Extasie*:
>> So must pure lovers soules descend
>>> T'affections, and to faculties,
>> Which sense may reach and apprehend,
>>> Else a great Prince in prison lies.

For all the differences between them, Spenser and Donne drew many of their ideas from a common source.

> and my glad mouth with her sweet prayses fill.
> Which when as fame in her shrill trump shal thunder
> let the world chose to enuy or to wonder. (LXXXV)

Here, it might be thought, the sequence could very appro-
priately end. Nothing more is needed to complete the tale of
successful courtship, to which the marriage ode bound up in
the same volume would provide a fitting finale. But there still
remain four sonnets. A sudden complication has arisen: some
wicked slander has been spread about which is poisoning the
lady's mind. Furiously the poet curses the 'venemous toung'
responsible for this breach in his 'sweet peace':

> Let all the plagues and horrid paines of hell,
>   vpon thee fall for thine accursed hyre:
>   that with false forged lyes, which thou didst tel,
>   in my true loue did stirre vp coles of yre . . . (LXXXVI)

Sonnets LXXXVII–LXXXIX lament the separation of the lovers,
and complain of weary days and nights passed in sorrow. The
'Idaea playne' of the betrothed remains vividly with her lover,
but it does not make up for her physical absence, and the last
sonnet of all offers no immediate grounds for hope.

> Dark is my day, whyles her fayre light I mis,
>   and dead my life that wants such liuely blis. (LXXXIX)

It may be asked whether Spenser was merely imitating the
example of Sidney, whose *Astrophel and Stella* had also ended on
a minor key. Taking into account the gulf between Sidney's
conception of courtship and Spenser's individual approach
throughout *Amoretti*, this seems quite untenable. Or it might be
thought that these last four sonnets have been misplaced in a
sequence whose defective arrangement has already been
noted. Yet, although sonnets LXXXVII–LXXXIX might perhaps
fit in at an earlier stage, LXXXVI would still be anomalous. It
clearly belongs in spirit to a late phase, some time after the
betrothal, and could not with any plausibility be fitted in elsewhere. Yet separated from the other three and left as the last
sonnet of all it would strike an even worse discord than before.
One can only suppose that LXXXVI–LXXXIX relate to some
actual occurrence in Spenser's life which, at the cost of impair-
ing the unity of the sequence, he felt obliged to mention. This

would certainly mean a departure from his usual practice and a break with the classical conception of poetry as a public offering rather than an outlet for private emotion. But there is a similar anomaly in the sixth book of *The Faerie Queene*. In this book the allegory works itself out to a conclusion. All evil conceptions have been exposed in their true light; only one adversary remains to be vanquished, the Blatant Beast of Slander. In the last canto the Beast is captured after a hard struggle and led in bonds through the land of Faerie. The reader expects the episode to end on this note of triumph: instead it is disconcerting to learn in the final four stanzas that the Blatant Beast has escaped and at the close of the book is still at large.

> So now he raungeth through the world againe,
> And rageth sore in each degree and state;
> Ne any is that may him now restraine,
> He growen is so great and strong of late,
> Barking and biting all that him doe bate,
> Albe they worthy blame, or cleare of crime:
> Ne spareth he most learned wits to rate,
> Ne spareth he the gentle Poets rime,
> But rends without regard of person or of time.[1]

The 'gentle Poet' is evidently the author, and the theme is, as in sonnet LXXXVI, the menace of slander. In *Amoretti* LXXX Spenser had mentioned the recent completion of Part II of *The Faerie Queene*: we may fairly assume that, if they are not misplaced, the last four sonnets of the sequence were written soon after the lines just quoted. It seems likely that the two outbursts were occasioned by a single, probably unforeseen event in Spenser's private life which seriously upset his plans.[2] If so, the *envoi* to *Epithalamion* may be read as an apology for the abrupt conclusion of the sonnet sequence:

> Song made in lieu of many ornaments,
> With which my loue should duly haue bene dect,
> Which cutting off through hasty accidents,
> Ye would not stay your dew time to expect, . . .

Had Spenser, like Sidney, based his poetry upon the represen-

1. VI. xii. 40.
2. The same bitter complaint against slander in high places also appears in *Colin Clout* (lines 688 f.) published in the same year as *Amoretti*. See p. 100, and note.

tation of experience as shaped by circumstance, he would not have found it hard to incorporate such incidents. But the pre-conceived doctrines on which both *Amoretti* and *The Faerie Queene* were built involved him, it seems, in major difficulties. The ending of the sequence is a flaw in the artistic design, and its full implications must necessarily affect one's final estimate of Spenser as a poet of the sonnet.

In *Amoretti* the use of imagery is almost as distinctive as the handling of content. Little need be said of the sonnets that have been set apart from the main body. Their technique, fashioned after the allegorical style, is based on calculated exaggeration, and the images employed, neither metaphors nor genuine similes, may perhaps be described as emblematic. The modern reader, unaccustomed to this technique, receives an unfavourable impression and so tends to dismiss the poems as 'conventional'. Actually they are a flagrant breach of con-vention: their fault lies not in timid conformity, but in the neglect of well-grounded sonnet traditions by an author used to working in a very different medium.

Spenser abandoned these methods in the sequence proper, but his characteristic treatment of courtship led to other pecu-liarities. Sidney had excelled in the use of personification and conceit to express subjective problems and emotional con-flicts. For Spenser, there was no question of dramatizing sense-perception; and it followed that the anacreontic fables and classical myths, with their personified eroticism, played no important part in *Amoretti*. Here the lady's eyes harboured no 'winged guest', and the angels who took Cupid's place were not susceptible to mythological treatment. Conceits are indeed to be found in these sonnets, but they are of minor importance in relation to the central issue. That of LXXI, with its spider and bee analogies, appears only after the real problem of the be-trothed lady's position has been settled, and amounts to little more than affectionate banter. The old tale of the sickness of the lady and the lover's impatience with her physicians had inspired the impassioned sonnet CII of *Astrophel and Stella*. It was borrowed again for sonnet L of *Amoretti*; but by giving the illness to the lover instead of his lady, Spenser transposed the conceit to a minor key. In general, personification and conceit, with their functions of introspection and self-analysis, become subordinate or merely decorative devices.

If conceit furthered the intellectual assessment of experience, metaphor involved an intuitive sense of affinities between nature and spirit more congenial to the Latin imagination than the English. The Italian writers who supplied Spenser with his models maintained in their imagery a continuity of outlook that went back to the pagan world. The myths of the classics became the personifications of romance allegory and the metaphors of the Renaissance sonnet. But the English tradition militated against such expressions of affinity. Mythological allusions often became ornamental embellishments or intellectual symbols, and the metaphors of Italian literature were usually rendered as similes or conceits. In writing his great allegorical poem Spenser had necessarily created superb myths of his own,[1] though subjecting them to a distinctly individual treatment: but in the personal medium of the sonnet the national tradition reasserted itself. LXXVI and LXXVII of *Amoretti* differed from their model in Tasso's poem by relegating myth to a minor place and dissociating the idea of the lady's physical maturity from that of vegetable growth and fruition. Only in XIX and LXX, celebrating the spring and calling on the betrothed to pay homage to the king of love, does myth predominate. But the two sonnets serve as occasional pieces to mark the passage of time, and contribute nothing to the unfolding of the main theme. The spring call is not answered, for it is irrelevant to the psychic issues which govern the lady's responses. Elsewhere the metaphors of the sequence have a special character, and serve to relate the lovers' mental states to observed cases of purposeful activity. Images are drawn from warfare, hunting, and seafaring. At his first rebuff, the poet thinks of the progress of a siege and the rallying of disgruntled forces (XIV); the ultimate success of his suit is expressed in the metaphor of a huntsman capturing his quarry (LXVII). In three important sonnets—XXXIV, LIX, and LXIII— the image of a pilot guiding a storm-tossed ship is applied respectively to his own plight, his lady's behaviour, and, after the betrothal, to his past anxieties. The conscious exercise of

1. An admirable account of Spenser's treatment of allegorical myths is given in C. S. Lewis's *The Allegory of Love*, Chapter VII.

F*

will-power, or patient endurance under acute strain, is the chief implication of all these metaphors. For a poet like Spenser, they shed far more light upon the realities of experience than any which drew upon unthinking and inanimate forces.

Simile, however, is the most usual type of imagery in *Amoretti*. The direct sensuous apprehension of likeness requires no deep commitments of intellect or imagination. Even so, it will commonly be found that the evocations of Spenser's similes are less perceptual than they at first appear.

> For loe my loue doth in her selfe containe
>   all this worlds riches that may farre be found,
>   if Saphyres, loe her eies be Saphyres plaine,
>   if Rubies, loe her lips be Rubies sound:
> If Pearles, her teeth be pearles both pure and round ... (xv)

Precious jewels exercise an immemorial fascination upon the mind. Traditionally they were the repositories of various virtues, so that mention of them suggested not so much any definite physical properties of colour and shape as the ideal qualities they embodied. Often, by placing his sensuous images in apposition to spiritual concepts or abstract states of being, Spenser invested them by association with a similar ideality:

> Fayre bosome fraught with vertues richest tresure,
>   The neast of loue, the lodging of delight:
>   the bowre of blisse, the paradice of pleasure,
>   the sacred harbour of that heuenly spright. (LXXVI)

At the same time, the extremer forms of spiritualization were generally avoided. Thus in sonnet LXIV the exotic aromas described in Canticles, symbolizing for the church the mystic rapture of the soul possessed by divine love, were replaced, not indeed by the sensualities of wild nature, but by the variegated scents of an English garden, the perfect expression of nature under the control and purposeful direction of mankind.[1] By such means the sensuous aspects of love were neither hypostatized nor completely abstracted from them-

---

1. The same biblical cadences return in *Epithalamion*, ll. 167–84, but the imagery now shows the fragrant flowers of courtship changed into the ripe fruits of marriage.

selves, but given their due subordinate place in the hierarchy of psychic values.

In the choice of words it had been, since Wyatt's time, the constant care of English poets to free the language from medieval encumbrances and to establish a contemporary diction. On the basis of Tudor achievements Sidney had evolved his flexible speech-rhythms, his colloquialisms and neologisms, which gave effect to every turn of the alert, quick-witted Elizabethan mind. Spenser, however, stood aside from this development and sought instead to incorporate in his diction the obsolete or obsolescent language of a bygone age. 'It was his aim,' wrote De Selincourt, 'to perfect for himself an instrument from which he could extract a music as subtle as Chaucer's, and by means of which he could create around his subject the atmosphere of an ideal antique world.'[1] The comment was made with reference to *The Faerie Queene* but it is also applicable to *Amoretti*. There is hardly a sonnet which does not contain words deliberately chosen for their strangeness. Medievalisms fast passing out of current use were revived and liberally introduced. We find 'mote' for 'might have', 'eke' for 'also', 'sith' for 'since', etc. Completely antiquated, almost forgotten words reappear, such as 'beseene', 'assoyle', 'stoures', 'amearst'. Side by side with these, Spenser introduced foreign loan-words, taking pains, when they had already been assimilated, to restore the marks of their alien origin. Such romance forms as 'semblant', 'pleasance', and 'richesse' replaced their familiar, anglicized variants. He chose, likewise, the romance spelling for 'ensample', 'pourtraict', 'noyous' and 'approch', applied the French stress to 'massacre', and French pronunciation to 'sacrifise'. Chaucer and the fifteenth-century allegorists showed precedents for many of these usages; but in their time the words were newcomers to the language and unavoidably conveyed an exotic flavour. Spenser's mannerisms, on the other hand, were a deliberate retrogression, aiming to associate with his treatment of courtship a sense of remoteness from the everyday world. From similar motives, he frequently departed from the customary sentence-order and used alien constructions, even at the risk of obscuring his meaning. A certain latitude in this respect has commonly been granted to

1. The *Oxford* Spenser (1912), Introduction, p. lxi.

poets; but Spenser made of it a regular practice and virtually disregarded the word-order of his own language. Such constructions as

> But they that skill not of so heauenly matter,
> all that they know not, enuy or admyre,
> rather then enuy let them wonder at her,
> but not to deeme of her desert aspyre (LXXXV)

almost justify Jonson's quip that 'in affecting the ancients . . . he writ no language'. In company with the 'aged accents and untimely words', they assist in estranging the diction of Spenser's sonnets from that of his time.

To some extent these retrogressive tendencies appear also in the use of alliteration. Wyatt and Surrey learned to abandon this device as a structural principle at an early stage in their development; and Sidney employed it mainly for its subsidiary value as a means of emotional emphasis. Spenser's approach was almost exclusively formal, aiming at the production of metrical harmonies unrelated to the immediate content of individual sonnets. No doubt he intended, as in his allegorical poetry, to suggest through this a preconceived and ideal interpretation of experience, which resolved its vicissitudes in a higher synthesis. But the formal consequences must be seen for what they were; and often enough Spenser's approach brought with it a relapse into the obsolete structural alliteration from which the sonnet had broken free. Such lines as 'in dread of death and daungerous dismay', or 'with louely light to cleare my cloudy grief' may have incidental beauty: but they show a dangerous tendency to abandon the necessary prosody of the sonnet as a personal medium.

The same principles may be found at work in Spenser's distinctive verse-form. Invented in his earlier experiments at sonnet-writing, it was essentially a system of interlacing rhymes suitable for a fourteen-line narrative or meditative stanza. Hitherto English poets had sought to escape from the narrative tradition in their sonnets, and to aim instead at a verse-form that would promote concise, inferential thinking based upon particular experiences. Spenser, however, deliberately weakened the capacity of his verse-form to suggest apposition, contrast, or logical correlation. His interlacing rhymes knit the whole sonnet into a seamless texture of sound, overlaying all verse divisions that correspond with separate links in a chain of logic, and setting up fourteen lines of un-halting, melodious exposition. The demonstrative exception was sonnet VIII, which, adopting the pure Surrey form, gave admirable expression to a moment of objective self-examina-tion. But in general Spenser, on conscious philosophical grounds, rejected this approach. He would not accept the in-trinsic validity of sense perception, and therefore could not admit logical inferences from perception as the informing principle of his love sonnets. True, courtship with its psychic discipline necessitated a measure of reflection and analysis of motives; true, too, that betrothal legitimately brought senses and affections into play. But these remained subordinate to a divinely appointed scheme, whose operations were indepen-dent of the fallible human faculties. The poet's task, as Spen-ser saw it, was not so much to shape through his art an ordered pattern from the flux of actuality, as to demonstrate a pre-ordained design; not to hold the mirror up to life, but to justify the ways of God to men. Spenser's attempt to perform this task through the sonnet medium is implicit in all aspects of his formal technique.

Some brief conclusions may now be drawn regarding Spen-ser's contribution to the Elizabethan love sonnet, regarded as a class of poetry with its own generic qualities rooted in the national literary tradition.

An ancient, instinctive dualism in the English conscious-ness, tending to the view that nature and spirit were funda-mentally opposed, distinguished the love poetry of this coun-try from that of Mediterranean lands. Its stamp is set upon the Elizabethan treatment of the sonnet, as appears frequently when comparison is made between a French or Italian original and its English rendering. This dualism shapes the whole character of Sidney's sequence, where a romance pattern of experience is re-lived by an outstanding representative of sixteenth-century English values. Spenser, approaching the dilemma on a far more speculative plane, evolved his own solution in terms of Neoplatonist metaphysics. While his philosophical theories were derived from a general European

school of thought, their application to creative literature
necessarily involved a treatment modified by specifically English intuitions. Consequently Spenser's poetry laid particular
stress upon psychic volition and practical virtue as the integrative factors capable of reconciling nature and spirit, rather
than upon the transcendental powers of the soul as celebrated
by Italian poets. Confirmation of this attitude was afforded by
Protestant teaching, with its emphasis upon the individual
conscience and on the merit of sacramental marriage. Thus
Spenser's poetry was largely concerned with a denigration of
the romance cult of courtly love and the substitution of a new
theme: the triumph of virtuous courtship in betrothal and
holy matrimony. It was an undertaking of great significance
for the whole future of English literature; and no small part
of Spenser's achievement was to have found expression for
it through the personal medium of the sonnet sequence.
Amoretti celebrated, often with striking beauty and delicacy, a
courtship in which spiritual aspiration and natural desire
were happily reconciled through a willed discipline of the
psyche. Instead of conflict in the soul, pangs of conscience, and
a final call for the renunciation of the flesh, love in these sonnets induced a growing measure of physical and spiritual ease.
In this respect Spenser's sequence amply vindicates his right
to be considered as one of the great masters of the English
sonnet.

Yet the fact must be faced that this success was bought at an
extremely high price, considered from the viewpoint of formal
values. As a sequence *Amoretti* was, as we have seen, structurally defective. Eighteen of the eighty-eight sonnets have
had to be segregated in order that justice might be done to the
remainder; the sole reason for their presence being, so far as
we can know, an attempt to overcome a deficiency arising
from the very nature of Spenser's theoretical approach. If self-
expression could only be sanctioned at a point where the
psychic and moral principles of the poet were endorsed, the
development of the sequence was bound to suffer; and to
patch it with conventional irrelevancies only made matters
worse. Furthermore, there was the aesthetic incongruity of the
last four sonnets, occasioned, it would seem, by some unanti-
cipated setback in Spenser's private life. It may be inferred

that the poet, under emotional strain, was after all unable to support a purely conceptual approach to his theme. Here the tradition of the sonnet, which aimed above all else at the voicing of personal perceptions, wrought a subtle revenge on the writer who rejected the prime validity of perception. Besides this must be set a retrogressive tendency in many aspects of formal technique that concerned the individual sonnet. Imagery lost the complex values of personification and conceit; the scope of metaphor was restricted; and similes, though sometimes of remarkable beauty, forfeited a wide range of sensuous appeal. Finally we may add the archaisms of diction, and the merely decorative or sonorous effects of alliteration and verse-form. All these divergencies from the main line of formal development were due to a common cause: Spenser's subordination of the traditional virtues of the sonnet-sequence to a preconceived interpretation of life that of its nature invalidated them.

Needless to say, many of the *Amoretti* sonnets offer a unique satisfaction for those who are willing to submit themselves to Spenser's individual genius. Nevertheless it cannot be denied that formally they stand apart from the main line of the sonnet tradition. However modified from age to age and country to country, the sonnet exists for the expression of personal and direct perception. It is not a valid defence to say that, because Spenser's form answered to his individual genius, his method stands above all further criticism. Creative originality and poetic tradition must interact positively for the healthy perpetuation of literature; and form in any medium carries with it the cumulative wisdom of past generations. For this reason Spenser's sequence, despite its many intrinsic merits, was to exercise virtually no influence upon the subsequent development of the sonnet in England.

The next chapter takes the case of a number of poets, less talented than Spenser, who instead of shunning the paths of sense-perception attempted to find their way by a wider exploration of its possibilities. In their work the phenomenal world was unconditionally accepted as the true field of the sonnet, and no limits were set to the scope of their discoveries or their modes of formal expression. The result was that, in

spite of much extravagance of style and a good deal of crude
or insipid writing, a contemporary vision of reality, at first but
momentarily glimpsed, came gradually to assume shape and
outline.

VI
THE LATE ELIZABETHAN SONNET

In the last years of the sixteenth century a new spirit, elusive but all-pervading, appears in English literature. It was the age of Marlowe's *Faustus* and Bacon's *Essays*, of Nashe's pamphlets and Donne's lyrics; above all, the age of Shakespearean drama. What common qualities of thought or imagination, we ask, underlie works of such amazing variety? It is evident that some profound ferment is at work. Yet the more closely we investigate this literature the greater the difficulties that face us in trying to assess its distinctive character. The enchanted wood, once entered, is seen to consist of all-too-familiar trees. Roman satires mingle with Italianate romances and homely English comedies. Images of intense evocative power, ideas which seem to have sprung fresh from the author's brain, dissolve under scholarly investigation into medieval commonplaces in disguise or classical tags adapted to new purposes. No wonder that modern critics show a growing diffidence in applying such European terms as 'humanism' or 'Renaissance civilisation' to an epoch so fitful and elusive.

Nevertheless, the literature of the late Elizabethans (including in this, too, that of the early Jacobeans) cannot be resolved back into its disparate parts. Certain unifying trends stand out unmistakably. The old interlude play with its personified virtues and vices, its type figures and didactic utterances, makes way for dramas enacting the conduct of individuals. In narrative poetry, allegorical and moralistic themes are superseded by the frank sensuousness of Ovidian romance or by versified history and politics. The lyric, though maintaining pastoral conventions, acquires a new grace and vividness; satires and epigrams, though imitating Roman models, show an acute observation of contemporary manners. No original system of ideas, no co-ordinating philosophy, is to be distilled from these works, which draw continually upon established precedents; but there is in fact a different mode of apprehension, a re-viewing of the old landscape from a changed perspective. The author took his theories wherever he found them, and preferably from the most ancient authorities; but whatever he borrowed was subtly transfigured. His approach might perhaps be described as a hyperacute curiosity concerning all forms of phenomenal behaviour, and especially of his fellow human beings; an eager desire to experience all knowledge upon his own nerve-endings. The metaphysical constructions of the universe, the moral categories of behaviour which were part of his intellectual inheritance, were constantly reaffirmed; but their hold on his imagination lay not so much in their intrinsic truth as in their power to illuminate the more obscure regions of personality. Man became in effect the measure of the universe, and it is especially notable that a drama whose protagonists were characters in their own right should emerge as the most typical art-form of the age. Before long, it may well be, scholarship will have traced every expression used by Hamlet, Bosola, or Epicure Mammon to its anterior 'source'; but the critical task will still remain of explaining how these ideas are, as it were, metabolized and made into one flesh with the living characters who voice them. Isabella's views on chastity, Hotspur's on honour, have familiar precedents: their poetic truth, however, can no longer be abstracted from the living persons of Isabella and Hotspur. Political and social concepts also appear in literature less as doctrines *per se*, than as second causes or derivatives from the character of the individual prince or governor, who is seen now as the repository of virtue, the arbiter of guilt, and successor to many of the attributes of divine justice and mercy. Even the forces of inanimate nature—time and the elements, the seasons of growth and decay, the revolutions of sun and stars—are drawn into the orbit of personality, and become extensions of the human predicament rather than its shaping factors.

In one sense this change of outlook may be said to have brought about a recasting of the traditional English attitude towards nature and spirit which, as we have seen, shaped Elizabethan poetry even at its most imitative. The familiar dichotomy could not operate along the usual lines in an age which conceived of nature in close association with humanity and interpreted spiritual or ideal principles primarily as attributes of character. Nevertheless this new tendency to integration did not involve a conversion to southern attitudes, despite the appeal of pagan mythology. Rather did the intuitive dualism of English tradition reassert itself in a new guise. By conceiving the universe in the image of man, the later Elizabethan poets focused on the individual its inherent antinomies. In the little world of man, the inimical powers of the elements and stars, the social anarchy of war and usurpation, the diseases and vices of body and soul, were co-present with ideal postulations of order and degree, of natural beauty and cosmic truth. Where then was integration to be found? For medieval Christianity, all the manifest contradictions of life were inevitable consequences of a fallen universe, which, under the guidance of holy church, would achieve their resolution on a supernal plane. Chaucer's Troilus, risen to the seventh sphere, could laugh as he looked down upon the 'erratic stars' and the 'wretched world' which was the scene of his own tragedy. For the sixteenth-century Protestant, the main burden of redemption was laid upon the individual conscience, to be supported through that psychic discipline and virtuous exercise of the will which was the central concern of Spenser's poetry. The writers of the new generation made no intellectual break with the essentials of Protestant teaching in its wider framework of Christianity. However, their creative impulses only functioned at their best through perceptual channels, only expressed themselves adequately through representations of observed character and conduct. Here no *a priori* explanations were valid to resolve universal antinomies. If these were indeed to be resolved, it could only be through the unaided power of the human spirit, triumphing over its innate flaws.

As the supreme and inalienable individual experience, love necessarily became the central theme of literature during this epoch. We have noted some of the modifications undergone by romance experience as expressed in the Elizabethan sonnet, and the conflicts to which it gave rise. With the notable exception of Spenser, the leading poets writing in the fifteen-nineties and after were attempting to evolve a treatment of love that accorded with the vision of their time. In pastoral lyrics and songs, as well as in such verse romances as *Hero and Leander* or *Venus and Adonis*, an unprecedented degree of sensuousness prevails. Desire is pre-eminently desirable, and calls forth no serious moral rejoinders. If the lovers of Shakespeare and Marlowe suffer death in these poems, it is not as the wages of sin, but as a result of inherent antipathies in nature. Leander is drowned because of the sea-god's jealousy; Adonis, who would have been safe had he complied with the desire of Venus, is gored to death through the motiveless malignity of the wild boar. On the Elizabethan stage particularly, love is presented as the ultimate good, in counterpoise to which all power, prestige, and even life itself are found wanting. The blood-guiltiness of Tamburlaine is purged away in the fire of his lament for Zenocrate; the Duchess of Malfi is beatified by her entirely human love, while the Arragonian brethren endure their damnation on earth. In Shakespearian comedy, love is the means of all human fulfilment, as it is the source of all natural fruition. Moreover, this orientation comes about without a spiritualizing of love's physical basis. Shakespeare's heroines are quite lacking in the saintly qualities of the Petrarchan mistress. Far from raising their lovers' thoughts above 'base desire', Rosalind teaches Orlando how to woo, and Juliet reciprocates Romeo's ardour so frankly that he promptly forgets the chaste attractions of his former lady. In the tragedies, suicide for love—a cardinal sin for all Christians—becomes an act of martyrdom in the new secular dispensation of poetry. Providence and salvation no longer operate from on high or await the soul in the outermost sphere of heaven: they emanate from the human spirit and function through the power of human love. Cleopatra's dream that she beheld an emperor Antony becomes the vision splendid of a kingdom which, though not of this world, is inconceivable save in terms of this world; an empire of the passions and poetic imagination which even in death is unconsumed by time.

This vision was most successfully projected through the drama, a medium offering the widest range for experiment in the presentation of character in action. It found significant expression in the narrative poem inspired by Ovidian erotics and heroics, which allowed for dialogues and quasi-dramatic

monologues of indeterminate length, composed in easy, flowing metres. But paradoxically the sonnet sequence, through
which the Renaissance poets first came to voice personality,
now proved the least amenable to new needs. By the end of
the sixteenth century, the sonnet was no longer an excitingly
modern form of lyric expression but a time-honoured institution. Practised by generations of writers for over two hundred years, modified by Serafino and his school, reconstituted
in French by Ronsard and his fellows of the *Pléiade*, revived in
Italy by the Neoplatonist poets, further rehandled by Desportes, and known in England since the time of Wyatt, the
sonnet carried a vast accretion of concepts, images, and traditional phraseology. Every detail in the pattern of courtship,
every simile portraying lover and lady, had already been prescribed. Just as communities which were the first to undergo
industrial revolution find their machinery the hardest to adapt
to new techniques, so for the poets of the fifteen-nineties the
sonnet, the original product of Renaissance literature, proved
the least flexible instrument. The difficulties were not indeed
apparent at first sight. Literary imitation was the accepted
doctrine of the age, and so long as no major shift of outlook
took place, verse precedents were less a bar than a stimulus to
poetic creation. To the reading public of 1591, the great success of *Astrophel and Stella* must have seemed a portent of yet
greater triumphs. An epoch which centred reality in the
experience of individuals understandably looked for a flowering of the sonnet. Only in the actual course of imitation would
the more discerning poets learn that Sidney's achievement
was in essence a culmination, not, as they thought, a fresh start.
In *Astrophel and Stella* the interplay of chivalric attitudes and
Elizabethan response had reached its maximum tension. A
peculiar set of circumstances, a particular cast of mind, had
sustained this tension throughout Sidney's sequence; but the
achievement could neither be repeated nor surpassed. Hence,
while more flexible mediums developed new modes of expression, the sonnet, which seemed to offer so much, failed by and
large in performance. Convention no longer evoked response,
and subject-matter sundered itself from form. Only through a
major creative effort, comparable to that of Petrarch himself
in his revitalization of the Troubadour inheritance, would the

sonnet once more answer fully to the needs of the age. Yet in partial and sporadic manifestations, certain positive factors will be found.

Little is to be gained from a close scrutiny of the minor sequences published after 1591. Rarely if ever, amid the voluminous outpourings of mock ardour and feigned torment, is the suggestion of a likely emotion conveyed. No figure of the beloved rises out of the sea of hyperboles; and from all the roses and raptures it is virtually impossible to piece together any coherent history of courtship. Imagery consists for the most part of a proliferation of conceits, employed not as a means of apprehending complex issues, but solely as an end in themselves. The Anacreontic fables of Cupid, Venus, Minerva, and other pagan deities supply decoration for sonnet after sonnet in the sequences of Barnes, Fletcher, and Constable. Their appearance reflects no intuitive sympathy with the classical view of life, nor are these fables endowed with the subjective symbolism that Sidney so brilliantly employed. Accompanying them are frequent allusions to alchemy, to the theory of humours, to astrology—a set of sonnets by Barnes was headed by signs of the Zodiac—to medical and legal practices, to heraldic devices, to euphuistic natural history. The more recondite and far-fetched these allusions, the more they commend themselves to their authors; and often ingenuity of this kind produces absurd effects. Fletcher sees what he thinks to be a comet in the west: on closer inspection it looks like a sun: at length it is revealed as Licia's eyes. Or he watches a spider running into Licia's house: while there it catches sight of her; and mistaking her for Minerva, sheds its poison. Constable's fancy is more extravagant. He is a murderer on trial for his life (x). Also he bears five wounds, like the stigmata of Saint Francis; but these are far more grievous, since they are located in his heart (xix). He bids his Diana go forth and establish the Fifth Monarchy, since she is a sovereign whom none can resist (xxxii). When the resources of Christian theology have served their turn, Islam provides further illustrations. He finds that Mahomet is 'but a morrall of loues Monarchie', and thrusts into a sonnet the prophet's miraculous coffin at Mecca (xxxiv). This does not seem to him out of place, since, of course,

That Mahomet is shee to whom I pray.

And from the coffin at Mecca to Caesar's tomb in Rome the mental journey is not far, since 'the richest relique *Rome* did euer view' is also an image of Diana's beauty (XXXVII). How much 'originality' may be found in such conceits is a pastime for men of much leisure; there can be no doubt that these gaudy plumes, whether borrowed or not, fail to disguise the meagreness of the underlying content. The same incongruity appears in the frequently strained diction, with its elaborate parallelisms and studied rhetorical devices, which elucidate no intricacy of thought, and suggest no depth of feeling. Typical of this is Barnes's noisy

> Ah pearse-eye pearsing eye, and blazing light
>> Of thunder thunderblazes burning vppe!
>> Oh sunne sunne-melting, blind and dazing sight!
>> Ah hart downe driuing hart, and turning vppe! (XLVI)

or Constable's dreary

> One Sunne vnto my liues day giues true light,
> One Moone dissolues my stormie night of woes.
> One starre my fate and happy fortune shoes.
> One Saint I serue, one shrine with vowes I dight.
> One sunne transfixt, hath burnt my hart outright.
> One Moone oppos'd, my loue in darknes throes.
> One star hath bid my thoughtes my wrongs disclose.
> Saints scorn poor swaines, shrines doe my vowes no right.
>
>> (LI)

Even the principles of verse-form worked out by Wyatt and Surrey, and formulated by Puttenham, are ignored in several of these sequences. Barnes's *Parthenophil and Parthenophe* contains fifteen-line sonnets and a medley of amorphous rhyme-schemes, Lodge's *Phillis* mingles regular sonnets with poems of twelve, sixteen, or sometimes twenty-four lines, which are in fact ordinary lyrics. Constable at first adopted Sidney's characteristic rhyme-patterns, but applied them mechanically and with no understanding of the subtle technique of inter-locking rhyme and syntax which gave them distinction. (His later sonnets, it is fair to add, showed some competence in the handling of the Surrey form.) In general it may be said that very few poems in these minor sequences show any real grasp of the formal virtues of the English sonnet.

But this negative estimate should not be made without qualifications. Regarded from another aspect, even the short-comings, which contrast so strangely with the rapid maturing of late Elizabethan poetry, were positive symptoms. While life had departed from the conventional themes of the sonnet, leaving only a husk of outworn devices, it was vigorously re-asserting itself in unexpected directions, and the very accelera-tion of decay was indicative of the pressure of new growth.

Turning to the preface of Giles Fletcher's *Licia*, we read:

> If thou muse what my Licia is, take her to be some *Diana*, at the least chaste, or some *Minerva*, no *Venus*, fairer farre; it may be she is Learnings image, or some heavenlie woonder, which the pre-cisest may not mislike: perhaps under that name I have shadow-ed *Discipline*. It may be, I meane that kinde courtesie which I found at the Patronesse of these Poems; it may be some Colledge; it may bee my conceit, and portende nothing.

In spite of the banter, this passage serves to indicate the approach of most sonneteers of the time. The theme of the heroine has become of minor importance; she is but a lay figure representing, according to the particular reader's taste, any person, idea, or institution that will serve for panegyrics. Since the conventions require a mistress, a lover, and some show of romantic ardour, these are provided. But neither the author nor his public regards such matters as of primary con-cern. Their attention is turned towards derivative aspects of the sonnet—the intellectual versatility and sensuous appeal of its imagery and diction—irrespective of any organic relation-ship between them and the ostensible theme. Like Romeo and Juliet on their first encounter, these poets play delightedly with the conceits of 'saints', 'pilgrims', 'palmers', and 'prayers', though the courtship they would seriously envisage has no-thing in common with such idealisms. The sonneteer only makes a pretence of experiencing romance in the high Petrar-chan fashion: his real desire is to be the king of infinite space in a nutshell; to set his mind ranging over the provinces of alchemy and astrology, of classical myth and oriental religion; to find brave new words and startling juxtapositions; and all this within the framework of a medium specially designed for the expression of personality.

This contemporary attitude cannot, of course, be seriously defended as a means to writing good poetry. It reflects a transitional taste, pending the reconstitution of the sonnet on a more vital basis. Sooner or later the interdependence of form and content must assert itself if any medium is to survive. Yet in spite of these fundamental limitations, the minor sonneteers occasionally produced attractive verse where the conceits lost their frigidity and took on a glow of lively fancy. Fletcher's treatment of a familiar Renaissance theme, the image of the lady graven on her lover's heart, is a good example:

> My love amaz'd did blush her selfe to see,
> Pictur'd by arte, all naked as she was:
> How could the Painter knowe so much by me,
> Or Art effect, what he hath brought to passe?
> It is not lyke, he naked me hath seene,
> Or stoode so nigh, for to observe so much,
> No, sweete, his eyes so nere have never bene,
> Nor could his handes, by art have cunning such:
> I showed my heart, wherein you printed were,
> You, naked you, as here you painted are,
> In that (My Love) your picture I must weare,
> And show't to all, unlesse you have more care:
>   Then take my heart, and place it with your owne,
>   So shall you naked never more be knowne. (*Licia* VI)

Even Constable achieved some pleasing effects, combining a graceful use of Anacreontics with a touch of Sidney's wit:

> Pitie refusing my poore Loue to feed,
>   a begger staru'd for want of helpe he lies,
>   and at your mouth (the door of Beautie) cries,
>   that thence some almes of sweete grants might proceed
> But as he waiteth for some almes-deed,
>   a cherrie tree before the doore, he spies,
>   Oh deare (quoth he) two cherries may suffise,
>   two onely may saue life in this my need.
> But beggers, can they naught but cherries eate?
>   Pardon my Loue, he is a Goddesse sonne,
>   and neuer feedeth but on daintie meate,
>   els need he not to pine as he hath done:

> For onely the sweete frute of this sweete tree,
> can giue food to my Loue, and life to mee. (*Diana* XVI)

At the same time, a parallel tendency which appears sporadically in these sequences was to have far-reaching consequences. If the intellectual unrest of the age—

> the English straine,
> That cannot long one Fashion intertaine

—drove the sonnet poet to multiply his conceits and elaborate
his diction, a heightened response to sense-perception, and a
new awareness of deep-seated consonance between human personality and the life of nature, found expression in metaphorical imagery. The English literary tradition had generally
eschewed this outlook, with its unconscious paganism; and the
Tudor poets, as we have seen, made it the occasion for their
first departure from Italian models. Now, however, the theme
of inanimate nature was a major concern of narrative verse,
pastoral lyric and drama; and the sonnet reflected this shift of
sensibility. The first evidence of change here was provided in
that small group of sonnets in *Astrophel and Stella* where Sidney
had turned aside from self-analysis to the sympathetic con-
templation of impersonal nature. Sidney was then a solitary
fore-runner; but in the last decade of the sixteenth century
practically all the sonnet-writers followed this trend. Often, it
is true, the allusions to nature were hyperbolical and vague;
often they drew upon no more than a slender stock of decorative images taken at second hand. Yet there are many instances
of a truly imaginative use of metaphor. Even Barnes could
produce such memorable lines as:

> The leauelesse branches of the liuelesse bowes
>   Carue winters out-rage in their withered barkes:
>   The withered wrinckles, in my carefull browes
>   Figure from whence, they drew those crooked markes:
>
> (LXIX)

Constable, leaving his arduous quest for new conceits, found
rare poise in a sonnet which influenced Shakespeare:

> My Ladies presence makes the Roses red,
>   because to see her lips, they blush for shame:
>   the Lyllies leaues (for enuie) pale became,
>   and her white hands in them this enuie bred.

The Marigold [her] leaues abroad doth spred,
    because the sunnes, and her power is the same:
    the Violet of purple cullour came, . . . (*Diana* (1592) XVII)

Fletcher too had his fortunate moments:

Heare how my sighes are ecchoed of the wind,
See how my teares are pittied by the raine . . .
                  (*Licia* XXXVI)

When as her lute is tuned to her voyce,
The aire growes proud, for honour of that sound:
And rockes doe leape, to shewe how they rejoyce,
That in the earth, such Musicke should be found.
                  (*Licia*, XXXI)

But perhaps the best examples from the minor sequences are to be found in Lodge's *Phillis*. Influenced by the poems in Sidney's *Arcadia*, Lodge conceived the idea of following up his own pastoral romance *Rosalynde* with a sequence of pastoral sonnets. In practice he did not sustain the plan, and *Phillis* taken as a whole does not greatly differ from the general run of sequences. Nevertheless the intended pastoral treatment called forth some admirable lines:

How languisheth the Primrose of loues garden!
How trill her teares th'Elixar of my sences, (VII)

The falling fountaines from the mountaines falling,
Cried out, ah-las, so faire and bee so cruel! (XIV)

I doe compare vnto thy youthly cleare
(Which alwaies bydes within thy flowering prime)
The month of Aprill, that bedewes our clime
With pleasant flowers, when as his showers appeare.
                  (XXX)

Such instances reveal a quiet competence in the use of alliteration and internal rhyme, a fresh responsiveness to words, and a fine sensibility, in marked contrast to the laboured effects of most of the sonnets. But the imaginative potency exhausts itself after a few lines, and is replaced by sterile ingenuities of the conscious mind:

Ah pale and dying infant of the springe,
How rightly now do I resemble thee:

That selfe same hand that thee from stalke did wringe,
Hath rent my breast and robd my heart from thee.
Yet shallt thou liue, for why thy natiue vigor
Shall thriue by wofull dew-droppes of my dollour:
And from the woundes I beare through fancies rigor,
My streaming blood shall yeeld thee crimson colour.[1] (v)

Lodge's predicament was that of all his contemporaries. His quite considerable literary talent was frustrated by the sonnet medium and its weight of conventions. Freedom came in the verse epistles of *A Fig For Momus* (1595), where his intellectual curiosity found proper expression in discussing such topics as dreams and their causes, the fallacies of alchemy, and the like. Here he could write with ease and vigour, not of his bleeding heart, but of a cure for his wife's obesity—

You pray me to aduise, and tell you what
Will take away your pursiness and fat,
You pray me without any let, or pause,
To write of both the remedie, and cause,
And in a short discourse to let you know
The *Antidote* of that mislikes you so.
Well, since your beautie may, & must command
Thus briefly will I answer your demand ... (Epistle vi)

Such commands of beauty could not be obeyed within the accepted framework of the sonnet sequence.

So far we have been concerned with the lesser poets, who were responsive to the new spirit of the age, but lacked the power to shape the sonnet form in accordance with its needs. In the work of Daniel and Drayton, however, there is a considerable advance towards the required synthesis.

Daniel's sonnets were probably the first of the new school, twenty-three of them appearing with the 1591 edition of *Astrophel and Stella*. Desportes was at that time his principal model and from the French poet he learned the virtues of simplicity and grace. These sonnets show a smooth and accomplished handling of verse, an avoidance of extravagant conceit, and a fastidious choice of words. Where, for example, Desportes wrote—

1. My emphases.

Je verray par les ans, vangeurs de mon martyre,
   Que l'or de vos cheveux argenté deviendra,
   Que de vos deux soleils la splendeur s'esteindra,
   Et qu'il faudra qu'Amour tout confus s'en retire. (*Cléonice* LXIII)

—Daniel produced the chaster rendering in *Delia*:

   I once may see when yeeres shall wrecke my wronge,
   When golden haires shall chaunge to siluer wyer:
   And those bright rayes, that kindle all this fyer
   Shall faile in force, their working not so stronge. (xxx)

Martyre is toned down to 'wronge', and *vos deux soleils* to
'those bright rayes'; while the Petrarchan image of Love re-
treating from the face, already used by Surrey, is entirely
omitted, at the cost of a rather awkward fourth line. The
theme of Desportes in this sonnet, with its stress on the fading
of beauty and its metaphors of sun and flowers, owed much to
Ronsard. When in 1592 Daniel brought out the first independent edition of *Delia*, twenty-seven new sonnets were added to
those published in the previous year, making up a sequence of
fifty sonnets; and in the new poems it was evident that he had
been led on to an earnest study of Ronsard's own work.
Instead of the usual ardours and complaints of courtly love, his
main concern was with the pathos of youth and beauty as victims of time. Women, like flowers, blossomed in the spring of
their maidenhood and withered in the autumn of old age. The
lady of the sonnets, however idealized by her lovers, was but
mortal: the day would surely come when her beauty would
decline and these very lovers forsake her—all save the poet,
who would commemorate her as she once had been. Such reflections were, of course, no more than variations on the pagan
theme of *carpe diem* to be found in Catullus and Horace; but in
the last phase of the Renaissance they acquired a special relevance. The glories and frailties of the individual, consummation
of all that was fair in the phenomenal world, yet subject, like
all phenomena, to time's depredation, stirred the deepest sentiments of the age. Conceived in terms of this vision, the sonnet
heroine appeared once more as an authentic being, endowed
with poetic universality; while the poet who claimed to immortalize her in verse, instead of being a mere mouthpiece for
decorative phrases, became the serious champion of positive

human values. The best of Daniel's new sonnets were devoted
to this conception. In the true sixteenth-century sense, he
'imitated' Ronsard—and Tasso, in so far as the Italian poet
showed Ronsard's influence; subduing his own genius so completely to the spirit of his originals that their poetry virtually
became his own. Every image, every turn of thought, was re-
created and re-experienced. The result was a formal perfection
unmatched in the work of any of his contemporaries, Shakespeare excepted. As mere fragmentary illustrations, we may
note the subtle variations of metre, acting in sensitive accord
with the inner implications of the theme, in the following
verses:

> No Aprill can reuiue thy withred flowers,
> Whose blooming grace adornes thy glorie now:
> Swift speedy Time, feathred with flying howers,
> Dissolues the beautie of the fairest brow. (XXXI)

> When men shall finde thy flowre, thy glory passe,
> And thou with carefull brow sitting alone:
> Receiued hast this message from thy glasse,
> That tells thee trueth, and saies that all is gone. (XXXIII)

> Care-charmer sleepe, sonne of the Sable night,
> Brother to death, in silent darknes borne:
> Relieue my languish, and restore the light,
> With darke forgetting of my cares returne. (XLV)

or these examples of metaphorical imagery, the effects of an
equally penetrating insight by the visual sense and the inner
eye:

> A modest maide, deckt with a blush of honour,
> Whose feete doe treade greene pathes of youth and loue
> (VI)

> Th'Ocean neuer did attende more duely,
> Vppon his Soueraignes course, the nights pale Queene:
> (XL)

In nearly all these sonnets, the diction is admirably simple and
pure, based upon monosyllables chosen with fastidious regard
for their sonorous quality. Daniel was a master in the evocative use of long vowels and in quiet harmonies of assonance and
alliteration. Without looking beyond the verses quoted, we
may note how the lines from XXXI range through a wide gamut

of vowel sounds and link these in a subtle music; or listen to the iterative vowels of *flowre*, *thou*, *brow* in xxxiii as they collaborate with the f-, l-, and th- alliterations; or trace the interweaving of s- and r- consonants in xlv. Nor was Daniel a slave to mere euphony: if this last sonnet is read as a whole it will be seen what power he was able to convey by interposing such strong, highly suggestive words as 'shipwrack', 'torment', 'passions', 'lyers', in the lulling, smooth invocation to sleep.

In addition to all this, Daniel should be credited with two major contributions to the formal development of the late Elizabethan sequence. His grasp of metaphorical imagery led to its employment as a structural principle binding together a run of sonnets, where the rose image of Ronsard and Tasso expanded, as it were organically, through a sustained metaphorical treatment of flowers, sun, and summer-and-winter contrasts. The nucleus of sonnets thus created, numbered xxxi–xxxv in the 1592 edition, had a new formal coherence, reinforced by the device of echoing the last line of each sonnet as the first of that which succeeds it, and the consequent iterations of rhyme-pattern. The effect was to restore in some measure the integral character of the sonnet sequence, which was in danger of being lost with the contemporary decline of interest in its traditional themes. Secondly, Daniel revealed the latent potentialities of the Surrey verse-form. With the exception of two sonnets in the 1591 edition, and five added after 1592 under the influence of Spenser, he consistently adhered to this in the *Delia* sequence. Surrey's form had been the staple of the English sonnet from the time of its inception; but hitherto its appeal had rested chiefly on its simplicity of rhyme and logic. Only once, in Sidney's 'Leaue me, ô Loue', had its wider possibilities been explored. Now at last it was recognized as a great reversionary inheritance for the new generation of poets. Devised by a writer more concerned with detached observation than ideal concepts, Surrey's sonnet-form perfectly corresponded with the needs of the later Elizabethans. Their thought-processes, if more speculative than his, were likewise experiential; built upon sense-perception; and functioning on empirical lines through the logic of apposition and contrast. *When* . . . *Then* . . . were the great structural words of their sonnets. However wide the range of their imagination, however profound their intuition, its basis remained the solid ground of physical reality. Daniel was the first of his generation to appreciate the contemporary significance of Surrey's form, which supplied the necessary foundation for all future developments in the sonnet medium.

There can be no doubting the crucial importance of Daniel's work. It was to exercise a far-reaching influence upon his colleagues, who all benefited from one or another aspect of his achievement. But at the same time these sonnets had their shortcomings, which were clearly recognized by the poets of his day. The trouble was that Daniel, while proving his mastery in his own chosen field, had failed sufficiently to widen the scope of his subject-matter. *Delia*, apart from its residuary features, was a sustained elegiac lament on the passing of youth and beauty, coupled with a declaration of faith in the survival of the poet's vision. It was undoubtedly a theme that touched chords of Elizabethan sentiment; but the contemporary spirit was nevertheless too positive and restless to be contained within such limits. Brightness might fall from the air; but the Elizabethans at the end of the sixteenth century were not disposed to sum up their total attitude to experience in terms of finely modulated pathos. Fortunately for the development of the sonnet, it had another outstanding practitioner whose strength lay exactly in the qualities where Daniel was most limited.

Drayton introduced the later editions of his *Idea* sequence with a warning to the reader who 'but for Passion lookes'. The recommendation to seek elsewhere might be extended to anyone looking for imaginative qualities in these sonnets. They show few traces of the fine sensibility and intuitive perception that mark Daniel's treatment of his themes. Whenever Drayton touched upon kindred subjects, the result was vulgarity and bathos. We may contrast the two poets in their description of the mistress in old age—

> When thou surcharg'd with burthen of thy yeeres,
> Shalt bend thy wrinkles homeward to the earth:
> When tyme hath made a pasport for thy feares,
> Dated in age the Kalends of our death.
> 　But ah no more, thys hath beene often tolde,

And women grieue to thinke they must be old.
(Delia, XLII)

That lovely, arched, yvorie, pollish'd Brow,
Defac'd with Wrinkles, that I might but see;
Thy daintie Hayre, so curl'd, and crisped now,
Like grizzled Mosse upon some aged Tree;
Thy Cheeke, now flush with Roses, sunke, and leane,
Thy Lips, with age, as any Wafer thinne,
(Idea (1619), VIII)

—or in their claims to immortalize her in verse:

This may remaine thy lasting monument,
Which happily posteritie may cherish:
These collours with thy fading are not spent;
These may remaine, when thou and I shall perish.
If they remaine, then thou shalt liue thereby;
They will remaine, and so thou canst not dye.
(Delia, XXXIV)

How many paltry, foolish, painted things,
That now in Coaches trouble ev'ry street,
Shall be forgotten, whom no Poet sings,
Ere they be well wrap'd in their winding Sheet?
Where I to thee Eternitie shall give,
When nothing else remayneth of these dayes,
And Queenes hereafter shall be glad to live
Upon the almes of thy superfluous prayse . . .
(Idea (1619), VI)

In treating such matters, Drayton sank far below his depth. He was not a very imaginative poet, and the finer shades of feeling escaped him. But he had keen powers of observation and a considerable store of knowledge. Even the lines just quoted, however ill-suited to their subject, show an alert eye and a flair for topicality. At their best, Drayton's sonnets were a kind of poeticized journalism that mirrored the everyday activities and intellectual interests of his time. From the first he made Sidney his model for wit, ingenuity of conceit, and idiomatic style. As in *Astrophel and Stella*, Cupid takes refuge in the poet's breast, and again sets his lodgings on fire ('Love banish'd Heav'n, in Earth was held in scorne', XXIII). There is another quarrel between Love and Reason, in which Love gains the upper hand ('Sitting alone, Love bids me goe and write', xxxviii). The poet again casts up his accounts, and finds himself a bankrupt through love:

> Taking my Penne, with Words to cast my Woe,
> Duely to count the summe of all my cares,
> I finde, my Griefes innumerable growe,
> The reck'nings rise to millions of Despaires. (iii)

And there are the same fervent protestations of untaught eloquence:

> See Miracles, ye unbeleeving, see,
> A dumbe-borne Muse made to expresse the Mind,
> A cripple Hand to write, yet lame by Kind,
> One by thy Name, the other touching thee. (xxxv)

All these Sidneian themes were treated with a liveliness and versatility beyond anything in Barnes, Constable, Giles Fletcher, and the rest; while in the fanciful dialogues between the poet and his lady, or the poet and his public, a vigorous colloquial diction came to be employed as skilfully as in Sidney's own sonnets:

> You cannot love, my prettie Heart, and why?
> There was a time, You told Me that you would,
> But now againe You will the same denie,
> If it might please You, would to God You could;
> What, will You hate? nay that you will not neither,
> Nor Love, nor Hate, how then? what will You doe?
> What will You keepe a meane then betwixt either?
> Or will You love Me, and yet hate Me too?
>   (xix) (first printed in 1599)

> I heare some say, this Man is not in love:
> Who? can he love? a likely thing, they say;
> Reade but his Verse, and it will eas'ly prove.
> O, judge not rashly (gentle Sir) I pray, ...
>   (xxiv) (first printed in 1600)

While *Astrophel and Stella* was Drayton's chief model, he was ready to imitate whatever appealed to him in the works of his contemporaries. A striking image from Marlowe's *Edward II* provided the opening of sonnet xl:

> My Heart the Anvile, where my Thoughts doe beate,
> My Words the Hammers, fashioning my desire, ...

Likewise a sonnet in Spenser's *Amoretti* suggested the theme of
IV:

> Bright starre of Beauty, on whose eyelids sit
> A thousand Nimph-like and inamor'd Graces, . . .

Sonnet XXXIII ('Whilst yet mine Eyes doe surfet with Delight'),
in which eyes and heart are jealous of each other's share in the
lady, and sonnet VII ('Love, in a Humor, play'd the Prodigall')
closely resemble two sonnets of Shakespeare, as does the conceit of the first four lines of XLIV:

> Whilst thus my Pen strives to eternize thee,
> Age rules my Lines with Wrinkles in my Face,
> Where, in the Map of all my Miserie,
> Is model'd out the World of my Disgrace.

Besides direct imitation, there are countless echoes of the conceits and phraseology of the European tradition, many of them,
it seems likely, unconscious. But Drayton's style, as it matured
through successive revisions of his sequence from 1599 onwards, tended increasingly to pattern itself on the qualities
of wit and apparent spontaneity introduced by Wyatt and
brought to perfection by Sidney. Twenty-one of the fifty-one
sonnets in the 1594 sequence *Ideas Mirrour* were excluded
from all later editions for various good reasons. Some were of
eighteen lines, in violation of the rules of verse-form; others
were renderings of now hackneyed sonnets of Petrarch. Drayton had learned that it was not in the best of taste to open a
love sonnet with the observation: 'Three sorts of Serpents doe
resemble thee';[1] or, having decided in another sonnet that his
lady was an angel, a goddess, and divine, to declare:

> And thus if thou be not of humaine kinde,
> A Bastard on both sides needes must thou be, . . .

In general, his revision was designed to eliminate the more
absurd hyperboles, and especially the once-fashionable kind
of adulation that verged on idolatry. Where sonnets were
allowed to survive into later editions, they were carefully chas-
tened in regard to such matters; as, for instance, in sonnet
XXXV, beginning:

---

1. Drayton intended this, it seems, as an improvement upon Desportes'
J'accompare ma dame au serpent furieux. (*Diane* I, LXVII.)

> Some misbeleeving, and prophane in Love,
> When I doe speake of Miracles by thee,
> May say, that thou art flattered by mee,

which in the 1594 version had been:

> Some Athiest or vile Infidell in love,
> When I doe speake of thy divinitie,
> May blaspheme thus, and say, I flatter thee:

Such improvements were directly in the line of English tradition.

The result of trial and error was a kind of sonnet which, without attempting high flights, succeeded very often in combining ingenuity, colloquial vigour, and balanced expression. Sonnet II, first printed in 1599, shows a deft use of legal terms:

> My Heart was slaine, and none but you and I:
> Who should I thinke the Murther should commit?
> Since, but your selfe, there was no Creature by,
> But onely I, guiltlesse of murth'ring it.
> It slew it selfe; the Verdict on the view
> Doe quit the dead, and me not accessarie:
> Well, well, I feare it will be prov'd by you,
> Th' evidence so great a proofe doth carrie.

Equally attractive is x ('To nothing fitter can I thee compare') appearing in the same year. Here the mistress is likened to 'the Sonne of some rich Penny-father', who, come into a large estate, dissipates his wealth amongst false companions and in the end is glad to have the return of a small loan once bestowed upon his only true friend, the poet. Sonnet XLVI ('Plaine-path'd Experience') recalls the common belief that a victim's corpse will bleed if the murderer is brought before it: in similar fashion the wounds in the poet's heart bleed at his lady's approach; and the couplet brings that final surprise inference which clinches the best conceits:

> But what of this? Should she to death be led,
> It furthers Justice, but helpes not the dead.

Other sonnets from 1599 onwards develop ideas as striking as any in the sequences of Drayton's contemporaries, but with an ease and economy these rarely achieved. Like a true journalist, Drayton had the knack of seizing upon the elements of a

'story' that would catch the reader's eye. Anecdotes of witch-
craft, of earth-spirits guarding treasure, of experiments in
vivisection practised upon condemned criminals—all became material for the sonnet; and so ably were these subjects
handled that their essential incongruity was hardly perceptible. There were classical allusions to Orpheus and Medea,
Styx and Phlegethon, to please the learned, and topicalities
that would appeal to the man in the street—

> And let the *Bards* within the Irish Ile,
> To whom my Muse with fierie Wings shall passe,
> Call backe the stiffe-neck'd Rebels from Exile,
> And mollifie the slaughtering *Galliglasse*. (xxv)

—sometimes of the kind that almost shape themselves into
newspaper headlines:

> Lastly, mine Eyes amazedly have seene
> Essex great fall, Tyrone his Peace to gaine,
> The quiet end of that Long-living Queene,
> This Kings faire Entrance, and our Peace with *Spaine*,
> We and the *Dutch* at length our Selves to sever;
> Thus the World doth, and ever more shall Reele . . . (li)

And once, as may happen in the career of a journalist, some
added stimulus of personal experience, some flash of inspiration, kindled Drayton's habitual virtuosity and his verse took
on the qualities of great drama:

> Since ther's no helpe, Come let us kisse and part,
> Nay, I have done: You get no more of Me,
> And I am glad, yea glad with all my heart
> That thus so cleanly, I my Selfe can free,
> Shake hands for ever, Cancell all our Vowes,
> And when We meet at any time againe,
> Be it not seene in either of our Browes,
> That We one jot of former Love Reteyne;
> Now at the last gaspe, of Loves latest Breath,
> When his Pulse fayling, Passion speechlesse lies,
> When Faith is kneeling by his bed of Death,
> And Innocence is closing up his Eyes,
>   Now if thou would'st, when all have given him over,
>   From Death to Life, thou might'st him yet recover.
>   (lxi)

In temperament, in approach to composition, in the respective tasks they set themselves, Daniel and Drayton represent the sharpest of contrasts. While Daniel's fastidious artistry wrought a limited perfection, Drayton's versatility, his agile wit and fluent pen enabled him to bring a wide variety of interests within the scope of the sonnet. Daniel's work was the fruit of fine intuition and acute sensibility; Drayton's was mainly concerned with the surface play of human activities, with subjects of contemporary intellectual appeal, with social and political happenings, with daily life and daily speech. Each man's achievement was the complement of the other's; and each in his own way gave expression to the elusive spirit of the age. Together, these two poets did much to revitalize the English sonnet tradition at a turning-point in its development. They showed that it was possible to bring impersonal themes and contemporary interests within the scope of the sonnet, yet without excluding the fundamental theme of personal experience. In form as well as content their achievements were positive and necessary. Daniel revealed to his generation the potentialities of Surrey's verse technique, and the resources of pure diction; Drayton resuscitated the wit and idiomatic force of Wyatt and Sidney. In spite of their obvious individual shortcomings, their joint work supplied the foundations for a far greater poet than either.

Before proceeding to a consideration of Shakespeare's sonnets, we may pause at this point to look back over the developments discussed in this chapter.

In the last decade of the sixteenth century the Renaissance ferment of ideas and emotional responses would seem to have reached its climax in England. Operating below the surface of professed beliefs, it profoundly influenced the imaginative creations of the age. While the flexible mediums of dramatic and narrative poetry were transformed during these years, the sonnet, indurated by a steady accretion of romance sentiments and idealizations, faced an apparent deadlock. Despite Tudor modifications of the European tradition, despite Sidney's brilliant individual achievement, the conventional theme of courtly love remained in essence unchanged, and of its very nature impervious to the new spirit. Hence the poets who wrote

their sonnet sequences after 1591—Spenser always excepted—
paid no more than lip-service to their ostensible theme and
gave their main attention to elaborating accessories. Their
sonnets inevitably suffered from the dissociation of form from
content; but this very defect was a necessity of growth. The
plethora of decorative conceits which marked the late Elizabethan sonnet reflected the intellectual curiosity of the age;
and the sporadic, usually ill-sustained metaphors from impersonal nature were prompted by characteristic perceptions.
Moreover, in the sequences of Daniel and Drayton these
accessories were gradually assimilated to the sonnet's formal
structure. Extravagances were mostly purged away, and new
potentialities revealed in the diction and verse-form evolved
by the English tradition. Daniel and Drayton gained their
successes in quite different styles, but their talents were complementary, and the combined effect was a reconstitution of
the sonnet medium. The task awaiting a poet of supreme creative power was to concentrate these formal qualities round a
new and vital theme infused with his own genius, thus drawing
the intellectual vigour and the intuitive sensibility of the age
into a great imaginative synthesis.

VII

SHAKESPEARE

'**P**ERSONALLY,' wrote Edward Thomas in one of his letters, 'I have a dread of the sonnet. It must contain fourteen lines, and a man must be a tremendous poet or a cold mathematician if he can accommodate his thoughts to such a condition.'[1] The same dread, or at least distrust, seems to have been Shakespeare's own reaction at one phase in his development. In *Love's Labour's Lost*, a select audience was entertained with a reading of three sonnets from the stage, accompanied by tart comments on their various shortcomings. The first, 'If Love make me forsworn', was dismissed with contempt by Holofernes the Pedant:

> Here are only numbers ratified; but for the elegancy, facility, and golden cadence of poesy, *caret*. Ovidius Naso was the man: and why, indeed, Naso, but for smelling out the odoriferous flowers of fancy, the jerks of invention? *Imitari* is nothing. . .[2]

Mere ratification of numbers, work for a cold mathematician, was not enough; and still more significantly, the advice to emulate Ovid led right away from the sonnet medium. Shakespeare was hinting broadly that the future of poetry lay along the lines of Ovidian romance, as in *Hero and Leander*, or his own popular narrative poems, rather than in more Petrarchan sequences. Lest Holofernes should not be taken seriously, the lesson was driven home by Berowne's scornful remarks on the other two specimens. A fine-spun conceit on tears carrying the image of the beloved, in 'So sweet a kiss', evoked the comment, 'Your eyes do make no coaches';[3] and the last of the three sonnets, 'Did not the heavenly rhetoric of thine eye', drew an attack on the whole convention of the idealized mistress:

1. John Moore, *The Life and Letters of Edward Thomas* (1939), p. 284.
2. *Love's Labour's Lost*, IV. ii. 126–31. All references to Shakespeare in this chapter follow the text of the Oxford edition unless otherwise indicated. The heavy punctuation has sometimes been slightly modified.
3. *Ibid.*, IV. iii. 155.

This is the liver-vein, which makes flesh a deity,
A green goose a goddess; pure, pure idolatry.
God amend us, God amend! We are much out o' the way.[1]

This violent reaction against the sonneteering fashion reflected a shift of taste towards classical models, resulting in the
combination of frank sensuousness and realistic satire to be
found in the work of Hall, Marston, and others during the last
years of the sixteenth century. Nevertheless we know that by
1598, the year in which *Love's Labour's Lost* was first published,
some of Shakespeare's own sonnets were circulating in manuscript. Next year two of them, now numbered CXXXVIII and
CXLV, found their way into print in *The Passionate Pilgrim*; and
ten years later still, in 1609, Thorpe brought out his large collection of 154 sonnets. Evidently Shakespeare had overcome
his distrust for this form, returning to it, indeed, as a 'tremendous poet'—and without controverting the views he had expressed in *Love's Labour's Lost*. Ovid, as we shall see, served his
purpose in a profounder sense than had been contemplated by
Holofernes. As for Berowne's mockery of 'the liver vein', it
was answered by the extraordinary character of these poems.
About five-sixths of them were addressed, neither to green
goose nor goddess, but to a young and eligible bachelor, who
was urged to marry, reprimanded for sensual faults—including an affair with the poet's mistress—warned against flatterers and rival poets, and promised immortality in verse. The
remainder of the sonnets, relegated to the last pages of the
Quarto, were a kind of sub-plot to the main series. They were
written, indeed, to a lady; but a lady by courtesy title only, as
black as hell, as dark as night, who was held to blame for corrupting both the poet and his friend. In its negation of conventional values, this second series defied tradition even more
outspokenly than the first.

This book is not concerned with the biographical information—nebulous at the best—which Elizabethan sonnets afford.
Doubtless Shakespeare, like all good poets, found enough
experience in his own life to supply him with the material he
needed. We may be equally sure that as a literary artist working through the sonnet medium, he selected, adapted, and re-

---

1. *Ibid.*, IV. iii. 74–6.

G*

shaped experience as judiciously as did every other great sonnet poet. Accordingly I shall take no part in chasing such wild
geese as the elusive Mr W. H., Willobie his Avisa, Chapman's
Familiar Spirit, and the rest. 'More folly has been written
about the sonnets than about any other Shakespearean topic',
as Chambers laconically observed;[1] and these questions have
no bearing on an appreciation of the *Sonnets* as poetry. But one
aspect of the personal relationships treated by Shakespeare
has relevance to the critic. Whoever the Friend of the *Sonnets*
may have been in life, the tone of deference in which he was
addressed, the importance attached to his begetting an heir,
the mention of rival poets who claimed his patronage, besides
frequent references to his wealth and position,[2] all indicate
that he was a gentleman of high rank. Friendship between
young men of noble minds was a major theme of Renaissance
literature and philosophy. With the new seriousness that
characterized sixteenth-century Italy, this male relationship
was more highly esteemed than at any time since the days of
Pericles. Bembo and Castiglione extolled it as the ladder leading directly to the Platonic *amor razionale*. In novels and pastoral romances, in poems and histories, noble friendships were
constantly held up as exemplary patterns of living. Lyly's
Euphues and Sidney's *Arcadia* provide familiar English illustrations, as do many of Shakespeare's plays. As usual, life and
literary fashions interacted, and so long as the culture of the
Renaissance prevailed, this idea of friendship exercised almost
as powerful an appeal to the imagination as the rival concept
of romantic love.

All the more binding was the tie when one of the friends was
a poet and the other his patron. Before the time of a mass
reading public, such patronage was an almost sacred bond.

1. E. K. Chambers, *William Shakespeare* (1930), I, p. 561. Such gothic
speculations have been provided with a handsome half-acre tomb in the
'Variorum' *Sonnets* (1944), II, pp. 177–313.
2. Cf. sonnet XXXVII:

> For whether beauty, birth, or wealth, or wit
> Or any of these all, or all, or more,
> Entitled in thy parts do crowned sit,
> I make my love engrafted to this store:

or XXXVI:
> Nor thou with public kindness honour me,
> Unless thou take that honour from thy name:

or XLI:
> Gentle thou art, and therefore to be won, . . .

We may recall the loyalty of Serafino to his Neapolitan duke, whom he followed into poverty and exile; Tasso's veneration as a young man for the Duke of Ferrara, and Spenser's life-long allegiance to Lord Grey. Years after he had been dis-illusioned, Tasso described his early sentiments towards his first patron in terms that closely parallel the attitude of Shake-speare in his sonnets:

> I confided in him, not as we hope in man, but as we trust in God. It appeared to me, so long as I was under his protection, that fortune and death had no power over me. Burning with devotion to my lord as much as man ever did to his mistress, I became, without perceiving it, almost an idolater.[1]

For a young writer of Shakespeare's genius, the combination of exalted patronage and close friendship may well have been a necessary pivot for the vast sweep of his creative energy.

Yet in itself this does not explain the choice of friendship as the major theme of a sonnet sequence. An individual's private experience was not enough, in the circumstances of Renais-sance literary composition, to overthrow the whole weight of a convention established for over two centuries. Courtship stood at the very foundation of sonnet tradition. It is true that friendship as a subsidiary theme was never quite excluded: Petrarch himself found a place for it. The sequences of Bembo, Della Casa, and others, as well as of the *Pléiade* poets, included individual sonnets of compliment to friends and patrons;[2] there are even examples of short runs of such poems.[3] But there is no parallel in the whole corpus of Renaissance poetry to Shakespeare's sustained exploration of the theme of friend-ship through more than a hundred and twenty sonnets. To explain it, we must consider not only the quality of his personal experience—however profound and formative—but also the

1. In a letter to the Duke of Urbino, quoted by Sidney Lee, *A Life of William Shakespeare* (1898), p. 11.

2. Analogues are mentioned by Lee in the *Life*, and others are given by M. J. Wolff, '*Petrarkismus und Antipetrarkismus in Shakespeares Sonetten*', *Englische Studien* (1916), XLIX. 161–89.

3. Etienne Jodelle in 1574 wrote a set of eight sonnets to his patron; in England, Richard Barnfield in *The Affectionate Sheperd* (1594) addressed pastoral verses to a beautiful boy he named 'Ganymede' urging him to marry. These and the other analogues have been set in their proper per-spective by Janet G. Scott, *op. cit.*, pp. 237–41. None of the sonnets I have read show more than remote generic resemblances to Shakespeare's.

nature of his literary development, and its significance with respect to the cultural background of his time. Spenser's evolution as a poet, rather than the private circumstances of his betrothal, was the key to our understanding of *Amoretti*. Similarly Shakespeare's development as a dramatist alive to the great spiritual issues of his age, rather than the accidents of personal friendship, must be our main guide to the *Sonnets*.

In the plays of his middle period Shakespeare was evolving a complex treatment of reality which, more comprehensively than any other writer's, voiced such issues. The contemporary outlook was essentially a dual vision, assuming a precarious co-existence of values; accepting at once the postulates of order and hierarchy, and the unmistakable evidence of conflict and transformation. In Shakespeare's dramas, love is at once an example of pre-ordained cosmic harmony and of the biological urge to increase, with significant analogies in society and economics. History is at once an object-lesson in political morality and a display of self-assertion on the part of individuals. The duality, moreover, is not static: the two sets of values interpenetrate. Sometimes the result is a kind of happy symbiosis, as in comedy, when, for instance, Portia's brains and enterprise (so unconventional and unfeminine) remove Shylock's threat to the romance harmonies; or in the culmination to the series of history plays, when Henry V's energy and *virtù* restore order to the body politic. But it may happen that these values prove mutually destructive, resulting in a negative vision of universal flux. The great arguments of history and romance become 'nothing but wars and lechery'. Crowned kings are corrupted by flatterers and vanquished by usurpers; Richard II, for all his conviction of divine right, is dethroned by Bolingbroke, who understands that nature's law is ruthless—yet Bolingbroke himself is increasingly haunted by the hollowness of his triumph. The negative vision is summed up in one great symbol: Time the Conqueror or Devourer, Ovid's *tempus edax rerum*, whose depredations are recounted in the last book of the *Metamorphoses*.

In Shakespearean drama this view of life was projected and made incarnate in living individuals. But the sonnet, so long as its central theme remained ideal courtship, could only treat such issues as peripheral: hence the failure, by and large, of the sequences considered in the last chapter. For Shakespeare, however, life supplied the occasion, which his genius knew how to seize, for revitalizing the sonnet medium through a transformation of the central theme. By substituting the patron-friend for the mistress of romance tradition, and by relegating the mistress to a merely subordinate rôle, he was able to resolve the major dilemma of the Elizabethan sonneteer. It was one thing for a lover to court his lady, and quite another for a poet to recommend marriage disinterestedly to his noble friend, speaking, as a romance lover could not without impropriety, of the natural functions of breed and increase. Moreover the friend, unlike the sonnet heroine, was a responsible leader of society, analogous to the Renaissance monarch in the wider sphere of state. He had his little court of admirers; he was a patron of the arts and an exemplar of virtue to lesser men. At the same time he was always subject to the hazards that assail the great. Sensuality might corrupt his virtue, flatterers and false admirers pervert his judgement. All these wider issues, which Shakespeare treated in his comedies and history plays, were now brought within the compass of the sonnet medium: yet none of its essential properties were lost. Love and honour, beauty and truth, were qualities as fitting for a noble friend as they were for an adored mistress. Even the traditional situations of courtship—absence, solitude, reflections in spring, memories and dreams of the beloved—might, with sympathetic adaptation, apply to a poet's friendship in the emotional climate of the age. At the same time it was possible to treat, in a subordinate series to a mistress, the negative aspects of erotic experience, where sensual desire and intellectual scepticism combined to induce a psychic disintegration such as no sequence in the romance tradition—not even Sidney's—could describe. Finally, the deepest concern of the age, mutability, could now be extensively explored. There was no need to cramp this, as Ronsard and Daniel had been obliged to do, within the narrow context of a rebuke to the proud fair—whose pride the poet was also supposed to admire—or of an exhortation to 'gather the rose', coupled with inconsistent praise of the lady's chastity. Time, the universal conqueror, might now be directly challenged in the poetry of personal experience.

It is usual to describe many plays of Shakespeare's middle

period as 'lyrical' dramas. The approach we are considering results in sonnets which may with equal right be called 'dramatic', using the term to signify, not merely an admixture of subject-matter, themes, and images drawn from the plays, but a thorough permeation of the sonnet-form with dramatic concepts. The process had in some respects been anticipated by Sidney, as we have seen in the monologues and morality-play conceits of *Astrophel and Stella*. But Sidney's temperament was too egocentric, and the theatre of his time still too immature, for the transformation to be complete. For Shakespeare's impersonal genius, one medium of expression necessarily influenced the other. The effects will be seen in the characterization of the poet, the mistress, and the friend in these sonnets, who are, like the protagonists of Shakespearean drama, at once individualized and given a poetic universality; as well as in the treatment of situations and themes, which sustain a complex and organically developing relationship.In part this proceeds through sonnets which display the dramatic qualities of monologues and soliloquies. Since, however, the sonnet as a literary form had to function without the elements of action and dialogue, its main scope for inner development lay in the use of imagery as a quasi-dramatic device. By way of illustration, we may note Shakespeare's characteristic treatment of one of Daniel's metaphors. In sonnet xxxiv, Daniel had envisaged Delia in her coming old age:

> When Winter snowes vpon thy golden heares,
> And frost of age hath nipt thy flowers neere:
> When darke shall seeme thy day that neuer cleares,
> And all lyes withred that was held so deere . . .

The poignancy of these lines derives from their contrast between the impersonal processes of nature and the plight of a single, hapless human being. On one side are ranged winter, snow, frost, and darkness: on the other stands a frail woman whose passive beauty is suggested in the associations of hair and flowers. No drama is possible in a situation that lacks the elements of conflict; there is only the pathos of human helplessness, melodiously suggested in smooth harmonies of metre and diction. Quite different is Shakespeare's rendering of the same imagery:

For never-resting time leads summer on
To hideous winter and confounds him there;
Sap check'd with frost, and lusty leaves quite gone,
Beauty o'ersnow'd and bareness every where: (v)

Here the transience of beauty is expressed in the military defeat of summer, with its vigorous sap and lusty leaves, at the hand of 'hideous' winter and 'never-resting time'. Impersonal nature has acquired human properties and volition without ceasing to be itself: time, winter, and summer are protagonists of a universal drama; and the metaphor is reinforced by such intentional discords of metre and diction as 'sap check'd with frost', and 'Beauty o'ersnowed'. In this sonnet the Friend is not directly addressed; he appears, however, in the next of the group, described through the same pattern of images:

Then let not winter's ragged hand deface
In thee thy summer ... (VI)

Just as nature has been humanized, so personality is assimilated to nature; and by means of the imagery both nature and man take their parts in a single drama which, dispensing with the need for a multiplicity of stage characters, centres upon the fate of the sonnet hero.

In view of such treatment, the question arises whether as a whole Shakespeare's collection of sonnets displays any structural coherence analogous to that of his plays. The sequences of Sidney and Spenser show a continuity of development, although—judging by *Arcadia* and *The Faerie Queene*—neither poet was distinguished for his architectonic powers. Moreover Daniel's use of iterative images in *Delia*, reinforced by other formal links, had set a precedent for runs of closely connected sonnets on contemplative themes, where the group rather than the individual poem stood as the primary unit. More subtle links and a more sustained organization of themes might be expected in Shakespeare's sonnets than in the work of these non-dramatic poets. Yet in fact the arrangement of the 1609 Quarto disappoints such expectations and shows very little cohesion. It is arguable, indeed, that Shakespeare, writing perhaps over a period of years, never intended to produce a formal sequence, or at any rate did not settle upon a satisfactory order. However, the confusion that prevails in the Quarto arises from other causes than hesitancy or lack of planning, and cannot be explained away in these terms.

The Quarto begins with a group of sonnets, continuing up to XIX, which are actually more closely integrated than any we have so far considered in this book. But after XIX the thread breaks and is only resumed at odd intervals. XX ('A woman's face with Nature's own hand painted') is an anti-climax to the serious tone of the previous group; and XXI ('So is it not with me') explicitly disclaims the use of images drawn from sun and stars, gems and flowers—many of which have already been applied to the Friend, and all of which will be associated with him later. Such anomalies are frequent in the Quarto arrangement. Sonnets closely linked in subject-matter, imagery, and diction are widely separated in the text—such as XXVII–XXVIII, XLIII, and LXI on visions of the Friend seen at night; or XXIV, XLVI–XLVII on the Friend's picture. Others are brought together through factitious resemblances—for example, XCVII ('How like a winter hath mine absence been') and XCVIII ('From you have I been absent in the spring').[1] And there are further inconsistencies in the unfolding of the story. XXXV alludes to the Friend's 'sensual fault', and XLI mentions his 'straying youth': yet in LXX the Poet declares that the Friend has 'pass'd by the ambush of young days, Either not assail'd, or victor being charg'd'. LV declares triumphantly that the Poet has now immortalized the Friend in verse: 'Not marble, nor the gilded monuments Of princes, shall outlive this powerful rhyme'. But forty-six sonnets later, in CI, the Poet blames his 'truant Muse' for neglect when it is in the Muse's power to make the Friend 'outlive a gilded tomb'. The theme of immortalization is treated in several intervening sonnets—LX, LXIII–LXV, LXXXI—and then in CIII–CVIII, CXV–CXVI, CXXIII–CXXV; but alternating with the latter are two runs of sonnets, CIX–CXII and CXVII–CXXI, where the Poet anomalously complains at

---

1. On which C. Knox Pooler remarked: 'This seems to have been placed here by someone who noticed that "absence" was referred to in the previous sonnet. Two sonnets on two different absences are unlikely to have been written without any other sonnet intervening.' (*The Sonnets*, 'Arden' Shakespeare (1918), p. 94.) T. W. Baldwin, *On the Literary Genetics of Shakespeare's Poems and Sonnets* (Urbana 1950), p. 302, disagrees, on the ground that this is an 'autobiographical' fallacy. But the time-scheme of a sonnet-sequence is as much a literary consideration as any other.

his estrangement from the Friend. As for the series to the Mistress, sonnets CXXVII–CLII, this lacks all coherence; the tone varies impredictably between decorous trifling and agonized soul-searching. And the concluding sonnets, CLIII and CLIV, toy with anacreontic conceits in a fashion unparalleled elsewhere in Shakespeare and without relevance to either series.

All this points to a disorder for which Shakespeare could not have been responsible; and the evidence of the text reinforces this impression. Its indifferent printing and bad punctuation stand in sharp contrast to the carefully set up, well-corrected quartos of *Venus and Adonis* and *The Rape of Lucrece*. Thorpe's edition appeared without either preface or author's dedication; and the almost complete absence of contemporary comment, at a time when Shakespeare was at the height of his fame, suggests some irregularity about its circulation. It may be added that Benson's quite arbitrary rearrangement in 1640 would hardly have been worth undertaking if in the opinion of his readers the 1609 edition was considered satisfactory. We must conclude that Thorpe's quarto was of the order of 'stolne and surreptitious copies', neither supervised nor approved by Shakespeare, who was not responsible for the arrangement of the text. This does not imply a deliberate mystification: if Thorpe had wished to obscure the details of the story, he would surely have omitted some of the more compromising sonnets rather than jumbled his collection. But the chances of accidental disarrangement in a large number of sonets were considerable, especially since, as we know, some at least had been passing from hand to hand several years before. Most average printers could rearrange the disordered sheets of a manuscript play by following the flow of dialogue; but although Thorpe seems to have made a perfunctory attempt, only the author himself could have succeeded in settling the order of over a hundred and fifty sonnets, once displaced.

If the arrangement of the Quarto, repeated for lack of a better in most collected editions of Shakespeare, has no authority, how is the reader to proceed? There can be no assurance that any reshuffling of the customary order will produce an ideally coherent sequence. None of the avowedly subjective arrangements by nineteenth-century scholars has found general acceptance; nor have the supposedly objective panaceas of the last generation solved the problem.[1] But even if we suppose that an 'original order' never existed, this does not mean that the collection given to the world in 1609 may be treated as a miscellany of individual sonnets, each to be read and judged in isolation from the rest. Whether or not they were meant to form a sequence comparable with those of Sidney, Spenser, and others, there are clear signs of planning and artistic organization. The absence of occasional or complimentary sonnets to any person except the Friend and the Mistress, or sonnets on any subject that does not closely concern them; the frequent cross-references and associations of themes and ideas; the countless links and modifications of structural imagery—all indicate organic unity and singleness of inspiration. A third alternative therefore suggests itself. On the analogy of scenes in a drama, it is possible to consider the *Sonnets* as a number of groups, like that formed by the first nineteen sonnets of the Quarto, each based upon some well-defined theme or situation, expressed through all the technical resources of this medium. Such groups would in turn form part of a composite sequence—using 'sequence' in a more flexible sense than has been considered hitherto—developing not in steady progression from beginning to end, but through the juxtaposition of themes and situations parted by intervals of time and modifications of outlook.

It is this third alternative that I propose to choose. The approach will be tentative and the results incomplete, for I

1. The most ingenious of these theories, based upon a system of rhyme-links, was put forward by Sir Denys Bray in *The Original Order of Shakespeare's Sonnets* (1925) and *Shakespeare's Sonnet Sequence* (1938). But it was pointed out by E. K. Chambers, *Shakespearean Gleanings* (1944), pp. 111-24, that Bray's arrangement unjustifiably separated a large number of sonnets clearly associated both in sense and subject-matter. The view that rhyme-link was one of a number of artistic devices in the Elizabethan sequence, and by inference, in Shakespeare's sonnets, is plausible. Bray's mistake was to impose a chain of rhyme-links mechanically binding every sonnet. A more recent theory is T. W. Baldwin's (*op. cit.*) who posits an almost vegetable growth of images throughout Shakespeare's work. Tracing these, with the help of carefully selected parallels from the narrative poems and plays, Baldwin finds perfect continuity (which somehow coincides artistically and chronologically) from the first sonnet to the last. 'Love is too young to know what conscience is' (CLI) would thus be a more mature sonnet than, say, 'Let me not to the marriage of true minds' (CXVI). Between the chain gang of rhyme-links and the jungle of 'genetic' images there seems little to choose in the way of poetic freedom.

shall not try to account for all the sonnets in the collection. Only those which seem to be intimately associated in theme and subject-matter will be taken into any group; but the group itself will be regarded as a unit and considered more closely than would be possible by other methods of approach. Although it will be necessary in some cases to rearrange individual sonnets, the cognate character of their themes will be a safeguard against serious faults of judgement. What is more, the iterative images will nearly always prove a sure guide. Far from being mere 'genetic' proliferations, the subliminal products of a poet's doodling, these images are part of a conscious structural design. Carefully patterned, shaping and shaped by the processes of creative thought, they infuse into the sonnet sequence the dramatic qualities by which it is distinguished, and subsume many functions of plot and characterization in Shakespeare's plays. With these groups as a basis, and the structural imagery to provide a wider integration, we shall gradually achieve an insight into the nature of the sequence as a whole.

As to the succession of the groups themselves, no serious difficulties arise. Allowing for the frequent anomalies, there remains a roughly progressive order in the main series to the Friend. The more trivial sonnets tend to come towards the beginning, the most serious ones towards the end of the series. The fragmentary story likewise advances as a whole from the Poet's first uncertain conception of his duty towards the Friend, through various episodes with their own quasi-dramatic development, to the final understanding which inspires the great immortalization group. On the other hand, no such order appears in the sonnets to the Mistress in the lesser series, which, while providing a sub-plot with close bearing upon the major themes, is directly concerned with a different experience and tells its own story.

It will prove convenient to give attention first to the Mistress sonnets. After this I shall follow the general progression in the main series to the Friend, considering in turn these groups: (i) *The Invitation to Marry*; (ii) *The Poet in Absence*; (iii) *The Friend's Fault*; (iv) *The Poet and His Rivals*; (v) *The Poet's Error*; (vi) *The Immortalization*.

SERIES I: THE MISTRESS

These sonnets, from CXXVII to CLII in the 1609 Quarto, are
an extremely disordered group. Clearly CXXIX ('The expense
of spirit') wastes its passions on the desert air between such
dwarf shrubs as CXXVIII and CXXX ('How oft when thou, my
music', and 'My mistress' eyes'). Nor has the painful self-
probing of CXLII ('Love is my sin') much in common with the
farmyard conceit and the 'Will' quibble of CXLIII ('Lo, as a
careful housewife'). Even the integrity of the series is doubtful.
In style, imagery and content, CXXXIX[1] and CXL[2] are more
closely related to the group in the main series on the Friend's
Fault; while XXI[3] continues the argument of CXXX[4] and is best
understood as part of the Mistress series. Since rearrangement
cannot be helped, I shall take the lighter eulogies of the Mistress
as beginning the series, and proceed by way of the 'Will' conceits to the sonnets of remorse and atonement which seem the
only possible ending to the story.

Satire governs the whole course of the series. Sometimes it
has a swift, rapier-like thrust; more commonly, it operates
like the heavy, old-English broadsword. Satire charged with
emotion brings together obscenity and earnestness, savage
invective and cynical humour; so that often the assailant is
liable to be injured as much as his antagonist. While the opening sonnets show a surface elegance, there is a rapid descent
to deeper and murkier levels. In outline the story is broadly
reminiscent of *Astrophel and Stella*, describing an infatuation
that is lightly entered upon, but leads to an ever sharper
cleavage between conscience and desire, until the affair is dissolved on a note of profound remorse. But Sidney was reinter-
preting the romance experience through contemporary life
and ideas; Shakespeare consciously aimed at negating all its
values. Therefore the resemblance of the Mistress series to
Astrophel and Stella was rather like that of a parody to its original, and the more nearly Shakespeare's sonnets came to
suggesting Sidney's, the more sharply their essential differences stood out.

1. 'Oh! call not me to justify the wrong'.
2. 'Be wise as thou art cruel'.
3. 'So is it not with me as with that Muse'.
4. 'My mistress' eyes are nothing like the sun'.

Tradition required that the sonnet sequence should open with a panegyric to the lady's beauty. In the sonnets describing the Mistress, each item in the usual catalogue of charms was coupled with a negative. Her eyes were nothing like the sun, her lips were not as red as coral, her cheeks had no roses, and her breath was not perfumed. Occasional burlesques of the Petrarchan heroine were nothing new; even Sidney, imitating Berni, included one in the *Arcadia*.[1] But for Shakespeare the real target was the fashionable minor sonneteer, Barnes or Lodge or Constable, not the Mistress herself, who was hardly to blame for their hyperbolical praises. Of course she was no Diana, or any other 'goddess' walking the sky: when *she* walked she trod the ground, as was merely natural. Sonnet cxxx ended with a deliberate paradox:

> And yet by heaven, I think my love as rare
> As any she belied with false compare.

Calling the Mistress as rare as anyone else was an Irishism, the Elizabethan equivalent of declarations that all animals are equal, but some more equal than others. Romance was democratized as never before—yet again the satire was directed at sham-Petrarchanism rather than at the Mistress. The lesson was driven home in xxi ('So is it not with me as with that Muse') and again in cxxvii ('In the old age black was not counted fair'). Constable's *Diana* certainly used heaven itself for ornament, and in their wider implication these sonnets damned the whole tribe of late-Elizabethan sonneteers. Shakespeare would not praise because he purposed not to sell: the word 'praise' having a secondary meaning of valuing or fixing a price: as much as to say that the conventional sonnet-writer was acting as a procurer for his painted beauty. In contrast to such ladies with their cosmetic charms the natural black colouring of the Mistress was a badge of mourning at the falsehood of the times. Sidney too had scoffed, though less cruelly, at the euphuists of the previous decade who 'with strange similes enrich each line'; but this had only demonstrated the supreme power of Stella, who was so direct an inspiration that no conscious art was needed:

---

1. *Supra*, p. 52, n. 1. A similar burlesque appears in Lyly's *Endimion*, v. ii.

> . . . in *Stellas* face I read
> What Love and Beautie be, then all my deed
> But copying is, what in her Nature writes.[1]

Shakespeare's conclusion to XXI made an instructive contrast:

> O let me, true in love, but truly write,
> And then believe me, my love is as fair
> As any mother's child, though not so bright
> As those gold candles fix'd in heaven's air.

His mistress was no 'poem', nor was she star-like—as Stella's name signified. Her beauty was a general earthly phenomenon, and his truthful description of it was also 'natural', since it made no claim to inspiration.

It is strange that the Mistress is frequently thought of as a painted courtesan, black as sin, but daubed and dyed with cosmetics, exercising an irresistible sensual appeal. This is surely an absurdity. The sonnets describing her all stress her unostentatious appearance and her contempt for artificial aids to beauty. Her main appeal for the Poet was indeed her 'naturalness'. She was as fair as any mother's child; no more, and also no less. It was the heroines encumbered with the attributes of ideal beauty who really depended on false adornment, as did the versifiers with their sham-Platonic claims to inspiration. Such is the initial case made out for the Mistress. Unfortunately for the Poet, this refreshing 'naturalness' has a deeper and more sinister meaning, and the satire against artificiality will prove to be double-edged.

The troubles begin as soon as the Poet turns from physical to moral considerations. The second pillar of the traditional sequence was always the lady's virtue, whether it was deemed transcendental or, as more often in England, judged empirically by effects. Here the premise of virtue itself is denied. Berowne's description of the dark lady he loved may be recalled:

> A wightly wanton with a velvet brow,
> With two pitch balls stuck in her face for eyes;
> Ay, and by heaven, one that will do the deed
> Though Argus were her eunuch and her guard.[2]

This was slanderously inappropriate to the Rosaline of *Love's*

1. *Astrophel and Stella*, III.   2. *Love's Labour's Lost*, III. i. 206 f.

Labour's Lost, but oddly relevant to the Mistress of the series. The transition from black eyes to black heart was made in cxxxi ('Thou art as tyrannous'). Sidney's Stella had shown 'how virtue may best lodg'd in beauty be', and 'all minds', drawn by her beauty, had been moved that way. In contrast, Shakespeare's Mistress only seemed fair to the poet's 'dear doting heart': for others, her face had not the power to make love groan. The Poet's defence of his own love was equivocal. A thousand groans bore witness that her black was fairest in his 'judgment's place'. Yet as everyone knew, the heart was not the place for true judgement. It was the seat of affections, actual or imaginary; it did not decide matters of fact.[1] The argument was entirely subjective and fallible, pointing to a condition where reason had absconded before passion; and the couplet stated the objective truth:

> In nothing art thou black save in thy deeds,
> And thence this slander, as I think, proceeds.

This sting in the tail, while leaving the Mistress's beauty for the heart to judge, admitted that her evil deeds were self-evident.

The satire now moves in a vicious descending spiral. The Poet's love for a mistress without beauty or virtue persists, though consciously based upon illusion. She does not even afford him sensuous pleasure: neither sight, nor any other of the five senses, receives any satisfaction from her presence (cxli). Yet his heart is enslaved, leaving him behind as the mere 'likeness of a man'. Here the traditional eyes–heart imagery serves to describe a hopeless state of inner conflict. The eyes deceive themselves; the heart's promptings run contrary to the heart's knowledge.

> If eyes corrupt by over-partial looks
> Be anchor'd in the bay where all men ride,
> Why of eyes' falsehood hast thou forged hooks,
> Whereto the judgment of my heart is tied?

1. '. . . the braine is the chiefe instrument . . . of thoughtes, and cogitations, perfourmed by common sense, and fantasie: . . . The hart is the seate of life, and of affections, and perturbations, of loue, or hate, like, or dislike; of such thinges as fall within compass of sense; either outward, or inward; in effect, or imagination onely.' T. Bright, *A Treatise of Melancholie* (1586), p. 47.

> Why should my heart think that a several plot
> Which my heart knows the wide world's common place?
>
> (CXXXVII)

When Shakespeare is caught in an emotional dilemma, his images become a medley of undisciplined associations. The archetypal female image of the bay represents the Mistress. While all men 'ride' there, coming and going freely (the verb has an obvious sexual innuendo), the Poet's eyes are anchored and he cannot float out to sea. His heart, submerged beneath the waters, is caught on hooks like a fish; finally the bay itself becomes dry land, a common which his heart had thought to be private ground. The main concern now is not the Mistress's beauty or virtue, but the Poet's awareness of his own psychical disruption.

With this awareness, a certain cool cynicism appears. Committed to 'nature', the Poet rationalizes his relationship at its lowest level.

> When my love swears that she is made of truth,
> I do believe her, though I know she lies . . .   (CXXXVIII)

She protests too much: he knows that she is lying; and she knows he knows. But he too has a secret fear. He is ageing, and his days are 'past the best'. Therefore he will act the ingenuous youth and pretend to believe her; while she, who can readily see through his pretence, will let herself be so deceived. On this new basis of mutual mistrust the idyll is resumed, and with tongue in cheek the Poet commends it as an example to others:

> Therefore I lie with her, and she with me,
> And in our faults by lies we flattered be.

The pun drives to the core of the whole affair. One lies and is thus lain with: falsehood and the act of love, described by one word, are made synonymous.

Moral nihilism passes over into deliberate obscenity in CLI where the Poet answers a reproach from the Mistress that he lacks 'conscience'. He chooses to give the word its special amoral connotation of 'knowing', and explains how this is bound up with the sexual act:

> My soul doth tell my body that he may
> Triumph in love: flesh stays no further reason . . .

The 'insurrection of the flesh', theme of many moral diatribes, here takes on an entirely forthright, priapic quality. Sidney's personified categories of the soul are transposed to the physiology of sex. According to this view of 'conscience', the function of intellect and soul is to act as bawds to the flesh.

To the nadir of the spiral belongs the masochistic satire of the 'Will' sonnets, cxxxv and cxxxvi. Courtship has become a joyless mating of human animals in rut. The Poet pleads with the Mistress: having had so many men, why not add one more? His name is Will, which means lust—why not accept him for his name's sake? The word is repeated like an obsessive formula that serves to obliterate personality. Both Poet and Mistress are reduced to featureless sex-partners, the forerunners of Apeneck Sweeney and the Lady in the Cape. Again the sea image appears, to suggest the primordial female, passive and undiscriminating.

> The sea, all water, yet receives rain still . . .

There is no question of being jealous of rivals, so long as the Poet is received with all the rest.

But in cxliv there is a major development. From the mass of unidentified sharers of the Mistress emerges one figure whose moral welfare is endangered.

> Two loves I have of comfort and despair,
> Which like two spirits do suggest me still:
> The better angel is a man right fair,
> The worser spirit a woman colour'd ill.

It is evidently the Friend,[1] and his appearance in this sonnet, as well as in cxxxiii and cxxxiv, provides the thematic link with the main series. The moral issues that the Poet had thrust out of sight in his own case at once present themselves when the Friend is involved. Instead of ambiguities there are clearcut distinctions: the man is fair, the woman dark, in deeds as well as appearance; and between his purity and her 'pride' is the difference between saint and devil. The Poet's suppressed

---

1. It is becoming the fashion to read into this sonnet a set of indecent innuendoes that originate in one of Boccaccio's tales. A little sensibility to Shakespeare's use of such words as 'better angel', 'saint', 'purity', would show the difference in tone between cxliv and cli with its unmistakable obscenities. Cf. *Othello*, v. ii. 205–6: 'This sight would make him do a desperate turn, Yea, curse his better angel from his side'.

self-hatred is now turned against the woman for corrupting the Friend to whom his better nature is committed:

> Beshrew that heart that makes my heart to groan
> For that deep wound it gives my friend and me!
> Is't not enough to torture me alone
> But slave to slavery my sweet'st friend must be?
>
> (CXXXIII)

Here and in CXXXIV there is an intrusion of dramatic conceits. The Poet asks to go bail for his Friend and be imprisoned himself in the Mistress's 'steel bosom's ward'; he claims that the Friend merely stood as surety for the bond with which, like a usurer, she now binds him. These conceits recall actual plot situations in *The Merchant of Venice*, and the analogy is hardly a coincidence, as we shall see when we come to the relevant group in the main series.

With this extension of the theme and its clarification of moral issues comes a painful return to normality. Desire is seen as a wasting fever, consuming both body and mind. The conventional image only serves to mark an essentially different approach. While the romance lover, sick for his lady, considered her the only doctor who could cure him, for Shakespeare's poet Reason is the true physician:

> My reason, the physician to my love,
> Angry that his prescriptions are not kept,
> Hath left me, and I desperate now approve
> Desire is death which physic did except. (CXLVII)

Actually the lucid diagnosis of his 'frantic mad' condition is a hopeful symptom, leading to a recovery of spiritual health.

The series ends with familiar palinodes. 'Desire is death'; and in a fury of invective the Poet purges himself of its bitter fruits:

> The expense of spirit in a waste of shame
> Is lust in action . . . (CXXIX)

Perjured, murderous, bloody, savage, rude—the epithets are flung out in a torrent, sweeping away the logic of the quatrain structure and shaping a new course in the verse paragraph. CXXIX is a dramatic monologue rather than a sonnet, with its rhetorical patterning of internal pauses and run-over lines, and its structure of assonance. The Christian antinomies, saint–devil, heaven–hell, spirit–flesh, have progressively asserted themselves in these last sonnets. In conclusion—for it is the one possible finale to the series—the Poet addresses his soul, 'the centre of my sinful earth', and bids it subdue his body:

> Then soul, live thou upon thy servant's loss,
> And let that pine to aggravate thy store:
> Buy terms divine in selling hours of dross;
> Within be fed, without be rich no more:
>> So shalt thou feed on Death, that feeds on men,
>> And Death once dead, there's no more dying then.
>
> (CXLVI)

In content, in form, and in their relation to the series, CXXIX and CXLVI are clearly analogous to Sidney's 'Thou blind mans mark' and 'Leaue me, ô Loue'. Desire is castigated in similar terms, and the contrast between sensual and divine love marked out with the same antithetical phrases. Yet the subordinate images of loss and store, buying and selling, with the final, Hamlet-like conceit urging the soul to feed on death (and so cheat the politic worm of its supper), are typically Shakespearean. They maintain the critical and satirical tone of the series to the last.

No ordinarily sensitive reader can doubt that these sonnets have roots in a real and painful experience. But it is by their poetic fruits that we must judge them; by their articulation of the mind of their age, and by their contribution to its outlook. The fierce diatribe against sexual infatuation only brought within the compass of the sonnet ideas which the Neoplatonists of the sixteenth century, notably Bembo and Castiglione, had already expressed in prose concerning *l'amor sensuale*, as compared with the higher relationships of love rational and love divine. Spenser, it might be claimed, had partly anticipated Shakespeare's approach in the sonnets to a Medusa-like mistress which were intermingled with the *Amoretti*, and which stood in much the same relationship to his sequence as these sonnets do to Shakespeare's main series. For Spenser as well as Shakespeare, the opposition of spirit and flesh, with its deep appeal to the English mind, lay below the stratum of contemporary ideas. It was easier for each poet in his own way to break from the romance tradition of the sonnet

than it was for the Italians, who for all their Platonist theoriz-
ing, continued to write sequences essentially in the Petrarchan
mould. Yet the conscious motivation of Shakespeare's Mistress series was neither Platonic doctrine nor Christian beliefs,
but a contemporary empiricism that rejected ideal premises,
and through the greater part of the sonnets was content to interpret love as a lust of the blood and a permission of the will.
Nature, unadorned and unashamed, was the true force that
instigated this courtship.

Nevertheless in Shakespeare's view of life two conceptions
of nature were equally valid, and one of them was creative and
benevolent. The nihilistic, descending spiral was not the only
possible course for love to follow: had it been so, his greatest
dramas could never have been written. We shall not fully
understand the Mistress sonnets unless we read them in association with the main series to the Friend, and it will meanwhile be wise to avoid too schematic a contrast between the
abstractions of 'love sensual' and 'love rational'. The love for
the Mistress, sensual as it may be, contains a large admixture
of cold intellectualism. Nor, as we shall see, is the friendship
wholly rational in its essence. Rather should we prepare to
find a dual interpretation of nature and human nature operative throughout the *Sonnets*, giving rise to contradictory and
changing responses, and deeply involving Shakespeare's total
attitude to life.

SERIES II: THE FRIEND

The true beloved of the sequence is the Friend, who is celebrated in over a hundred and twenty sonnets. All praises accorded to former sonnet heroines are his by right, and all the Poet's bygone loves find their being again in his person. The cynosure of nature and mankind, he is 'the world's fresh ornament And only herald to the gaudy spring' (I), as well as 'beauty's pattern to succeeding men' (XIX). He combines the promise and fulfilment of spring and autumn, like trees of the earthly paradise bearing both flowers and fruit; and is the original of both Helen and Adonis, the paragon of the two sexes (LIII). Nor is this a merely subjective estimate, like that of the Mistress as seen by the Poet's 'dear doting eyes': all humanity concurs in the same judgement. Should the Friend die without issue, the world will mourn him 'like a makeless wife' (IX). The future holds nothing that can replace him—

> hear this, thou age unbred:
> Ere you were born, was beauty's summer dead. (CIV)

—and past eulogies in verse merely foretold the actuality of the present day:

> So all their praises are but prophecies
> Of this our time, all you prefiguring. (CVI)

On a transcendental plane, the Friend thus becomes all that was, is, and shall be. The very values of the universe are bound up with his life, and must perish together with him:

> Thy end is truth's and beauty's doom and date. (XIV)

This Shakespearean concept must be accepted boldly from the start, if the sonnets are to have any meaning to the reader. Remembering the satire against 'idolatry' in the Mistress series, such attachment of superlatives to any human being is all the more surprising and incongruous at first sight. George Wyndham, one of the more sensitive critics of Shakespeare's sonnets, was deeply troubled by these panegyrics, and sought to explain them as echoes of Renaissance Neoplatonism.

The mystical confusion with and in the Friend of all that is beautiful or lovable in the Poet and others is a development from the

Platonic theory of the Idea of Beauty: the eternal type of which all beautiful things are but shadows. It is derived from the Poet's prior identification of the Friend's beauty with Ideal Beauty.[1]

Such prior identification is certainly a factor in the love sonnets of Spenser, as we have seen; but it does not explain Shakespeare's approach. In all the varied eulogies of the Friend there is no suggestion of eternal types, divine manifestations, or emanations from the realm of pure ideas. There are no absolutes from which the Friend's perfections are derived; there is no reality—unless it be the power of human love itself —which stands beyond the phenomenal universe. Wyndham indeed was led to admit this anomaly, which he attributed to 'rhetorical' exaggeration:

> Shakespeare in certain passages does but lay under contribution the philosophy of his time. . . So far indeed is he from pursuing, as Spenser did pursue, a methodical exposition of the Platonic theory that *he wholly inverts the very system whose vocabulary he has rifled*. The Friend's beauty is no longer Hoby's plate of fine gold, which reflects Eternal Beauty more brilliantly than aught else. . . For a greater rhetorical effect, it becomes in Shakespeare's hand *itself the very archetypal pattern and substance of which all beautiful things are but shadows*.[2]

The explanation requires us to take Shakespeare's intellectual integrity rather lightly. He need not have been a trained philosopher, but it is improbable that he would turn upside-down a universally respected system of thought for the sake of a few high-sounding phrases. Great poetry is not written in this way. It is better to take Shakespeare at his word and assume that he meant what he said; that he seriously intended the Friend's beauty, and his truth as well, to appear as 'the very archetypal pattern and substance' which the sonnets declared them to be.

Here is a treatment of character which presents a mortal man, subject to the universal laws of change and decay, who is yet the *fons et origo* of all positive values in nature and society. The conception is indeed anomalous in terms of logic or metaphysics; but this need not impair its imaginative validity.

1. *The Poems of Shakespeare*, edited by George Wyndham (1898), Introduction, p. cxviii.
2. Wyndham, p. cxxii. (My emphases.)

It effectively crystallizes the late Elizabethan vision of an an-
thropocentric universe, experienced by the poet in the act
of creative composition. Though consciously he may have
assented to all the orthodoxies of the age, in his poetry they
became contingent upon sensory experience and individual
response. The traditional assumptions were not explicitly rejected, as they might have been by a modern rationalist; but
they were reconceived with ultimate reference to the individual, sentient human being, who epitomized all the virtues and
energies diffused throughout the cosmos. Inevitably the vision
carried within itself its own negation, and the virtual apotheosis of man was coupled with a vivid awareness that he was
exposed to all the hazards of mutability and corruption that
were latent in the phenomenal world. Shakespeare's achievement in the *Sonnets* was to focus this duality upon the person of
the patron-friend, who now stood in the place of the conventional romance heroine. In doing so he coupled his eulogies
with an explicit acknowledgement that the new hero was the
potential victim of every mortal chance.

Complementary to the Friend is the Poet, whose part in the
sequence is equally important and equally striking in conception. Like the romance lover, the Poet undergoes the tribulations of courtship. Absence and sleeplessness torment him; he
is solitary in the spring, troubled with jealousies, abashed at
his own shortcomings. Upon these customary themes, however, some distinctive variations are played. The Poet's most
outstanding trait is his extreme capacity for self-effacement.
This is not merely an echo of the sonnet lover's avowed humi-
lity. Sidney had always had his Protestant conscience and the
dignity of his rank for ultimate solace; Spenser, regarding
courtship as a preliminary to the sacrament of marriage and
the subordination of wife to husband, had stooped to conquer.
Even Petrarch had sacrificed himself on the altar of love with
a certain hauteur—*E voglio anzi un sepolcro bello e bianco*. But the
self-effacement of Shakespeare as poet of the sonnets is total
and unreserved. He has no place in nature or society save that
accorded him by the Friend. He is in the autumn of his years,
'lame, poor, and despised', 'in disgrace with fortune and men's
eyes'. Repeatedly he confesses to his artistic failings. He thinks
good thoughts while others write good words; his verse is bar-

ren of new pride; he envies this man's art and that man's scope. Far from planning, like Petrarch, a memorial of white marble to commemorate his love,[1] he pleads to be left forgotten and unmourned, lest the world should mock the man who once befriended him:

> No longer mourn for me when I am dead
> Than you shall hear the surly sullen bell
> Give warning to the world that I am fled
> From this vile world, with vilest worms to dwell:
> Nay, if you read this line, remember not
> The hand that writ it . . . (LXXI)

There is a kind of criticism, sometimes amusing, that would treat such attitudes as material for a clinical vivisection of Shakespeare's sub-conscious; exposing (it may be guessed) his death-wish, frustrated homosexuality, and so on. But the Poet who speaks in the sonnets is no longer the 'I' of an autobiography or private diary. He is transmuted, like Sidney's Astrophel, by the exigencies of the literary medium, so that he has become himself a poetic creation, presented in significant contrast to the Friend, and conceived, like him, with the universality of imaginative characterization. What distinguishes Shakespeare's *persona* from that of Sidney is his completely extraverted approach to life. Without self-regard or desire to analyse his own psyche, his preoccupation is wholly with the phenomenal world and especially with other human beings. It is a generic quality, not of all poets, perhaps, but certainly of those whose genius leads them on to narrative and dramatic composition, and as such has been best described by Keats:

> A Poet is the most unpoetical thing in existence; because he has no identity—he is continually informing and filling some other Body—the Sun, the Moon, the Sea and Men and Women who as Creatures of impulse are poetical and have about them an unchangeable attribute—the poet has none; no identity—he is certainly the most unpoetical of all God's Creatures.[2]

The poet, as Keats and Shakespeare saw him, brings to the world nothing but his own love for it. The more dedicated he

---

1. Compare Wyatt's treatment of this sonnet, pp. 24–6 *supra*.
2. *The Letters of John Keats*, edited by Maurice Buxton Forman (2nd edition 1936), p. 228.

is to his creative task—the more he strives towards impersonality—the less palpably he appears in his own eyes as a real individual. His virtues and energies are drained off into his works; youth, beauty, social aspirations are exchanged for the capacity to represent these; and he is progressively reduced to the mere shadow of himself.

But this too is not the whole truth. There are moments when the poet obtains such rewards as drive from his mind any thought of what has been foregone. There is the sudden upsurge of joy—

> Yet in these thoughts myself almost despising,
> Haply I think on thee,—and then my state,
> Like to the lark at break of day arising
> From sullen earth, sings hymns at heaven's gate... (XXIX)

In the intense realization of his theme he participates in its very nature, and gains for himself a more vivid sense of life than normal human activities could afford:

> So then I am not lame, poor, nor despis'd,
> Whilst that this shadow doth such substance give
> That I in thy abundance am suffic'd
> And by a part of all thy glory live. (XXXVII)

This is the experience that makes amends for every loss; what has been jettisoned in the lifelong struggle for expression is recovered, rich and strange, in the new-found world of the poetic imagination.

Thus while the Friend's character is presented as the epitome of universal beauty and truth, the Poet's character sums up the essential qualities of the creative artist. It is on this polarity that the sequence turns. The Poet's love of the Friend traverses a different range of experience from that known to the romance tradition. It is the crystallization, in terms of a personal medium, of the artist's love of life on all the planes of phenomenal being—the microcosm of the individual; society, of which the Friend is the paragon and uncrowned king; the natural realm, where he flourishes as beauty's rose; the macrocosm of the sun and stars, whose truth he concentrates in his own personality. And this love, like that of the body, is creative, so that the Poet of the sonnets performs a unique function

H

in the world to which he belongs. He, and he alone, can resolve the antinomy of being. No force in the universe can hold back Time or lift the weight of sad mortality; only the miracle of the human spirit, manifested in black ink, through which love may still shine bright.[1]

Such is the significance of these sonnets on what may, perhaps, be termed their anagogical level. But it would certainly be wrong to view Shakespeare's characters as types or abstractions. The relationship between the Poet and the Friend is neither static nor preconceived; it undergoes considerable change in accordance with the theme's inner development. As we read on from sonnet to sonnet, the friendship appears to us as many-sided, kinetic, and at times inconsequential, as any subsisting between two human beings. The characters themselves, for all their universality, are progressively individualized with their full share of faults and inconsistencies. In the successive groups about to be considered, the governing principle will be seen as an essentially dramatic evolution, operative in every aspect of formal technique; almost certainly not as a result of prior planning, but by virtue of the relationship itself. In the first group the Poet will be led, in the very act of composition, to an understanding of the true nature of his task, even though this realization runs counter to his preconceived intention. This will be followed in later groups by the revelation of his own imaginative powers; by a period of disillusionment and recoil from friendship; by an act of truancy with subsequent grief and repentance; finally, by a resolution of all conflicts through a faith which enables him to effect the long-promised immortalization.

1. ['All those qualities which make a person lovable, all those, perhaps, which for Shakespeare made life itself lovable and livable, are particularised, incarnated, in an individual, and that individual is generalised into their unique but alas! so transient incarnation. It is as though Shakespeare could only apprehend the meaningfulness of life when it was, for him, incarnated in a person, and as though he could only love a person as the incarnation of that meaningfulness.']
J. B. Leishman, *Themes and Variations in Shakespeare's Sonnets* (1961) p.51.

(a) *The Invitation to Marry*

The first nineteen sonnets of the 1609 Quarto form the most coherent group in Thorpe's collection. They are composed with a remarkable mastery of verse technique, which combines all Daniel's virtuosity in the euphonious marshalling of vowels and consonants with a truly Shakespearean subordination of words to the very nature of the subject-matter. The most casual reading will permanently impress upon the mind lines of such felicity as

> When I do count the clock that tells the time,
> And see the brave day sunk in hideous night

> Devouring Time, blunt thou the lion's paws,

> Against the stormy gusts of winter's day
> And barren rage of death's eternal cold

Beneath the fine nap of sensibility, however, is a firm texture of reasoned exposition, proceeding by analogies and reinforced by the logic of the Surrey sonnet-form. Unlike the Mistress group, whose satirical effects were based upon simple paradox and antithesis, these nineteen sonnets show a complex intellectual foundation. What is more, the reasoning itself is progressively modified by the imaginative processes generated in the course of invoking analogies, until the initial thesis of the group is transformed into a new poetic concept. Rarely in Shakespeare's writings do we find so complete a demonstration of the working of his mind in the course of composition.

Marriage is the explicit theme of this group, as it was of the greater part of Spenser's work. But Shakespeare's Poet, unlike Spenser, is indifferent to the psychic or even the physical benefits of married love. Nowhere in the group does he concern himself with the character of the wife the Friend might choose, or spare a thought for her qualifications in the way of beauty or virtue. In sonnet I, the generalization concerning 'fairest creatures' evidently alludes to the Friend and not to any prospective bride. The mention of 'maiden gardens yet unset' in XVI avoids the conventional association of maidens and flowers, and substitutes for flowers mere vacant seed-beds as a symbol of potential fertility. The end of marriage is simply and solely procreation: a definition in one sense restrictive, since it precludes any treatment of courtship, but in another sense remarkably flexible, since it allows Shakespeare to express through the sonnet medium one of the most vital and comprehensive doctrines of the age.

So much attention has been given to the medieval commonplaces which underlay the Renaissance outlook that the more dynamic aspects of its thought are in some danger of neglect. The doctrine of Increase, with its stress upon breed—in nature, in society, and in the life of the individual—was as valid for the expanding world of the sixteenth century as the concept of order and degree, and may at times have exercised a more cogent appeal. If nature supplied illustrations of an ideal order, it was nature's very essence to be *naturans*, bringing forth new life. The middle ages had indeed recognized this primary function, personified by the allegorists as the goddess Kind. But it was Erasmus, the great humanist scholar, who first had the audacity to make nature the touchstone of sexual morality and to praise breed above virginity. In the epistle *Encomium Matrimonii*, translated and made accessible to the Elizabethan common reader in Wilson's *Arte of Rhetorike*, he struck out fearlessly as an advocate of the virtue of procreation:

> This is the law of nature, not written in the Tables of Brasse, but firmly printed in our mindes, the whiche Lawe, whosoeuer doeth not obeye, he is not worthie to be called a man, muche lesse shall he be coumpted a Citezen. . . For there is nothyng so naturall, not onely vnto mankinde, but also vnto all other liuing creatures, as it is for euery one of them, to keepe their owne kind from decaie, and through increase of issue, to make their whole kind immortall. The whiche thyng (all men knowe) can neuer be doen without Wedlocke, and carnal copulation.[1]

Some grudging tributes were paid to virginity as 'a heauenly thyng' and 'an Angels life'. But wedlock was 'a manly thyng' of far more practical concern to humanity and the commonwealth. The disparagement of sex, a function as natural as eating and drinking, was merely perverse:

> But shall I tell you at a worde, we make that filthy by our owne imagination, whiche of the owne Nature is good and godly . . . how chanceth it, that we thinke it less filthie to eate, or chewe, to

1. p. 47 (1584 edition).

digest, to emptie the bodie, and to slepe, then it is to vse carnall
Copulation, suche as is lawfull and permitted. Now sir (you
maie saie) wee must followe vertue, rather than Nature. A gentle
dishe. As though any thing can be called vertue, that is contrary
vnto Nature.[1]

Such arguments were a counterblast not only to the teachings
of the Catholic church on virginity, but also to the romance
conception of courtly love. The epistle of Erasmus, with its
profusion of rhetorical analogies, furnished Wilson with a
model for his text-book, and later writers with a pattern for
literary imitation. Sidney drew upon it twice in his *Arcadia*,
summing up the theme in the verse dialogue of Geron and
Histor,[2] and elaborating on the analogies in the prose discourse of Cecropia urging Pamela to break her vows of chastity.[3] Sidney showed himself in this discourse somewhat appre-
hensive of the immoral inferences that might be drawn: he
gave the speech to a scheming old woman and deliberately
impaired her case. Nevertheless his flaws of logic were atoned
for by many fanciful illustrations which other poets gratefully
attached to those they found in Wilson. Finally Marlowe in
Hero and Leander extended the doctrine of Increase to include
not only human procreation and natural fertility but likewise
all forms of commercial expansion. Accordingly his Leander,
as a 'progressive' thinker, sought to woo Hero with a lecture on
the economics of value in use:

> What difference betwixt the richest mine
> And basest mould, but use? for both not used
> Are of like worth. Then treasure is abused
> When misers keep it; being put to loan

1. pp. 50–1.
2.   Nature above all things requireth this
   That we our kind doo labour to maintaine;
   Which drawne-out line doth hold all humane blisse.
         Thy father justly may of thee complaine,
   If thou doo not repay his deeds for thee,
   In granting unto him a grandsires gaine.
         Thy common-wealth may rightly grieved be,
   Which must by this immortall be preserved,
   If thus thou murther thy posteritie.
         His very being he hath not deserved,
   Who for a selfe-conceipt will that forbeare,
   Whereby that being aye must be conserved. (Vol. i, p. 139)
3. Vol. i, pp. 379–80.

> In time it will return us two for one . . .
> Who builds a palace, and rams up the gate
> Shall see it ruinous and desolate.
> Ah simple Hero, learn thyself to cherish:
> Lone women, like to empty houses, perish.[1]

According to this view, beauty was a capital asset, analogous to bullion and real estate. The miser's hoard and the celibate's body were to be contemned as sterile; but the investor's loan-capital and wedlock were fruitful and therefore required by the law of nature.

The doctrine of Increase was a major concept of Shakespearian drama, carrying a significance that has yet to be investigated. It made its presence felt too in the narrative poem *Venus and Adonis*, where Venus begged Adonis to be her lover:

> Upon the earth's increase why shouldst thou feed,
> Unless the earth with thy increase be fed?
> By law of nature thou art bound to breed,
> That thine may live when thou thyself art dead;
> And so in spite of death thou dost survive,
> In that thy likeness still is left alive.[2]

Shakespeare may already have been seeking to fashion a young patron in virtuous and gentle discipline, despite the voluptuous setting of his poem. But a doctrine ill suited to the mood of Ovidian romance found its true expression in sonnets addressed to a male friend urging the benefits of matrimony. Such had in fact been the original occasion of *De Conscribendis*, styled by Wilson 'An Epistle to perswade a yong Gentleman to mariage, deuised by Erasmus, in the behalfe of his freend'. Undoubtedly Shakespeare had this epistle in mind while writing his sonnets, and was likewise indebted to the arguments he found in *Arcadia* and *Hero and Leander*. But he did not limit himself to the mere versification of other men's reasoning. The sonnet-form permitted him to conceive his friend as the perfection of genial nature, and accordingly rational exposition was drawn into a wider imaginative ambience. The legend of Narcissus, Ovid's Time the Conqueror, the traditional similes taken from the corresponding planes of being, were brought into association with the analogies of Erasmus,

---

1. *Hero and Leander*, 231–42, sest. 1.   2. *Venus and Adonis*, 169–74.

the illustrations of Sidney's Cecropia, and Marlowe's parallels from the economics of rent and investment, until all were synthetized in a composite vision.

The opening sonnets of this group show images of varied provenance ranged in loose apposition. Immediately after the general statement of the theme in the first line of sonnet I, 'From fairest creatures we desire increase', the Friend is represented as 'beauty's rose': a metaphor drawn from the traditional correspondences, where the rose is paragon of the vegetable world. This will emerge as one of the main structural images of the sequence. At the same time the Friend resembles Narcissus, in being 'contracted to his own bright eyes', whose light feeds upon his physical substance. This further suggests the economic concept of capital depreciation; so that the Friend is reproached for 'making a famine where abundance lies'. And the last quatrain brings together the two principal ideas of the sonnet: as a rose, the celibate Friend buries his content in his own bud, and as a thriftless hoarder of beauty, he 'makes waste in niggarding'.—In II ('When forty winters') Time the Conqueror makes a spectacular entry. His troops of years, who will dig their trenches in beauty's field, are ingeniously associated with the rose metaphor through a play on the double meaning of the word 'weed', as both clothing and plant. The enemy Time must win the battle against beauty, with the result that youth's gay livery and beauty's rose will together be reduced to 'a tattered weed, of small worth held'. Relationship between roses and weeds will be explored in another group: here the destruction of beauty's worth leads back to the opening images of I:

> Then being ask'd where all thy beauty lies,
> Where all the treasure of thy lusty days,
> To say, within thine own deep-sunken eyes,
> Were an all-eating shame and thriftless praise.

These 'sunken' eyes contrast with the bright eyes of Narcissus, and suggest the now sinking flame of youth that lived on self-substantial fuel. But the image is here overlaid by the more important one of the miser's sunken hoard of treasure, consumed by time. After this telescoping of the two images, the

Narcissus conceit disappears from the group: and the sonnet ends by again advocating beauty's use through the propagation of a child.

A more rational association than the fanciful play on 'weed' was afforded by the word 'husbandry', semantically of the same origin as 'husband'. In III ('Look in thy glass') natural fertility and human procreation were yoked together:

> Thou dost beguile the world, unbless some mother,
> For where is she so fair, whose unear'd womb
> Disdains the tillage of thy husbandry?

For this image, Shakespeare was directly indebted to Wilson's Erasmus:

> ... it is for the common weales behoue, that euery manne should well and truely houseband his owne. If that manne be punished, who little heedeth the maintinance of his Tillage, . . . what punishment is he worthie to suffer, that refuseth to Plowe that lande whiche beyng Tilled, yeldeth children.[1]

Modern economics return in IV ('unthrifty loveliness'), where Nature's legacy of beauty is seen as a loan granted for investment. For his reluctance to marry, whereby he merely uses up this loan, the Friend receives the striking epithet of 'profitless usurer': an implied acceptance of commercial usury which is curious even in the form of a conceit, and not without its relevance to Shakespeare's general outlook. The second structural image of the sequence, Time the Conqueror, returns in V ('Those hours that with gentle work'), associated as in II with the rose metaphor. And here, instead of word-play on tattered weeds, a more imaginative way of linking war and roses was suggested by one of Cecropia's illustrations in *Arcadia*:

> Have you ever seene a pure Rosewater kept in a christal glas; how fine it lokes, how sweet it smels, while that beautifull glas imprisons it? Breake the prison, and let the water take his owne course, doth it not imbrace dust . . . ? Truly so are we, if we have not the stay, rather then the restraint of Cristalline mariage.[2]

Marriage as a woman's moral stay was not at all Shakespeare's concern in these sonnets, but the image of rose-water in a glass admirably expressed the idea of progeny that would preserve

1. Wilson, p. 54.   2. Vol. I, p. 380.

the father's youth. In the lost battle with Time, in which all beauty is destroyed, the distilled rose may survive as 'a liquid prisoner pent in walls of glass'. Finally in VI all three concepts, from nature, economics, and warfare, unite: so that the distilled rose and the thrifty investor represent the Friend as a married man withstanding the onslaught of Time:

> Then let not winter's ragged hand deface
> In thee thy summer, ere thou be distill'd:
> Make sweet some vial; treasure thou some place
> With beauty's treasure, ere it be self-kill'd.
> That use is not forbidden usury
> Which happies those that pay the willing loan;
> That's for thyself to breed another thee,
> Or ten times happier, be it ten for one . . .
> Be not self-will'd, for thou art much too fair
> To be death's conquest and make worms thine heir.

So far we have traced the interweaving of analogies for the doctrine of Increase, expressed through the recurrent images of treasure hoarded or invested, flowers fading or distilled, human beauty perishing or perpetuated; while set against these has appeared the hostile figure of Time. There follow a number of subordinate conceits, generally derived from Sidney's *Arcadia* or Wilson's *Arte of Rhetorike*, which are tried out once or twice, and prove less capable of development. *Arcadia* supplied the comparison of marriage to a concord of well-tuned sounds ('Music to hear', VIII) and the suggestion that on the Friend's death the world would wail him 'like a makeless wife' ('Is it for fear to wet a widow's eye', IX). From Wilson's Erasmus came the conceit that a celibate committed 'murderous shame' (IX) and was 'possessed with murderous hate' ('For shame deny that thou bear'st love to any', X)[1] as well as the reflections in XI ('As fast as thou shalt wane'):

> If all were minded so, the times should cease,
> And threescore year would make the world away.[2]

[1]. 'Other shal be thought to seke a purenesse of life, you shal be compted a *Parricide*, or a murtherer of your stocke' (Wilson, p. 62).
[2]. 'Lette it bee forbidde that man and woman shall not come together, and within fewe yeres all mankind must needes decaie for euer. When Xerxes Kyng of the *Persians*, beheld from an high place that greate armie of his, such as almost was incredible: Some saied he could not forbeare weeping, consideryng of so many thousandes, there was not one like to bee

H*

The 'murderer' conceit was accompanied in x by the more serviceable image of the neglected house—

> Seeking that beauteous roof to ruinate
> Which to repair should be thy chief desire.

This may also have been taken from Wilson,[1] or perhaps from *Hero and Leander*. And in xiii ('O! that you were yourself') the time and winter metaphors of previous sonnets were finely fused with it through the flexible word 'husbandry':

> Who lets so fair a house fall to decay,
> Which husbandry in honour might uphold
> Against the stormy gusts of winter's day
> And barren rage of death's eternal cold?

Progressively, by juxtaposition, by word-play, and finally through an intuitive penetration to their essential oneness, the seemingly disparate images are made to coalesce. However, there is a limit to the scope of suitable analogies for increase, and the attempt to recruit them from every plane of being in honour of the Friend's perfection leads finally to an intellectual crux. Already in vii ('Lo in the orient') the sun metaphor, for the first time introduced into the group, had proved less tractable than the others. Rising like a young monarch admired by his subjects, but declining unobserved at the end of its course, the sun appeared to be an excellent analogy to the Friend in his splendour and mutability. Yet it could only be associated with marriage and procreation through an unsatisfactory pun in the final couplet:

> So thou, thyself outgoing in thy noon,
> Unlook'd on diest, unless thou get a *son*.

The truth was, that only in the sublunary realm of mankind

---

aliue within seuentie yeres after. Now, why should not wee consider the same of all mankinde, whiche he ment onely of his armie' (p. 60).

1. 'seyng also you are a man of grate landes and reuenues by your aūcestors, the house whereof you came beeyng bothe right honourable, and right aunciente, so that you could not suffer it to perishe, without your great offence and greate harme to the common weale' (p. 63).

Cf. pp. 52–3: 'you notwithstandyng can not want great rebuke, seeyng it lieth in your handes to keepe that house from decaie, whereof your lineally descended, and to continue still the name of your auncesters . . .'

and organic nature did the principle of reproduction apply. Suns did not beget sons, and the word-play was not rationally defensible, like that on husband and husbandry. Beyond earthly beauty, which died and was reborn in progeny, stood the seven stars, or planets, also exposed to mutability— such was the universal law—but lacking the power of self-regeneration granted to sublunary things.[1] In so far as the Friend epitomized the more sublime aspects of the universe, he was subject to their fate, and procreation would not revive his distinctive glories.

In xiv ('Not from the stars do I my judgment pluck') the problem is even more acute as the Poet seeks his supreme analogy in the fixed stars. An incidental conceit in *Arcadia* described Philoclea's 'heavenly face' as her lover's astronomy, and her 'sweet virtue' as his philosophy.[2] In *Love's Labour's Lost* the idea of a cosmic wisdom contained in the lady's eyes provided the text for Berowne's elaborate discourse on love:

> From women's eyes this doctrine I derive:
> They are the ground, the books, the academes
> From whence doth spring the true Promethean fire. . .[3]

A far deeper note was struck in the sonnet:

> But from thine eyes my knowledge I derive,
> And, constant stars, I read in them such art
> As, Truth and Beauty shall together thrive,
> If from thyself to store thou wouldst convert;
> Or else of thee this I prognosticate:
> Thy end is Truth's and Beauty's doom and date.

The category of Truth, now for the first time added to Beauty, follows from the correspondence of the Friend's eyes with the stars. This is not, as in the minor Elizabethan sequences, a mere hyperbolical effect: it is declared in complete serious-ness, the fixed stars being traditionally the source of all higher knowledge, which they diffuse upon earth through their mys-terious influence. Personality also, which is manifested in the

1. This is well put in John Frampton's *Arte of Navigation* (1595), trans-lated from Peter de Medina (fol. 3, sig. B2): 'The heauen is ingenerable inaugmentable, it cannot receiue strange impressions, it [is] neither light nor heauie, hotte nor colde, drie nor moiste, formall or royall, but ver-tuous...'

2. Vol. 1, p. 375.   3. *Love's Labour's Lost*, IV. iii. 302-4.

eyes of human beings, contains truth; this is the quality man shares with the higher intelligences of the outer spheres. But for the late-Elizabethan poet, the stars, and with them truth itself, which Christianity and Platonism would regard as the spiritual part of the universe, have become virtual extensions of the individual. Upon the Friend's death, his eyes, which diffuse 'the true Promethean fire', will perish: hence the prognostication from *these* stars is that their extinction will involve the end of truth. The alternative is indeed put forward, that the Friend will redeem truth and beauty by converting himself to 'store'. But in reality only beauty can be thus revived, as a mundane category perpetuated through offspring. The unique personality of the Friend, the truth shining in his eyes, must perish, and breed cannot restore it. This dilemma, growing unforeseen out of the very process of poetic thought, will assert itself inexorably from now on, and compel a new assessment of the initial theme. The last five sonnets of the group show, through a tangle of logical contradictions and confused metaphors, the path by which the Poet is brought to understand his own indispensable part in the Friend's survival.

xv ('When I consider every thing that grows') apparently retreats from the untenable positions of the last sonnet. The stars are now back in their inscrutable spheres, whence 'in secret influence' they comment on human affairs. They are the spectators, mankind the poor players, of the sublunary drama. The thought leads to familiar, safe premises: men 'as plants increase Cheered and check'd e'en by the self-same sky'. One expects the usual argument for marriage and procreation; but instead a concealed sun metaphor begins to obtrude upon the imagery. Lines 7–8 declare that men, again like plants,

Vaunt in their youthful sap, *at height decrease*,

The description is not an apt figure for men or plants; they may shrink in age, but do not 'at height decrease'. The half-conscious analogy is with the sun's course, as described in vII:

But when from highmost pitch with weary car
Like feeble age, he reeleth from the day.

And in the third quatrain the suppressed image becomes explicit:

> Then the conceit of this inconstant stay
> Sets you most rich in youth before my sight,
> Where wasteful Time debateth with Decay
> To change your day of youth to sullied night;

Then, for the first time in this group, the concept of immortalization through verse is announced:

> And all in war with Time, for love of you,
> As he takes from you, I engraft you new.

Normally grafting pertains to husbandry, and so by analogy to human reproduction; but now the image is abstracted from its natural context and made to indicate poetic creation. The former process of manipulating sun and star metaphors to fit the arguments for increase has been reversed: instead, the analogies for increase are themselves made to support intellectual premises in keeping with the new trend of thought.

Further efforts are made in XVI and XVII to continue the advocacy of increase. It is a 'mightier way' of fighting Time than 'barren rhyme'. An ingenious attempt is made to recruit the sun (which in any case will not stay out of the picture) as a reinforcement to the argument. Since the sun is the fecundating force which breeds earth's flowers, its function is supposedly comparable with the Friend's:

> Now stand you on the top of happy hours,
> And many maiden gardens, yet unset,
> With virtuous wish would bear you living flowers
> Much liker than your painted counterfeit . . .

But even this will not do, for the last line spoils the metaphor. Flowers do not reproduce the likeness of the sun as a portrait does its original. The sun is not compensated for the fertility it bestows, and again the meaning contradicts the intention of the sonnet. In the last six lines natural metaphors are abandoned, and instead the Friend's 'sweet skill' at drawing the lines, or lineaments, of life in offspring is contrasted with the lines of verse of the Poet's 'pupil pen', as well as the lines of his 'painted counterfeit' or portrait.[1] Neither poetry nor painting

---

1. Line 10 of sonnet XVI, given in the Quarto as
> Which this (Times pencil) or my pupil pen
clearly requires emendation. A misplaced comma after 'this' has been converted, with the correct comma after 'pencil', into parentheses which con-

can give such life to the Friend as lies in his own power, whether it be 'inward worth' or 'outward fair'. Attention is clearly shifting towards the problems of artistic creation; and xvii is wholly concerned with the Poet's qualifications to treat his theme. The grounds for his diffidence are revealing:

> If I could write the beauty of your eyes,
> And in fresh numbers number all your graces,
> The age to come would say, 'This poet lies;
> Such heavenly touches ne'er touch'd earthly faces.'

This was precisely Shakespeare's own reaction in the Mistress series and elsewhere to the 'goddesses' and 'saints' of minor sonneteers. The notion of 'immortalization in verse' immediately prompts the fear of committing another *Phillis* or *Diana* sequence: and the Poet shudders with strange prescience at the remarks of some present-day commentators. The upshot is a compromise: he will write, but the Friend must also produce a child.

It is the last time that marriage will be advocated. In xviii poetic creation has won decisively, and the sonnet shows a greatly enhanced sensibility and control. 'Shall I compare thee to a summer's day?' takes into its scope with complete facility and grace all the main images of the group. The rose metaphor is deftly humanized in the phrase 'darling buds of May'; 'summer's lease' adds the concept of property with such quiet euphony that its association with flowers seems quite inevitable; and 'the eye of heaven' introduces the correspondence between personality and the higher spheres with equal ease. All beauty, 'every fair', declines—a word primarily suggesting the course of the sun, but open to more flexible interpretation than *decrease* in xv. In contrast stands the Friend's

---

fuse the entire meaning of the image. The line should be read as it must have stood in manuscript:

> Which, this time's pencil, or my pupil pen, . . .

'This time's pencil' thus refers to a portrait, or 'painted counterfeit' of the Friend, representing the best art of the present age (an idea which is further developed figuratively in xxiv). In contrast is the Poet's 'pupil pen': but the lines of portraiture and verse are both inferior to the 'lines of life'. This play on 'lines' for features and writing had already been made in Sidney's 'Who will in fairest booke of Nature' (*Astrophel and Stella*, LXXI):

> Let him but learn of *Loue* to reade in thee
> *Stella*, those faire lines, which true goodnesse show.

'eternal summer', which does not 'fade', like the rose, nor 'lose possession', as one may forfeit a lease, nor wander in death's shade, like the sun in the Antipodes. This eternal summer, with its classical evocations of an earthly paradise, will be created by the Poet's 'eternal lines'; yet even *their* eternity depends on the continuity of the human race—

> So long as men can breathe or eyes can see,
> So long lives this—

For in these sonnets mankind is, in the last analysis, the sole tribunal of all values.

xix is the finale to the group. The dilemma has been resolved and the theme of immortalization by verse decided upon: only a rhetorical flourish of trumpets is required as a challenge to the conqueror Time. For this Shakespeare returned to his Ovid, choosing a passage from the *Tristia* that described the characteristics of the arch-foe.[1] This was also used in *The Rape of Lucrece*, with a good deal of narrative elaboration.[2] Here the immediacy of the sonnet-form preserved, perhaps even intensified, its classical force and compression:

> Devouring Time, blunt thou the lion's paws,
> And make the earth devour her own sweet brood;
> Pluck the keen teeth from the fierce tiger's jaws,
> And burn the long-liv'd phoenix in her blood.

In the latter part of the sonnet, Time's 'antique' pen is seen as drawing lines on the Friend's brow; a figure corresponding to the trenches dug by Time's soldiers in ii, and contrasting with the 'pupil pen' of the Poet in xvi. The conceit prepares the way for a promise to defy Time with this same inexperienced pen that will nevertheless perpetuate the Friend's youth:

> Yet do thy worst, old Time: despite thy wrong,
> My love shall in my verse ever live young.

This pledge concludes a group which may be thought of as the introduction, and propounds the main theme of the whole sequence.

1. *Tempore paenorum compescitur ira leonum*
   Nec feritas animo, quae fuit ante manet . . . (*Tristia*, iv. 6)
The opening phrase of the sonnet, 'Devouring Time', is, of course, the *Tempus edax rerum* of the *Metamorphoses*.
2. Lines 953–9.

(b) *The Poet in Absence*

The sonnets taken into this group comprise a number of variations on the theme of the Poet's absence from his Friend. The subject-matter is traditional—conceits on the eyes and heart, laments at separation, accounts of the sleeplessness or troubled dreams of the beloved. Shakespeare leaned far more heavily on contemporary models than in the Marriage group and signs of the 'pupil pen' are to be seen in over-laboured conceits, over-rigid rhetorical patterns, and an uneven style. But although some of these poems have a conventional base, it would be wrong to dismiss them summarily. Imitation soon paves the way to self-expression and a discovery of new potentialities; well-worn conceits on absence become instruments for investigating the workings of poetic thought, its power to transcend space, its visionary quality; so that in relation to the Poet's part in the sequence the function of this group is comparable with that of the marriage sonnets on the Friend, and almost as serious a work of exploration.

XXIV, XLVI, and XLVII form a trio of sonnets based on aspects of the eyes–heart conceit. The first of these, 'Mine eye hath played the painter', is perhaps the most pointlessly elaborated sonnet that Shakespeare wrote. It was a commonplace of romance that Love entered through the eyes and penetrated to the heart. Renaissance fancy, probably expressed most gracefully by Ronsard,[1] developed the conceit, with love engraving upon the heart the lady's image. The engraving became for Constable a portrait, with the eyes as windows through which it could be seen:

> Thine eye, the glass where I behold my heart;
> Mine eye, the window through the which thine eye
> May see my heart, and there thyself espy
> In bloody colours, how thou painted art.[2]

Shakespeare, while leaving out the personification of Love,

1.   *Il ne falloit, Maistresse, autres tablettes*
            Pour vous graver, que celles de mon cœur,
            Où de sa main Amour nostre vainqueur
            Vous a gravée, et vos graces parfaites. (*Amours Diverses,* IV)
The analogue was first pointed out by David Klein, *Sewanee Review* (1905), XIII, p. 460f.
     2. *Diana* (1592), I. 9.

produced a complete painter's shop, with the Friend's portrait hanging in the Poet's bosom, his body as the frame, and the Friend's eyes for shop-windows 'where-through the sun Delights to peep'. For a special touch of modernist complexity, the portrait was 'perspective'—a fashionable device of sixteenth-century painting, whereby the likeness could only be discerned when the picture was viewed from a particular angle.[1] For this painting, however, 'through the painter must you see his skill'; the image of the Friend in the Poet's heart could only be viewed by the Friend himself, looking into and through the Poet's eyes. In this sense, the Friend's eyes became the windows to the Poet's bosom; and the portrait enjoyed a privacy unfortunately denied to that of Giles Fletcher's Licia.[2] Ingenious enough to make Berowne's coach conceit pedestrian, the sonnet's one hint of seriousness lay in the final couplet:

> Yet eyes this cunning want to grace their art,
> They draw but what they see, know not the heart.

XLVI ('Mine eye and heart are at a mortal war') takes up an equally time-honoured subject, the dispute of eyes and heart; but the treatment already begins to show signs of independence. Following up the last lines of XXIV, the sonnet is concerned with the difference between outer form and inner reality. To whom does the 'portrait' of the Friend truly belong —eyes or heart? There is litigation to decide the title; but the jury is packed with thoughts, all 'tenants to the heart', and the court's decision is biased:

> As thus, mine eye's due is thine outward part,
> And my heart's right, thine inward love of heart.

This law-suit conceit was probably based upon *Astrophel and Stella* LII, where the poet acting as judge awarded Stella's soul to Virtue and her body to himself and Love. Shakespeare

1. See Kathleen Tillotson's note to Drayton's *Mortimeriados*, 2332–8 (*The Works of Michael Drayton*, ed. Hebel, 1941, V, p. 43), which cites another reference to the 'perspective' picture in *Twelfth Night*, V. i. 227–8:

> One face, one voice, one habit, and two persons
> A natural perspective, that is, and is not.

Mrs Tillotson also refers to 'the well-known portrait of Edward VI in the National Portrait Gallery . . . where the picture seems distorted until looked at from one particular point'.

2. See p. 147 *supra*.

avoided abstract categories, and substituted appearance, seen by the 'clear' eyes, and reality, known by the 'dear' heart, for Sidney's body-soul antithesis.[1] The conceit was equally witty, and served similarly to advance the poet's understanding of himself, derived not from ideal principles but from observation and intuition. XLVII ('Betwixt mine eye and heart a league is took') adds a sequel, with eyes and heart now reconciled and doing good turns to each other. Sometimes the eye feasts upon the Friend's picture and invites the heart as his guest; sometimes the heart calls the eye to share his thoughts of love. Instead of the fierce inner conflicts of both faculties described in the Mistress series, here there is co-operation and goodwill. This is simpler and more pleasing than the previous conceits, and it will be noticed that instead of the fanciful picture on the heart's 'table', a real portrait is indicated. Serious investigation of the Poet's thoughts may now develop unhindered by the need for mere cleverness, and the gain is to be seen in the last six lines of the sonnet, with their quiet beauty of diction and their flexible verse structure:

> So either by thy picture or my love,
> Thyself away art present still with me;
> For thou no further than my thoughts canst move,
> And I am still with them, and they with thee;
>   Or if they sleep, thy picture in my sight
>   Awakes my heart to heart's and eye's delight.

Here the true subject of the group is for the first time enunciated: the power of poetic thought to overcome space, and its visionary character. The sonnets that follow present these questions in terms of particular situations.

L ('How heavy do I journey on the way') opens with a description of the Poet on horseback riding away from the Friend. He plays with the notion that his heavy heart weighs upon the beast, which 'plods dully on' and merely groans in response to the spur. The precedent for this conceit was in *Astrophel and Stella* XLIX:

1. The subtle shift of emphasis indicates clearly an absence of physical homosexuality in the friendship. This is confirmed rather than contradicted by sonnet XX, which declares that nature has 'defeated' the Poet in making the Friend a man—i.e. *had* the Friend been a woman, the Poet's love would have been sexual.

> I on my horse, and Love on me, doth trie
> Our horsmanships . . .

Sidney's comparison was elaborated on symbolical lines, with
his thoughts as the reins, reverence as the bit, will as the whip,
and so on. The method was a survival of the image-forming
process in allegory, which expands a simile in all directions to
accord with a preconceived pattern of experience. Shakespeare's treatment correspondingly typified the experiential
mode of thought that results in metaphor. He sought to avoid
personified abstractions; instead, a couple of actualities were
noted: slow horse and sad rider. The beast's sympathetic
'instinct', and its groan that seemed to utter the Poet's own
grief, suggested an underlying resemblance, but so far the two
figures remained distinct. Then in LI ('Thus can my love excuse the slow offence') they suddenly fused to precipitate a new
image. Anticipating a joyous return the Poet saw his desire as
a Pegasus whose spirited neighing contrasted with the dull
groan of the actual horse on the outward journey:

> Then can no horse with my desire keep pace,
> Therefore desire, of perfect'st love being made,
> Shall neigh, no dull flesh, in his fiery race;

This winged steed of desire was a veritable child of the imagination, neither horse nor thought, but an originally created
compound of the two.

The process of self-examination continues without interruption in XLIV–XLV. Here the relationship between horse and
man is located within the Poet's own being. It is his own 'dull
flesh', his own 'fiery race' of desire, that these sonnets now con-
template. If the dull substance of his flesh were thought, then
space would no longer exist—

> For nimble thought can jump both sea and land
> As soon as think the place where he would be.

Both thought and desire now correspond to the magic horse
traversing sea and land with instantaneous leaps, while flesh
remains earth-bound. The terms 'dull' for flesh and 'fiery' for
desire, with air-borne thought, suggest the elements, while the
Poet's tears complete the scheme, with the fourth or watery
element. While desire and thought, composed of fire and air,

surmount physical distance and rejoin the Friend, the Poet remains with his flesh and tears, the heavy elements of earth and water, which weigh him down with sadness and bring him almost to death. To modern readers this may seem like a return to mere ingenuity; we forget that the correspondences of humours and elements were considered authentic science, so that the train of thought in XLIV–XLV was clearly distinguished from the pure exercise of fancy that produced Love the horseman or the portrait painted on the heart.

But orthodox science, however reputable, was still not as convincing as personal discovery, and self-examination only came to a satisfactory end in the four sonnets XXVII, XXVIII, XLIII, and LXI, on the Poet's thoughts at night. What they reveal had already been foreshadowed in the couplet of XLVII:

> Or if they sleep, thy picture in my sight
> Awakes my heart to heart's and eye's delight.

Now the original concept is modified—it is thoughts that portray the Friend when the picture, through darkness, is no longer visible to the eye. In XXVII ('Weary with toil') the Poet, fatigued after his travels, hastens to bed. But instead of true rest, a journey of the mind begins. His thoughts make 'a zealous pilgrimage' to the Friend, and he lies awake, staring into the dark. In this condition, his 'soul's imaginary sight'

> Presents thy shadow to my sightless view,
> Which, like a jewel hung in ghastly night,
> Makes black night beauteous and her old face new.

There is a suggestion, as Malone noticed, of Romeo's first glimpse of Juliet at the ball of the Capulets—

> It seems she hangs upon the cheek of night
> Like a rich jewel in an Ethiop's ear.
> (*Romeo and Juliet*, I. v. 49–50)

But the fanciful details, with their 'fixities and definites', have fallen away before 'imaginary sight', which is not governed by simple association or unconscious memory. What distinquishes this vision from a hundred others in romance literature is that it is the projection of an alert mind and heightened sensibility. Sidney's dream of Stella had been the effect of sleep

and subconscious desire;[1] Spenser's description of his lady's
bosom had been given the properties of a dream;[2] as far back
as the Troubadours the nocturnal vision had served to express
the poignancy of desire uninhibited by waking thoughts.[3]
Shakespeare's Poet alone is concerned with the workings of
the imagination, its transcending of sense-perception, its power
to generate an inner light.

In comparison with this crucial sonnet, XXVIII and XLIII
show a slackening of tension. 'How can I then return in happy
plight' continues the lament on absence along conventional
lines, with Day and Night personified as rival tyrants 'shaking
hands' to afflict the Poet, and some decorative panegyrics
comparing the Friend with sun and stars, which fall far below
the metaphorical seriousness of the Marriage group. 'When
most I wink' likewise adds nothing to the inner development
of the series, with its Arcadian play on the simple juxtapositions
day–night, bright–dark, light–shade. The compelling vision
of XXVII has degenerated into a dream, as it was for other poets,
and one so indistinct that no genuine image arises. But LXI
('Is it thy will thy image should keep open') returns to the
original experience. Here the Friend's 'shadow' takes on a
volition of its own, less agreeable for the beholder: it seems to
gaze back at the Poet; regarding him with mockery; prying
into his idle hours and secret shames. For eight lines the sonnet
conjectures that the Friend's will, impelled by jealousy, has
overcome the barriers of space by a mental telepathy analogous to the Pegasus leaps of the Poet's thoughts. Then, in the
third quatrain, the possibility is dismissed.

> O no! thy love, though much, is not so great:
> It is my love that keeps mine eye awake;

1. Cf. This night, while sleepe begins with heavy wings
To hatch mine eyes, and that unbitted thought
Doth fall to stray . . . (*Astrophel and Stella*, XXXVIII)
2. *Amoretti*, LXXVI–LXXVII. See pp. 110–13 *supra*.
3. Compare in this respect the verse epistle of Folquet de Romans to his
lady—a typical expression of Troubadour sentiment—*Que la nueit, quan
soi endurmiz*. H. J. Chaytor translated the passage: 'For at night when I am
asleep, my spirit goes forth to you, lady; then such happiness is mine that
when I wake and memory returns, I scarce believe my eyes . . . for I would
like to sleep ever so that I might hold you in my dream' (*The Troubadours
and England*, 1923).

> Mine own true love that doth my rest defeat,
> To play the watchman ever for thy sake.

This rational interpretation, which replaces the former Chapman-like toyings with the occult, is strikingly bold. The Poet's own sense of guilt, his personality divided between an everyday self and a sublimated lover's self, have projected the menacing quality of the vision. And a further consideration enters into the couplet:

> For thee watch I whilst thou dost wake elsewhere,
> From me far off, with others all too near.

The Poet's higher self must watch, not only over his own baser nature, but also over the Friend, who may at that moment be 'waking' in a double sense: keeping wakes with rival companions, or perhaps waking in his bed 'all too near' to 'others' not specifically named. If there is a quality of guilt in the Poet, there is also a quality of corruptibility in the Friend.

Other sonnets may well belong to the group, but I have preferred to mention only those most closely linked. There is a clear unity of development from the first heart-and-eyes conceit of xxiv, with its superfluous cleverness, to the psychological penetration of this last sonnet. The fanciful picture on the heart becomes first a real portrait, then a vision of the inner eye. The debate between eyes and heart becomes a study of the processes of thought, formulated in terms of contemporary science, and followed by an intuitive revelation of the soul's imaginary sight. In effect, this group complements the previous one: what time signifies to the beauty and truth of the Friend, space signifies to the eyes and heart of the Poet, and both antinomies await their resolution through the functioning of the Poet's imagination, inspired by his love. But in the last sonnet there are suggestions of latent guilt and corruptibility which, though partly accounted for by the Mistress series, will call for full investigation in the coming groups before this resolution can be brought about.

(c) *The Friend's Fault*

Structurally at the hub of the whole sequence, stand a number of sonnets concerned with the sensual character or conduct of the Friend. Every issue treated so far leads up to this crux: the complications of the Mistress series; the question of the Friend's survival; the function of the Poet with respect to his living theme. And from the revelations of this group flow the profound changes that will appear both in the nature of the friendship and in the poetical conception of the sequence. Indeed the conflict expressed here may have left an indelible mark upon Shakespeare's total interpretation of life and personality.

The sonnets in which the Friend's sensuality is suspected but denied, admitted but excused, and finally accepted as one more contradiction in a bewildering universe, are spread through the main body of the collection from XXXIII to XCVI. There has certainly been disarrangement. The Poet, having said in XXXIII with reference to the Friend that 'suns of the world may stain', was not likely to declare in LXX that the Friend presented a 'pure unstained prime'. Nor could he fairly claim in this latter sonnet that the Friend had 'pass'd by the ambush of young days Either not assail'd or victor being charged', after making the statement in XLII: 'That she hath thee is of my wailing chief.' These anachronisms, which might pass in the theatre, can hardly be disregarded in poems addressed to a reader, perhaps the Friend himself; and equally apparent is the incoherent succession of ideas and images in the Quarto order. Here again I have no alternative but to set up a new order of reading—which, of course, need not be regarded as either definitive or complete.

The subject matter of the group has no precedent in traditional sonnet themes, and is more closely linked with certain plays of Shakespeare's middle period than with any other sequence. The connection appears on the surface in quite fanciful transpositions of plot relationships to poetical conceits. We have already noticed sonnets in the Mistress series which recalled the story of *The Merchant of Venice*:[1] a similar echo may be heard in the following conceit from LXVII:

1. *Supra*, p. 180.

> Why should he live, now Nature bankrupt is,
> Beggar'd of blood to blush through lively veins?
> For she hath no exchequer now but his,
> And proud[1] of many, lives upon his gains.

This may be set beside Shylock's description of Antonio after the loss of his ventures:

> a *bankrupt*, a prodigal, who dare scarce show his head on the Rialto;
> a *beggar*, that used to come so smug upon the mart; . . .
> *(The Merchant of Venice*, III. i. 48 f.)

In the sonnet, Nature has been placed in the situation of Antonio, with Portia, whose abundant wealth was the only exchequer to meet his obligations, paralleled in the Friend. But the connection between *The Merchant of Venice* and the group operates at a deeper level than the above exercise of fancy. Both works are governed by the same moral attitudes to life, and it is at the point in the play where they become explicit that the major analogy with the sonnet group will be found. In Bassanio's long moralizing soliloquy of Act III, scene ii, the great theme of Ornament which, with Increase, animates both the characterization and the plot of *The Merchant of Venice* is set forth in detail. Placed at the exact climax, just before the choice of the leaden casket, this speech establishes a fixed point from which the values of the drama may be reviewed.

> So may the outward shows be least themselves:
> The world is still deceiv'd with ornament.
> In law, what plea so tainted and corrupt
> But, being season'd with a gracious voice,
> Obscures the show of evil? In religion,
> What damned error, but some sober brow
> Will bless it and approve it with a text,
> Hiding the grossness with fair ornament?
> There is no vice so simple but assumes
> Some mark of virtue on his outward parts. . .
> Look on beauty,
> And you shall see 'tis purchas'd by the weight;
> Which therein works a miracle in nature,
> Making them lightest that wear most of it:

1. This word seems to be a misreading in the Quarto of '*priud*', i.e. 'prived', or deprived.

So are those crisped snaky golden locks
Which make such wanton gambols with the wind,
Upon supposed fairness, often known
To be the dowry of a second head,
The skull that bred them, in the sepulchre.
Thus ornament is but the guiled shore
To a most dangerous sea; the beauteous scarf
Veiling an Indian beauty; in a word,
The seeming truth which cunning times put on
To entrap the wisest. (III. ii. 73–82, 88–101)

Here the contraries of show and reality, artifice and nature,
semblance and truth, are brought together in a general diatribe against Ornament. These same concepts, as well as the
images through which they are expressed, lie at the core of the
group of sonnets on the Friend's fault; and we shall watch
them evolving and acquiring new significance as they progressively interpret the particular situation of the sonnets.

I take LXVII ('Ah wherefore with infection should he live')
and LXVIII ('Thus is his cheek the map') as introducing the
group. The Friend is reproached in LXVII with keeping doubtful company. Impiety and sin are graced by his society: he is
in fact the 'sober brow' and 'gracious voice' that sanction them,
and he encourages the evils of ornament, since the true rose of
his cheek supplies a model for false painting and its roses of
shadow. Next comes the commercial conceit already quoted,
where the Friend is seen as nature's only exchequer; but
LXVIII returns to the essential issues of truth and ornament.
The rose of the Friend's cheek survives from a past era when
beauty was as natural as flowers are now, which 'live and die'
without a spurious perpetuation through cosmetic art. There
follows a simple transition from rose cheeks to golden hair with
its pristine natural beauty:

Before the golden tresses of the dead,
The right of sepulchres, were shorn away
To live a second life on second head,
Ere beauty's dead fleece made another gay.

The dead fleece of false hair recalls by contrast Portia's sunny
locks which hung on her temples like a golden fleece; but
the main image is evidently a parallel to that of Bassanio's
soliloquy:

> So are those crisped snaky golden locks
> Which make such wanton gambols with the wind,
> Upon supposed fairness, often known
> To be the dowry of a second head,
> The skull that bred them in the sepulchre.

In the drama the major theatrical symbol for ornament was the golden casket with its skull, which Bassanio rejected for the living portrait in the plain casket of lead. Like this portrait is the beauty of the Friend, 'without all ornament, itself and true'.

From the simple warning lest the Friend's naturalness give aid to society's artificiality develop the complications proceeding from his fault. The imagery now centres upon the rose–cheek association which is specific, abandoning the more generalized association gold–hair, which did not (perhaps could not) directly describe the beauty of the Friend. In LIV ('Oh how much more doth beauty beauteous seem') the metaphor of the rose begins to grow out of its first static symbolism. The Friend's beauty, at first characterized as without ornament and true, is here said to be *enhanced* by the 'sweet ornament of truth', distinguishing it from the scentless canker-blooms—or wild roses—which are outwardly as fair:

> The canker-blooms have full as deep a dye
> As the perfumed tincture of the roses,
> Hang on such thorns, and play as wantonly
> When summer's breath their masked buds discloses:

It will be noticed that the Friend's distinctiveness is now no longer his natural beauty, which is common to the wild roses, but an abstract, intangible perfection. While the inferior canker-blooms 'live unwoo'd' and 'die to themselves', the immortal perfume of the rose will be preserved.

> And so of you, beauteous and lovely youth,
> When that shall vade, my verse distils your truth.

The image of the rose distilled, used tentatively in the Marriage group to signify offspring, takes definitive shape here as the symbol of perpetuation in verse.

But, side by side with the metaphor of the rose with its perfume as the ornament of truth, now appears the new, anti-

thetical image of the scentless canker-blooms. The words
'play', 'wantonly', 'hang on', are charged with sexual suggestion. Every motion of these flowers is a provocation: they
are the Cressidas of the garden, the ladies of fashion whose
masks[1] are a mere show of virtue intended to stimulate desire.
With the mention of masked buds a different kind of ornament has been introduced into the sonnet: that of seeming virtue, or *faux-semblant*, that half-conceals, half-discloses, the
natural sensuality of the Friend's companions.

In his early plays Shakespeare had thought of masks,
whether on ladies or on roses, as quite innocently attractive.
But in differentiating the one rose whose perfume was to be
distilled, he now found it necessary to debase all others to the
level of the despised dog-rose, and to discover a sinister quality
in their masked buds. Nor was this all. It will not be considering
the image too curiously if we note that the Poet is guilty of
some falsification. The distinction in LXVIII between nature
and artifice, true roses which 'live and die', and painted ones
which are spurious though perpetual, might logically be extended to point a contrast between increase and sterility:
painted roses indeed cannot propagate like real ones. But
canker-blooms are not artificial flowers; they belong to nature
as much as the cultivated stock. And in nature, wild roses do
not 'live unwoo'd'; they propagate freely: in Elizabethan
society too, the fashionable masked ladies and their escorts
soon settled down to prolific parenthood. It was the Friend
rather who, in choosing to remain celibate, would 'die to himself'. Such falsifications do not come about in serious poetry
unless some emotional disturbance has occasioned them; and
the Poet's over-laboured attempt to attach the concept of
sterile ornament to natural modes of conduct rather suggests
an unresolved conflict in his attitude to the Friend.

LXIX and LXX turn from generalities to particular and personal issues. In consequence these sonnets assume a dramatic
character, using the rhetorical devices of circumlocution,
illustration by familiar proverbs, and aphorisms to clinch an
argument. At the same time the structural images are kept,
and continue to develop according to their own inner logic.

1. 'Mask' signified, of course, any covering for the face, such as a veil,
and could apply suitably to the leaves enclosing a flower bud.

LXIX ('Those parts of thee that the world's eye doth view') opens with a good deal of embarrassed hesitancy, and winds rather wordily to a point that is not made until the final couplet. All men praise the Friend's external beauty, and indeed their praise is only the bare truth. Yet their tongues confound this praise by 'seeing further than the eye hath shown'. (A measure of the Poet's awkwardness may be found in this Bottom-like absurdity of tongues that see too far.) They look into the beauty of his mind, and estimating this according to his deeds, add to his fair flower the 'rank smell of weeds'. This is uncomfortably reminiscent of the Mistress in CXXXI, who was black in nothing save her deeds. The couplet instead of rebutting the slander merely adds a reproach:

> But why thy odour matcheth not thy show,
> The soil is this, that thou dost common grow.

The Rose, it cannot be denied, has begun to grow wild, and is in course of degeneration to the common scentless canker-bloom. The blame is still chiefly laid upon the society he keeps, but the contact is more than incidental; he is rooted in the same soil. As usual, slander goes further than fact; not content that he has lost the odour and ornament of truth, it must associate him with the rank smell of weeds, Shakespeare's favourite image for the grosser sensualities of propagation.[1] The very fact that the canker-rose should thus be confused with rank weeds shows how baseless was the attribution of sterility in LIV. Evidently the distinction between wild rose and wild garlic is not absolute: both have their roots in the common earth. What is more, so has the cultivated rose.

Having conceded that the slanders are not wholly baseless, the Poet is driven to employ some rather transparent casuistry. LXX ('That thou art blam'd shall not be thy defect') declares that suspicion is in fact a kind of compliment:

> The ornament of beauty is suspect,
> A crow that flies in heaven's sweetest air.

Here the rose concept is completely transformed, with suspicion taking the place of truth as the Friend's 'ornament', which

---

1. Cf. *Othello*, IV. ii. 66–7: 'O thou weed! Who art so lovely fair and smell'st so sweet'.

is also described as a mask. The crow as the symbol of suspicion may recall the 'raven black' with which the Mistress's brows were 'suited' in CXXVII: certainly the new ornament of a mask associates the Friend with the masked canker-blooms, and all they signify in the way of deceit. Nevertheless, the Poet reaches back at the original image of the Friend as true rose. Because he presents 'a pure unstained prime', Time woos him: the canker vice loves the sweetest buds. This last observation, though pessimistic enough, at least distinguishes the Friend in essence from his companions and restores the hero of the Marriage group, assailed by Time. No mere social infection, but a disease of the spirit afflicts him, represented by the image of the canker that feeds from within. It is a cosmic evil, the invisible worm of Blake with its dark, secret love; and such a wooing is more terrible and tragic than the unrespected fading of the canker-rose. But the sonnet explores the idea no further; instead it ends with a return to casuistry. The rose only wears the mask of suspicion to conceal what might otherwise conquer all hearts. The argument is entirely without conviction, and merely employs flattery to cover the Poet's retreat from the moral dilemmas into which he has been driven by the Friend's conduct.

There is some easing of tension in XCV and XCVI, which continue the sycophancy of the last lines of LXX. The Poet, making no serious attempt to reprove the Friend, is concerned to humour him in his present way of life. So resolutely does he pursue this course that he virtually acts Pandarus. It cannot be denied that the rose is cankered; but how sweet and lovely is the shame that spots his bud! In what sweets he encloses his sins! The effect is rather gruesome, like complimenting a consumptive on his flushed cheeks. A 'kind of praise' is found in the lascivious gossip current about the Friend's behaviour; even the spectacle of his physical beauty undermined by vice is made a theme for congratulations: 'O what a mansion have those vices got . . .' Yet this was the same house of the body which the Friend had been enjoined to keep in good repair through marriage.[1] The warning in the couplet to 'take heed' is a completely ineffective attempt to qualify such encouragement, and the cynicism continues unchecked in the next son-

1. In sonnet III. See p. 194 *supra*.

net. According to XCVI, society approves both the Friend's
graces and his faults; finds them indeed to be one and the
same. Just as the basest jewel becomes precious when seen on
a queen's finger, so errors, if discovered in the Friend, are
made into truths. Values thus become merely relative, determined by public esteem. Again a mild appeal is made for the
Friend to control his powers of harm. It is put in the form of a
parable,[1] as homely as the proverb of the ill-used knife that
ended XCV.

> How many lambs might the stern wolf betray,
> If like a lamb he could his looks translate!
> How many gazers mightst thou lead away,
> If thou wouldst use the strength of all thy state!

Such flattery of the Friend's exploits as a seducer could hardly
serve as a serious deterrent.

Read in the context of this group, XCIV proves less enig-
matic than is sometimes supposed. It draws together, with a
recrudescence of seriousness, the various strands of thought
that have become so entangled, and results in a certain clarification of the main issues.

> They that have power to hurt and will do none,
> That do not do the thing they most do show,
> Who, moving others, are themselves as stone,
> Unmoved, cold, and to temptation slow;
> They rightly do inherit heaven's graces,
> And husband nature's riches from expense;
> They are the lords and owners of their faces,
> Others, but stewards of their excellence.
> The summer's flower is to the summer sweet,
> Though to itself it only live and die,
> But if that flower with base infection meet,
> The basest weed outbraves his dignity:
>   For sweetest things turn sourest by their deeds;
>   Lilies that fester smell far worse than weeds.

This sonnet, which at no point addresses the Friend directly,
stands back from the group much as a contemplative soliloquy

1. This originates in Matthew vii. 15, as a description of false prophets.
But its relevance here seems to derive from Lyly's *Euphues*: 'The Wolfe
weareth a false face to deuour the Lambe.' See M. P. Tilley, *A Dictionary
of Proverbs* (1950), W 614.

does from the dialogue of a play. Like the soliloquy, it provides a generalized consideration of themes elsewhere stated from an individual viewpoint; but (again like the soliloquy) it should not be abstracted from its setting. Properly considered, sonnet XCIV will be found to bear a close and detailed relationship to its group in the sequence.

The first eight lines of the poem may be read as a purely political statement, summing up the main qualities the sixteenth century looked for in a model prince or ruler. Again and again these qualities are set forth in the political tracts, sermons, and reflective poems of the age. The true prince exercises supreme power; but he tempers justice with mercy. He is the prime mover, or *primum mobile*, of society, while remaining himself unmoved.[1] His virtues arise through a profound self-knowledge; his reason is in full control of his desires, or 'motions of the mind', and he is well able to withstand their temptations. Such a ruler is graced by God, and is the careful guardian of his country.—But these generalities do not wholly explain the phrases and images used, nor have they much relevance to the latter part of the sonnet. To understand the poem as a whole we must consider it as part of the group. A valuable pointer to its personal plane of reference will be found in the derivation of the first line, 'They that have power to hurt and will do none'. It is well known that this echoes Sidney's observation in *Arcadia*:

> but the more power he hath to hurte, the more admirable is his praise that he will not hurt.[2]

What has not been considered is the very significant occasion of this remark. It concerns the young Prince Plangus, whose story is told in Book II, chapter 15:

> This Prince (while yet the errors in his nature were excused by the greenenes of his youth, which tooke all the fault upon it selfe) loved a private mans wife of the principal Citie of that King-

1. Cf. John Norden: 'Therefore must euery inferior haue an eye vnto the superiour: so by degrees shall there be true obseruation of dutie in euery place: her Maiestie and Counsell is as it were *primum mobile*, whateuer moueth must begin from thence, and by direction from thence, must all the rest moue as vpon the axletree, which carieth about al the gouernment of this commõ-wealth'. *A Christian Familiar Comfort* (1596), p. 59.

2. I, p. 246.

dome, if that may be called love, which he rather did take into
himselfe willingly, then by which he was takē forcibly. It suf-
ficeth, that the yong man perswaded himself he loved her: she
being a woman beautiful enough, if it be possible, that the outside onely can justly entitle a beauty. But finding such a chase as
only fledde to be caught, the yong Prince broght his affectiō with
her to that point, which ought to engrave remorse in her harte,
& to paint shame upon her face. And so possest he his desire
without any interruption; he constantly favouring her, and she
thinking that the enameling of a Princes name, might hide the
spots of a broken wedlock.[1]

Sidney goes on to relate how the Prince's father, in his son's
absence, fell in love with the same woman, and how the Prince,
on his return, forebore out of filial respect from continuing the
intrigue. It is in reference to this triangular affair that the
remark was made which Shakespeare took for the opening
line of his sonnet; and one can hardly doubt that it came to
mind through the association of the episode from romance
with the circumstances of the Friend's fault, as well as with
the situation in the Mistress series.[2] By these tokens we may
be prepared to find, in the other political commonplaces of
sonnet XCIV, parallel meanings which have a direct bearing
upon the personal issues of the present group of sonnets.

From this aspect, the first line recalls the figure of the 'stern
wolf' in XCVI. The Friend to be desired, who is implied in the
general pronoun 'they', will retain the power to hurt that his
beauty gives him, but will decline to exercise that power. The
'thing' that he most 'shows' is equally allusive, recalling
beauty's ornament of suspicion in LXX, the 'suspect of ill' that
'masks his show'—and, like all decorative masks, draws attention to it. Thus the ideal Friend will continue to arouse suspicion, but the suspicion will never be confirmed by his deeds.
In 'moving others' (the argument returns to XCVI—'How
many gazers mightst thou lead away, if thou wouldst use the
strength of all thy state') he will himself remain steadfast and
untempted. Such persons, the sonnet continues, are the rightful inheritors of 'heaven's graces'—in contrast to society's conception of grace ('Some say thy grace is youth and gentle

1. I, p. 243.
2. It is also to be noticed that in sonnet XXXIII the relationship of Poet
and Friend is treated figuratively as that of father and son. See pp. 221–3.

sport')—and are the fit guardians of nature's riches—in contrast to society's artificial values, whereby the basest jewel
becomes precious if seen on a queen's finger. Accordingly
these persons possess and exercise their powers as their own
conscience directs; while 'others'—be they the slanderers, or
the unprincipled admirers, or the Poet himself—are reduced
to the status of subordinates, mere stewards of their lord's
excellence.

This is the explicit reasoning of the first part of the sonnet;
for the deeper implications we must look to the imagery. And
here some critics detect an undertone of ambiguity. The suggestions latent in the epithets 'cold', 'slow', 'as stone', amount,
it is said, to a subtle irony directed against the Friend.[1] Comparisons have been drawn with Angelo of *Measure for Measure*,
whose blood was very snow broth; who scarce confessed that
his appetite was more to bread than stone.[2] But such irony, if
deliberate, would surely miss its mark, since the description is
not a characterization of the Friend, but an ideal portrait of
what such a man *should* be. What occasions these epithets is
rather an involuntary obtrusion of personal bitterness, due to
the predicament of the Poet himself. The phrase 'as stone'
breaks in upon the catalogue of ideal virtues with inapposite
recollections of the discourse on marriage in *The Arte of Rhetorike*:

> such a one as hath no mind of mariage, seemeth to be no man but
> rather a stone, an enemie to nature . . .[3]

And again, there is the metaphorical expression of line 6: 'husband nature's riches from expense'. Throughout the Marriage
group the concept of husbandry had signified procreation and
natural increase. The Friend had been warned not to waste
nature's wealth by hoarding it in celibacy, but to invest it in
offspring. Instead he has chosen to remain celibate—and to
squander his beauty and truth in dissipation. The Poet, arriving, after a considerable imaginative readjustment, at the
conception of his task as a perpetuating of the Friend's values
in verse, is left to eat his words, with no better function than
that of literary sycophant, uttering now and then some in-

1. William Empson, *Some Versions of Pastoral* (1935), pp. 89–115.
2. L. C. Knights, *Explorations* (1946), pp. 53–4.
3. Wilson, p. 48.

I

effective moral platitude. It is better, indeed, for the Friend to
be chaste than profligate, and as a lesser evil continency might
be considered a 'husbanding' of nature's riches. But the praise
of cold chastity, with its negative virtues, can hardly be sustained without an ill-concealed regret that the warmth and
geniality of normal wedded life could not have sufficed, and a
growing chagrin at the vicious substitute the Friend has preferred.

In the latter part of the sonnet, this suppressed regret is
explored, still not overtly, but through the undertones of
imagery, which range back over the group. In LXVIII the
Friend's rose-like cheek had been seen as a relic of the lost
state of human innocence—'When beauty liv'd and died as
flowers do now'. The concept was then free from the special
pleadings of LIV, with its false dichotomy of sterile canker-
blooms and celibate yet immortal roses. It signified, not the
conscious virtues of chastity, but a simple and spontaneous
beauty of living, and this simplicity of nature is nostalgically
evoked in the present sonnet:

> The summer's flower is to the summer sweet,
> Though to itself it only live and die . . .

Let the pretended distinctions between wild and cultivated
roses lapse, and the Friend live merely as one of nature's
flowers, sharing the common fate of all creation. For although
many a flower is born to blush unseen, its sweetness is not
wholly wasted; it has its part in the phenomenal world and
the summer welcomes it—even if summer itself must die. And
at the conclusion of the sonnet all the traditional hierarchies
are thrown down. The rank smell of weeds may offend the fastidious, but Nature is a leveller, who accepts the rankest weed
with the most chaste of lilies. An image from Greene suggested
the conclusion of the whole matter:

> The fairest flowre nipt with the winter's frost,
> In shew seemes worser than the basest weede.[1]

1. Greene, *Alcida* (1588), IX. 88. Cf. Lodge, *Rosalynde* (1590), ed. Greg,
(Shakespeare Classics, 1907), p. 7:
> Lilies are fair in show, but foul in smell.
From the next verse of this poem comes the reference to sirens mentioned
on p. 242 *infra*. The last line of sonnet XCIV recurs in *Edward III*, II. i, which
may point, with other indications, to Shakespeare's part authorship in

But frost was a clean death, and show might itself deceive. Only corruption was entirely abhorrent, the inner festering of life. Such was the profligate celibacy of the Friend, far worse than the coarse philoprogenitiveness of the common man.

Sonnets XXXIII–XXXV are still concerned with the Friend's fault, but treat it from another aspect: its influence upon the personal relationship between Poet and Friend. The interplay of character adds a new factor, which in the course of three sonnets will appreciably modify the conclusions of XCIV. This extension of the theme is accompanied by a different order of images, which finally blend with those of the previous sonnets of the group.

The main figure of XXXIII–XXXIV had been anticipated in the sun and king metaphors of the Marriage group, but its present form was the result of parallel developments in the plays. The Marriage group had revealed how unsatisfactory was the sun image as an illustration of the doctrine of increase. Rather it suggested universal mutability, with clouds and eclipses corresponding with anomalies in the body politic and the microcosm of the individual. But while the sun could not beget a son, the analogy between the sun of heaven and earthly sons held good in their common imperfection. In the medium of drama this analogy supplied tragical undertones to several of Shakespeare's history plays. It gave special poignancy to Talbot's farewell to his son in *1 Henry VI*:

> Then here I take my leave of thee, fair son,
> Born to eclipse thy life this afternoon. (IV. v. 52–3)

In *King John* too, the description of the treacherously brilliant morning sun carried a concealed irony:

> To solemnize this day the glorious sun
> Stays in his course and plays the alchemist,
> Turning with splendour of his precious eye
> The meagre cloddy earth to glittering gold:
> (III. i. 77 f.)

Here the *sun* shone out upon a disgraceful peace whereby

---

this play. See Kenneth Muir, 'A Reconsideration of *Edward III*', *Shakespeare Survey* (1953), VI, pp. 39–48.

Arthur, the *son* of Constance, was betrayed. But in *Richard II*, instead of an association through word-play explicit in the dialogue or implied in the action, the sun about to be obscured by inferior clouds was metaphorically identified with the King as tragic hero:

> See, see, King Richard doth himself appear,
> As doth the blushing discontented sun
> From out the fiery portal of the east,
> When he perceives the envious clouds are bent
> To dim his glory and to stain the track
> Of his bright passage to the occident. (III. iii. 62 f.)

Richard II, who fatally mistook show for reality and indulged his 'rash fierce blaze of riot', was in this very scene to descend into the 'base court'. The situation of the stage king closely paralleled that of the sonnet Friend, and XXXIII opened with an interweaving of the images from *King John* and those in the lines just quoted:

> Full many a glorious morning have I seen
> Flatter the mountain tops with sovereign eye,
> Kissing with golden face the meadows green,
> Gilding pale streams with heavenly alchymy;
> Anon permit the basest clouds to ride
> With ugly rack on his celestial face,
> And from the forlorn world his visage hide,
> Stealing unseen to west with this disgrace. . .

The complete metaphorical identification of Sun, King, and Friend was an achievement of the sonnet-form, and typical of this form too was the personal treatment of the theme. The Poet is not only a witness of the sun's 'disgrace', but a party directly involved. Gradually through the double sonnet this becomes the main issue.

> Even so my sun one early morn did shine, . . .

It is the Poet's own spiritual son who has been 'mask'd' by cloud, not an objectively conceived tragic hero. Hence at the end of XXXIII the sun–son homonym induces a further development in the Poet's experience:

> Yet him for this my love no whit disdaineth;
> Suns of the world may stain when heaven's sun staineth.

The universal levelling of this conclusion completes the renun-

ciation in xcIV of false distinctions in nature. The cankered
rose and the festering lily are no better than the basest weed:
the stained sun of the macrocosm is in the same plight as kings
and common men, alike sons of the world. But this is not all:
the very completeness with which the hierarchies are broken
down leaves no standard of values for exercising judgement.
The health of the weed and the sickness of the rose are as one
in a corruptible universe. Therefore a new, merciful response
is called for. If the sun of heaven is itself not immaculate, the
beloved Friend, as a son of the world, may be acquitted. With
this revolution in standards, leaving personal relationships as
the only valid ones, xxxiv ('Why didst thou promise such a
beauteous day') shows an unprecedented forthrightness of
address. Even while the Friend is identified with the sun, he is
spoken to quite directly, on a footing of equality:

> 'Tis not enough that through the cloud thou break,
> To dry the rain on my storm-beaten face,
> For no man well of such a salve can speak,
> That heals the wound and cures not the disgrace . . .

Here is in effect a dramatic monologue, where the presumed
responses of the person addressed form part of the poem. The
Friend has evidently sought to make amends for the wrongs he
has done to the Poet through his fault. But his expressions of
renewed kindness are not sufficient: they do not cure the disgrace of the man who has travelled without a cloak—who has
trusted the sun and become involved in the sun's shame. Some
further token—this time, of heartfelt contrition—is needed.
These reproaches are not inconsistent with the form of exon-
eration which ended xxxiii: indeed there could be no call for
an act of penance, but only eternal casuistry, perpetual flattery, until the Friend was accepted with all his imperfections.
Paradoxically it is through the supreme eulogy, the identification of the individual with the paragon of the universe, that
this acceptance has come about; just as in the Marriage group
it was through the introduction of the sun metaphor, following
that of the rose, that the true means of perpetuating the Friend
was apprehended. And in the last lines of the sonnet it is made
known that the required act of penance has been performed.
The Friend weeps in genuine remorse; and his tears pay the
price of his fault:

> Ah! but those tears are pearl which thy love sheds,
> And they are rich, and ransom all ill deeds.

It is a momentous utterance; although, as other sonnets indicate, neither party is completely aware of all it signified. While the symbolism of these lines is drawn from the Christian ethos of redemption through suffering, the rationale of forgiveness is based on wholly inductive premises. Analogies and inferences drawn entirely from the phenomenal world, operating through the structural images of the sequence, have prompted the Poet to forgive. Charity proceeds not from belief in the equality of all men under God, but from evidence of the equality of all beings in Nature.

Yet just because no systematic philosophy, whether idealistic or sceptical, underlies the sequence, this impulsive declaration runs counter to the Poet's conscious pattern of beliefs. Accordingly xxxv, the last sonnet of this trio, is a painful and unsuccessful attempt to comprehend the position to which he has been led. It opens with a set of balanced antitheses which sum up the main images of the group: the stain in the macrocosm, the canker in the rose, the faults of individual men:

> No more be griev'd at that which thou hast done:
> Roses have thorns, and silver fountains mud;
> Clouds and eclipses stain both moon and sun,
> And loathsome canker lives in sweetest bud.
> All men make faults, and even I in this, . . .

But the order collapses suddenly in the fifth line, as the Poet turns upon himself and his own process of thought.

> For to thy sensual fault I bring in sense,—

He discovers that he has been judging the faults of sense by sensory knowledge, instead of by spiritual criteria; that his reasoning, wholly experiential, admits no moral absolutes. The rest of the sonnet is inchoate, the formal quatrain units dissolving and one image incoherently succeeding another. The Poet sees himself as defending just the sins he set out to condemn—'Thy adverse party is thy advocate'—and attacking his own professed moral code by so doing—'And 'gainst myself a lawful plea commence'. There is civil war in his love and hate: his 'sense'-induced mercy towards the man who is at fault conflicts with the spiritual love that should rebuke him. In the end, he is neither prosecutor nor defendant, but the mere accessory to a thief at once sweet in his appearance and sour in his deeds.

It is as well at this point to look back at the development of ideas in the Mistress series, to which this group is in many respects a counterpart. Below the conventional opposition of sensual love for the Mistress and rational love for the Friend is a common pattern of experience. Both Mistress and Friend have been loved for their naturalness; both of them, black in nothing save their deeds, have evinced a core of corruption. The Poet in his relations with each has been led to jettison the moral precepts of his age and creed. But at the end of the Mistress series he has undergone a sharp revulsion and has consciously returned to the familiar Christian antinomies of spirit and flesh, good and evil. In the present group there is no simple return. The logic of the Poet's own metaphors, drawn from the phenomenal world, has driven him on to a vision of universal corruption, and thence to an impulsive affirmation of individual forgiveness which militates against the very moral standards he consciously desires to restore. Why then is the Mistress condemned and the Friend forgiven? There is only one answer, and no preconceived doctrine will provide it. The answer lies in the power of human love as it subsists between the Poet and the Friend. The very condemnation of the Mistress which, with the resurgence of traditional morality, ended the Poet's infatuation, only came about through the shock of discovery that the Friend's virtue was being corrupted by her influence; similarly the pardon given to the Friend's faults resulted from the impulsive reaction to his tears of remorse at the wrong he had done to the Poet. Herein lies the essential difference between the developments of the minor and major series. Both unfold in terms of a poetic interpretation of nature or 'sense'; but while the minor series breaks nature down into sterile negations, the major one redeems it through the positive functioning of human love. Thus far, indeed, the process is not wholly conscious, and therefore the Poet's state remains one of intellectual confusion. The true consummation will not be achieved at the present level of the friendship, but will have to await further tests.

XL–XLII turn to the particular exigencies of the intrigue between Poet, Mistress, and Friend. The centre of poetic concern is elsewhere, and little need be said about these sonnets, which show a marked relaxation of tone and emotional tension. Were the 'story' of the sequence essentially a conflict between love and friendship, after the manner of nineteenth-century romanticism, the stiff patterns of formal rhetoric with their mechanical syllogisms would be hard to account for. But here such a conflict is almost non-existent; there can be no possible weighing of the Poet's passion for the Mistress against his love for the Friend. Even the suffering mentioned in XXXIV is not occasioned by jealousy, but by a sense of humiliation at the Friend's disgrace. The Mistress's eyes are nothing like the sun: what matters is that the Sun should be enamoured of them.

> That thou hast her, it is not all my grief,
> And yet it may be said I lov'd her dearly;
> That she hath thee, is of my wailing chief,
> A loss in love that touches me more nearly. (XLII)

Since the implications of this loss in love have already been investigated as far as the Poet's self-knowledge extends, nothing remains save to gloss over the whole problem with the trite Platonic conceit of identity. The Poet and Friend are one person; therefore the Poet's love cannot be stolen from him:

> But here's the joy: my friend and I are one;
> Sweet flattery! Then she loves but me alone.

Such casuistry can add nothing to the sequence, and the sole literary value of sonnets XL, XLI, and XLII is in their specific allusions to the Mistress, which provide the factual link between the theme of this group and that of the minor series.

The fault of the Friend, regarded in the present group from its sensual aspect, has wider ramifications in the field of social relationships and literary patronage. It is not only as a lover that the Poet finds the Friend 'with others all too near'; and while these blemishes do not stir the Poet's emotions at so deep a level, they affect his external conduct more closely. The next group, therefore, brings to a climax the strain to which the friendship is exposed, leaving in abeyance the imaginative factors which operate to maintain it.

(d) *The Poet and his Rivals*

Gaunt. Though Richard my life's counsel would not hear,
My death's sad tale may yet undeaf his ear.
York. No; it is stopp'd with other flattering sounds,
As praises of his state: then there are fond
Lascivious metres, to whose venom sound
The open ear of youth doth always listen:
Report of fashions in proud Italy,
Whose manners still our tardy apish nation
Limps after in base imitation.

(*Richard II*, II. i. 15–23)

Richard's character vividly calls to mind the fashionable young nobleman of Shakespeare's time, with his Italianate manners and his taste in verse for Ovidian erotics. The theme of ornament which underlay *The Merchant of Venice* is transposed in *Richard II* from romance to politics and social conduct, with disastrous results for the brilliant *roi fainéant*. A similar transposition of theme from sexual to social faults takes place in the sonnets of the present group, whose core is LXXVIII–LXXX and LXXXII–LXXXVI, according to the reasonably coherent Quarto numbering. Already in the previous group casual mention had been made of

That tongue that tells the story of thy days,
Making lascivious comments on thy sport . . . (XCV)

Now this is expanded into a full consideration of the writers whose poems or dedications flatter the Friend. A literary parallel may be drawn between the situation in *Richard II* where Gaunt, representing the old order, is supplanted by modish young courtiers, and the situation in this group of sonnets where the Poet is displaced by the modernists of the fifteen-nineties.

The form of these sonnets is essentially rhetorical, and the dominant technique is irony. While the ostensible tone remains courtly and deferential throughout, again and again the imagery and diction carry double meanings or have ambiguous implications. These are part of the conscious intention, and the reader may legitimately set out to detect their presence without much fear of importing irrelevancies.

In LXXVIII ('So oft have I invoked thee for my Muse') the
1*

Poet, while identifying his Muse with the Friend, points out that now every 'alien pen' has got his 'use', and 'disperses' poetry under this inspiration. The term *alien* suggests not merely another writer, but an outsider who has no birth-right to such aid; while the Poet's 'use', besides the use of his pen, carries an implication of interest or gain. Other writers, that is, have both stolen the Poet's occupation and appropriated the Poet's share of reward; while in *dispersing* their poetry they are not only publishing it but at the same time dissipating its value. They are, in fact, squandering the benefit accruing to them from their intimacy with the Friend—an intimacy which by right belongs to the Poet. The mention of 'alien pens' leads by a common Shakespearean association to the image of a bird in flight:[1]

> Thine eyes, that taught the dumb on high to sing,
> And heavy ignorance aloft to fly,
> Have added feathers to the learned's wing,
> And given grace a double majesty.

Now in xxix ('When in disgrace with fortune'), the Poet's own powers had been described by a different bird image. While 'desiring this man's art and that man's scope', recollection of the Friend had sent his imagination soaring like a lark away from sullen earth. For the rival poet, in contrast, the Friend has performed a different kind of service. He has added feathers to the rival's wings—the reference being to a practice of hawking, whereby 'feathers missing or broken were replaced by sound ones or spliced'.[2] The rival is thus associated with a hawk, belonging to a predatory species, alien to the Friend's congenital disposition; an incapacitated hawk, moreover, aided by the imping out of his wing with borrowed plumes. The Poet's verse, on the other hand, owes its very life to the Friend; it is conceived under his influence, 'thine and born of thee'; created therefore *ab ovo* a veritable lark; while in the works of others the Friend can but 'mend the style', patching up by his presence the deficiencies of a foreign genius.

This sonnet is a fine example of Shakespearean irony, with every significant word and image chosen for its undertones of

1. See Edward A. Armstrong's discussion of image clusters in chapter ii of *Shakespeare's Imagination* (1946).
2. C. Knox Pooler, *The Sonnets* (Arden edition, 1918), p. 79.

meaning. Two concepts emerge from it, which are already familiar, in a different guise, from previous groups. One is the contrast in poetry between natural breeding—the process of authentic inspiration—and usurious gain—the 'use' or exploitation of a theme by a writer of a different bent. The other is the contrast between truth in poetry—the natural flight of the lark—and ornament—the hawk's flight assisted by extraneous trappings. LXXIX ('Whilst I alone did call upon thine aid') continues the ironical method and extends the scope of these concepts. Here the Friend ceases to be identified with the 'Muse', which term instead becomes a synonym for the Poet's own genius; the reason being that the sonnet is primarily concerned with stressing, not so much the alien qualities of the rivals, as their imitativeness. The Poet's Muse is said to be 'sick'; she has given place to another. He grants that the theme of the Friend deserves the 'travail' of a worthier pen—'travail' signifying a true state of poetic gestation, as when Astrophel was 'great with child to speak';[1] but instead there is only a kind of shabby commercial trick, the rival poet first robbing the Friend of his attributes, and then returning them to him as a gift:

> He lends thee virtue, and he stole that word
> From thy behaviour; beauty doth he give
> And found it in thy cheek; he can afford
> No praise to thee but what in thee doth live.

Not only does no natural increase ensue from this mode of writing; the rival even expects to take a breed of thanks for his barren metal:

> Then thank him not for that which he doth say,
> Since what he owes thee thou thyself dost pay.

The payment may indeed be actual as well as figurative: a cashing in of the Friend's excellence which is met out of the Friend's own pocket. We are reminded of the Poet's claim in XXI: 'I will not praise that purpose not to sell'.

On the other hand, the lavish praise of the rival in LXXX ('O! how I faint when I of you do write') serves to destroy this writer's reputation by its very hyperbole. A 'better spirit' makes the Poet tongue-tied—not by the quality of his verse,

1. *Astrophel and Stella*, 1.

we note, but by merely speaking of the Friend. The two writers
are next represented as ships sailing the ocean of the Friend's
worth; the Poet a 'saucy bark', the Rival a man-of-war 'of tall
building and of goodly pride'. Superficially the comparison is
to the Poet's detriment; but to the Elizabethan reader the
image immediately suggested the little English ships that
fought the Armada. Nashe compared himself with Gabriel
Harvey in a similar conceit; and Fuller, describing the wit-
combats of Shakespeare and Jonson, would again employ
the figure.[1] The proud Spanish galleon was a fit transposition
from the 'alien pen', as predatory as the hawk (and as liable,
it might be inferred, to be incapacitated). But there was yet a
lower level of meaning. In sonnet convention the ship represented the lover, with the beloved as the harbour to which it
sailed. Here the Friend was the ocean itself, with the Rival
'riding' on its 'soundless deep'. For all the apparent dignity of
the metaphor, it was basically the same as that applied to the
Mistress, 'the bay where all men ride'.[2] If she was physically
accessible to all, the Friend by his acceptance of flattery was
spiritually just as promiscuous. The innuendo is, of course,
private, perhaps not wholly conscious, and certainly not dis-
cernible to the Friend as a reader of the sonnet; but it points
to a new element in the Poet's irony which will become
gradually more apparent in other sonnets of this group.

The contrast of use and natural increase shades off in LXXXII
to the second antithesis of ornament and truth. This sonnet
opens with an apparently humorous concession to the Friend's
point of view: 'I grant thou wert not married to my Muse'.
The Poet's Muse, we remember, is sick: indeed she is not, at
any point in this group, a very robust figure to choose as a life-

1. Nashe wrote: 'As much to say as why may not my Muse bee as great
an Appollo or God of Poetrie as the proudest of them? but it comes as farre
short as . . . a Cocke-boat of a Carricke' (McKerrow, III, p. 104). The conceit is used, as in Shakespeare, for sarcastic effect. It was expanded by
Fuller as a description of Shakespeare himself: 'Many were the *wit-
combates* betwixt him and Ben Johnson, which two I behold like a *Spanish
great Gallion* and an English *man of War*; Master Johnson (like the former)
was built far higher in Learning; *Solid*, but *Slow* in his performances.
Shake-spear, with the *English-man of War*, lesser in *bulk*, but lighter in *sailing*,
could turn with all tides, tack about and take advantage of all winds, by
the quickness of his Wit and Invention.' (Worthies of England (1622),
Warwickshire.)
2. See pp. 177-9 *supra*.

companion. But the comment is also a reminder of the Friend's own plight. Who then is he to marry? He has rejected a union of kind that would perpetuate him in the flesh; his one hope of immortality lies in marriage to a 'Muse'. But if indeed he is resolved to stay fancy-free, then he extends his sterile dalliance from body to spirit. Like Richard II once **again**, he is in love only with novelty—

> Where doth the world thrust forth a vanity—
> So it be new there's no respect how vile—
> That is not quickly buzzed into his ears? (II. i. 24–6)

but he will find that 'rhetoric' is no substitute for being 'sympathized' in 'true plain words'. Finally rhetoric, as the meretricious opposite to true poetry, is identified with ornament, the painting that imitates beauty's cheek—

> And their gross painting might be better used
> Where cheeks need blood: in thee it is abus'd.

The conclusion is amplified in LXXXIII '(I never saw that you did painting need') and coupled with an attempted defence of the Poet's own silence:

> I found, or thought I found, you did exceed
> The barren tender of a poet's debt.

Painting and barren payment are now brought together as substitutes, in the false world of ornament, for the sympathetic insight and creative travail of true poetry. Hence the declaration:

> For I impair not beauty, being mute,
> When others would give life and bring a tomb.

The central symbol for ornament in *The Merchant of Venice*, the golden casket enclosing a skull, is latent in these lines. But this negative stance does not fully explain the Poet's own failure to engage in creative writing. It is better, no doubt, to say nothing than to offer the golden casket: but why does he refuse a more positive rôle? The answer is insinuated, seemingly by accident, in the quiet parenthesis of line 3: 'I found, *or thought I found* . . .'. Perhaps, after all, the Friend is intrinsically worth no more than the barren offerings he welcomes. If so, to be dumb must be the only response of a poet concerned with the truth.

It becomes increasingly evident that the Poet's fight is on two fronts: against his rivals on the one side; on the other, against the Friend's own spiritual fault that brought the rivalry into being. Any show of passion in either instance would expose the Poet to the charge of vulgar jealousy; hence the subtleties of ambiguous praise or mock-deference in referring to the rivals. But in addressing the Friend such irony is barred. The only means of expression is a series of indirect hints that the Friend's acceptance of insincere eulogies undermines the whole relationship and deprives the Poet of his very theme. This is the true meaning of the Poet's silence, as well as of the notable omission of any pledge to immortalize the Friend. Even in LXXXIV ('Who is it that says most?') where the phrasing and imagery look back unmistakably to the issues of the Marriage group, the promise is withheld. The supreme praise, 'that you alone are you', does not answer the warning of XIII:

> O that you were yourself; but love, you are
> No longer yours than you yourself here live.

And there is an ominous implication in the word 'immured' as applied to the Friend's person—

> In whose confine immured is the store
> Which should example where your equal grew.

If the Friend's store is walled up in his own body, the prediction of sonnet IV will come true:

> Thy unus'd beauty must be tomb'd with thee,
> Which, used, lives th'executor to be.

Finally, instead of the necessary pledge of immortalization, the sonnet ends with a carefully planted ambiguity:

> You to your beauteous blessings add a curse,
> Being fond on praise, which makes your praises worse.

This can mean that the praise given by rival poets only derogates from the Friend's true fame; but the comma after 'praise' carries the graver insinuation that it is the Friend's own 'fondness', or folly, that lessens his repute.

LXXXV opens with further humorous deprecation of the

Poet's own Muse. She is 'tongue-tied' and 'in manners holds her still', overawed by the whole troop of muses summoned by the Rival Poet. It is evident that besides the minor sycophants there is one rival with pretensions to learning, whose 'precious phrase' is adorned by history, astrology, mathematics, and the other arts. In comparison, the Poet of the sonnets is reduced to the position of an 'unlettered clerk' who can only add his 'Amen' to another's hymns. Yet despite his ignorance and his Muse's bashfulness, the Poet's thought deserves priority over the Rival's words, as far as unspoken love is superior to glib erudition. The sonnet ends with a contrast between the 'breath of words' and 'dumb thoughts' in which the bubble of the Rival's self-importance is lightly but effectively pricked—learning without true sympathy being reduced to a mere wordy breath.

The more extreme the afflatus given to the Rival, the lower he is made to fall. But with him too falls the Friend. There is a return in LXXXVI to the metaphor of the tall ship, which is combined with the tomb association of 'immured' in LXXXIV:

> Was it the proud full sail of his great verse
> Bound for the prize of all too precious you,
> That did my ripe thoughts in my brain inhearse,
> Making their tomb the womb wherein they grew?

The Friend is now the objective of the great galleon, not the ocean on which it sails; he is the precious silver of the new world in danger of being captured as prize. Not only is the Poet, his thoughts inhearsed in his brain, frustrated as a creative artist, but the Friend, with his store immured in his body, is correspondingly frustrated in his hope of increase. The expedition may be profitable for the Rival Poet; but the image reduces the Friend to the condition of barren metal, useless to itself, and merely passive to exploitation by another. Yet why has the Poet's verse been rendered still-born? He was not 'struck dead' by the Rival's 'spirit, by spirits taught to write'—a word-play linking spirit (which could mean personality) with the mention of all the muses as the Rival's aids. This play is presently reinforced by the ambiguity of 'his compeers by night', who may be the muses of inspiration, but who are more likely to be the Rival's own clique of versifiers. Finally these mysterious visitors are particularized in one figure—

> that affable familiar ghost
> Which nightly gulls him with intelligence.

A 'familiar' might be a spirit—or a boon companion. 'Intelligence' signified both secret information and mental proficiency. And the word 'gulls'—as the birds that in folklore incarnated the spirits of the dead, but also with the colloquial meaning of fraud—exploded the Rival's pretensions in one shattering monosyllable.[1] No flyting of a learned poet could be more destructive than to say that he was gulled with intelligence. Yet all this is only incidental to the sonnet's main argument. None of the Rival's humbug, the Poet continues, has caused his silence or given him any ground for fear:

> But when your countenance fill'd up his line,
> Then lack'd I matter; that enfeebled mine.

It is not merely that the Friend's beauty, his physical countenance, has gone to 'fill up' the line, to complete a dunce's metre or provide a stock simile. But the Friend's *moral* countenance, his commendation and patronage, have swelled the Rival's exsufflicate verse. And this being so, the very theme of the sonnets, the truth of the Friend, has evaporated. He is lost to the Poet who could have immortalized him; he belongs to the Bushys and the Greens in their world of ornament.

The process of disillusionment that began with the revelation of the Friend's sensual fault is brought to a conclusion in these sonnets. They do not sound the emotional depths touched in the previous group, and only criticize the Friend by implication or oblique reference. But the rupture of the relationship is all the more evident for being expressed on an intellectual plane. Previously the Poet had flattered and re-

---

1. It is interesting to compare Shakespeare's thought processes in this conceit with those described by a modern psychopathic patient, writing, as he declares, in a state of manic hyper-aesthesia. '. . . the gulls terrified me for two reasons: firstly because I thought of myself as a sort of super-gull who had been "gulled" into selling his soul; and secondly because I thought I was responsible for all the death and evil in the world and that the spirits of all the lost seamen since the world began were in those gulls calling for vengeance on me.' (John Custance, *Wisdom, Madness and Folly* (1951), pp. 33-4.)

proved; he had oscillated between the parts of pander and father-confessor; he had torn up his Elizabethan world picture in the course of excusing sensual faults by sense. Nothing remained of the great hierarchy of perfections which the Friend had summed up in human form; instead there was the universal levelling of corruption, the stained sun of heaven equated with the stained son of the world. All this ensued from imaginative speculation on a cosmic plane; now, in terms of practical man-to-man relationships and problems of literary composition, the friendship is accurately weighed—and found wanting. The irony directed at the rivals may be crushing in its easy mastery; but it does not restore the creative power that has been baulked by the Friend's desertion. In consequence a parting is inevitable, and a long pause may be taken to follow the end of this group.

Yet even these sonnets, like those that treated the Friend's sensual fault, contribute a certain positive element to the sequence. The encounter with the rivals has crystallized the distinction in poetry between ornament and truth, 'painted rhetoric' and true, plain words. Authentic poetry is seen as a creative function, operating from within through sympathy with its subject. The sham substitute is barren and commercial, exploiting the subject for the sake of fame and profit. Ultimately sympathy, not superimposed erudition, is the true mettle of the imagination, which begets children of the heart and brain. But for the present this necessary sympathy has been lost, and mere wishing will not restore it. Time must pass, until the Poet has himself undergone the same test as was applied to the Friend, and the process of self-knowledge has completed its course with the writer as well as his theme.

(e) *The Poet's Error*

The Poet's return after a long absence and his plea for re-conciliation with the Friend are the subject-matter of CIX–CXII and CXVII–CXX. These sonnets are highly dramatic in con-ception, developing their argument in the context of a tensely emotional situation, and the reader must approach them as he would a dramatic monologue, interpreting what is said by reference to the situation and state of mind of the speaker. Once more Shakespeare's plays afford closer parallels in the treatment of theme and character-relationships than may be found in the sonnet tradition.

The structural images of this group are also best understood by reference to the drama. In the later plays of his middle period, Shakespeare increasingly drew upon verified obser-vations rather than upon ideal concepts and *a priori* assump-tions. This was to result in the presentation of realistic char-acters in action, shaping their own ethos and analysing their own motives through technical images drawn from medicine and psychology, horticulture and handicraft, political science and geographical discovery. Certainly the new style came fully into its own in the second part of *Henry IV*, where political struggles are represented not so much as breaches of order and degree as symptoms of physical disease, the effects of surfeit and impurities of the blood:

Archbishop.—Briefly to this end: we are all diseas'd;
              And with our surfeiting and wanton hours
              Have brought ourselves into a burning fever,
              And we must bleed for it: of which disease
              Our late king, Richard, being infected, died . . .
              I take not on me here as a physician . . .
              But rather show a while like fearful war,
              To diet rank minds sick of happiness
              And purge the obstructions which begin to stop
              Our very veins of life. (IV. i. 54–66 *passim*)

The Archbishop is a rebel, and his proposal for wholesale blood-letting would make too drastic a purge. Milder treat-ment at the hand of a skilled physician is recommended by the loyal Warwick.

K. Henry. Then you perceive the body of our kingdom,

How foul it is; what rank diseases grow,
And with what danger, near the heart of it.
Warwick.   It is but as a body, yet, distemper'd,
Which to his former strength may be restor'd
With good advice and little medicine. (III. i. 38 ff.)

Warwick and the Archbishop, the loyalist and the rebel, are at
one in their diagnosis: they differ only in their conceptions of
a cure. The rank diseases endangering the heart of the kingdom are throughout the play embodied in Falstaff, and the
first action of Prince Hal on coming to the throne will be to
apply the 'little medicine' to his old companion, who is sent
away to leave gormandizing and reform himself before again
approaching the royal presence.

   The sonnets of this group present, through the medium of
personal experience, some interesting analogies to this situation, expressed through the same complex of images. If previously the Poet stood in much the same relationship to the
Friend as Gaunt to Richard II, here he acts Falstaff to the
regenerate Prince. He is as old, surfeited, and diseased as that
corruptor of youth. But he is far more penitent, and his end
will be correspondingly more happy.

   CIX ('O never say that I was false of heart') may be taken to
commence the group. The Poet, seeking a reconciliation, fer-
vently protests that his absence did not indicate any cooling
of affection. His 'home of love' is in the Friend's breast, where
his soul is fixed; he could no more depart from this than from
himself. The conventional exchange of hearts is joined to an
old popular conceit found also in *Romeo and Juliet* and *A Midsummer Night's Dream*, representing the beloved as the true
home of the lover.[1] This proverbial conceit will be further
adapted in the finale to the sequence; here, quite typically, it is
concretized in a realistic and physical image. The Poet has returned, as travellers must, and in keeping his pledge to come
home 'just to the time, not with the time exchanged', he claims
that he himself brings the water that will cleanse his stain.

---

   1. *Romeo and Juliet*, II. ii. 174–5: 'And I'll still stay, to have thee still
forget, Forgetting any other home but this'. *Midsummer Night's Dream*, III.
ii. 171–2: 'My heart with her but as guest-wise sojourned, And now to
Helen it is home returned.' The proverbial expression was: 'The lover is
not where he lives, but where he loves.' (See Tilley, *op. cit.*, L 565.)

But the figure of the returned traveller at once involves a contradiction:

> Never believe, though in my nature reign'd
> All frailties that besiege all kinds of blood,
> That it could so preposterously be stain'd
> To leave for nothing all thy sum of good.

The Poet's stain is thus not merely skin-deep, the blameless result of a long journey. All the frailties of mankind mingle in his bloodstream; a little water will not clear him of his deed. His acute awareness of this underlies the extreme panegyric of his address to the Friend:

> For nothing this wide universe I call,
> Save thou, my rose; in it thou art my all.

There is a difference between this and the eulogies of the early groups. The Friend is not the paragon of the universe but the exception to its sum-total of negations, invested with a supreme reality of his own. This complete polarity between Poet and Friend has nothing to do with the Friend's character, actual or literary, as it has appeared in the development of the sequence. Its purpose is to supply a dramatic contrast suggesting the Poet's extreme revulsion from the world with which he is contaminated. Just such a polarity of characters appears in the last scene of *Henry IV*, Part 2, where Falstaff, dishevelled and exhausted, arrives at the coronation of the new king:

Fal.   But to stand stained with travel, and sweating with desire to see him; thinking of nothing else; putting all affairs else into oblivion, as if there was nothing else to be done but to see him.

Pistol.   'Tis *semper idem*, for *absque hoc nihil est*:
'Tis all in every part. (v. v. 26 f.)

Falstaff too is not rejected because he is travel-stained, but for a more organic defilement. As for Henry V, the Conqueror King, Pistol's description of him in garbled philosophical tags —which continue the *nothing-all* antithesis of Falstaff's words —endows him with the same transcendent qualities as are given to the Friend.

The process of confessional atonement is continued in cx

('Alas! 'tis true I have gone here and there'). The Poet's absence has not been a mere physical separation; he has spiritually degraded himself, making himself 'a motley to the view'. Whatever was the precise connotation of motley to the Elizabethans, it was certainly associated in their minds with exhibitionism and buffoonery. The new-crowned king's reply to Falstaff contained almost the same accusation:

> How ill white hairs become a fool and jester![1]

Neither Falstaff nor the Poet were, of course, professional fools: their wildness was assumed for their own pleasure and expressed a craving to recover vanished youth. 'These blenches', declared the Poet, 'gave my heart another youth'; while Falstaff justified his conduct on the same grounds:

> . . . we that are in the vaward of our youth, I must confess, are wags too.[2]

What sharply distinguishes the two figures in their respective relationships is the Poet's abject repentance. He will no longer grind his appetite to try an older friend or seek new acquaintances to gain added relish from the Friend's company. There is no trace of such remorse in Falstaff's bearing, and one is led to ask whether the strange pathos of the rejection scene, running counter to the obvious thematic developments of the play, did not half-consciously reflect the intense emotions of the present sonnet group. However that be, such emotions certainly explain here the hyperbolical eulogy of the Friend, which parallels that of CIX:

> A god in love, to whom I am confin'd.
>> Then give me welcome, next my heaven the best,
>> Even to thy pure and most most loving breast.[3]

Judged by the normal standards applied to lyrical poetry, this is intolerably strained and clumsy. But as expressing the overwrought vehemence of the speaker in a tense dramatic situation it becomes intelligible and effective.

If the Poet's motley is only figurative, his profession of paid entertainer is actual enough; and its requirements are made

---

1. *2 Henry IV*, v. v. 53.   2. *Ibid.*, i. ii. 201–3.
3. Which may also be compared with Falstaff's 'My king! my Jove! I speak to thee, my heart' at the coronation of Henry V.

the excuse for his desertion in CXI ('O! for my sake do you with Fortune chide'). Public means breed public manners, and only fortune is to blame that the Poet must seek a living. The effects of contact with the vulgar are described in a technical simile: his nature is subdued to what it works in, like the dyer's hand. Therefore the stain he bears is an occupational mishap; it cannot be lightly washed away, but it also does not make him morally culpable. In terms of the new imagery the dyer's hand expresses the notion of contamination from social contact just as the metaphor of the canker-rose and the rank smell of weeds had done through the traditional correspondences. Here, as when the Friend was at fault, the plea for forgiveness is based on the principle of excusing sensual faults by sense. Should the Friend require it, the Poet will act the 'willing patient' and drink potions of eisel or vinegar to cure his infection. Acid may work where water fails; he will undergo any penance laid upon him, however sour it may taste. But pity is still the best of all cures:

> Pity me then, dear friend, and I assure ye
> Even that your pity is enough to cure me.

As with the state of England, so with personal friendship, the chief need is for 'good advice and little medicine'.

The recurrence of the word 'pity' in the first line of CXII ('Your love and pity doth the impression fill') was sufficient inducement for Thorpe to place this sonnet next in his arrangement. Marking as it does the resolution of the issues, it is certainly premature, for the crisis continues unabated through CXVII–CXIX. In the first of these three ('Accuse me thus') the Poet, speaking on the Friend's behalf, sets forth a complete list of charges. He has 'scanted all' that the Friend deserves of him; he has forgotten to invoke the Friend's love; he has 'frequent been with unknown minds', and has 'given to time' the Friend's right to his company. These charges parallel, in the Poet's circumstances, all the previous faults of the Friend. The neglect of the Poet by his patron is matched by the Poet's own recent neglect of the Friend. Whereas the Friend has exchanged his immortality for time in preferring 'alien pens', the Poet has served time in frequenting 'unknown minds'. He has, he now admits,

> hoisted sail to all the winds
> Which should transport me furthest from your sight.

The ship metaphor recalls that of LXXXVI: while the Rival's galley was bound for the prize of the all-too-precious Friend, the Poet has hoisted sail in any direction that would lead away from him. Objectively there is little to choose between the two wrongs. None of these charges is denied; the only defence now offered is that

> I did strive to prove
> The constancy and virtue of your love.

It is not very convincing and suggests a precarious relationship very unlike that of the early groups. But the amplification of the argument in CXVIII exposes even worse discrepancies:

> Like as, to make our appetites more keen,
> With eager compounds we our palate urge;
> As, to prevent our maladies unseen,
> We sicken to shun sickness when we purge;
> Even so, being full of your ne'er-cloying sweetness,
> To bitter sauces did I frame my feeding;
> And, sick of welfare, found a kind of meetness
> To be diseas'd, ere that there was true needing.

This is the same conceit as that of the Archbishop, who urged revolt in order to diet rank minds sick of happiness; and it has the same ring of absurdity. The Poet, in his own words, has needlessly rebelled against friendship; his absence has amounted to a drastic course of homœopathic treatment to anticipate a disease that did not occur. But if the period before his lapse was one of ne'er-cloying sweetness, and his absence a purge and a feeding on bitter sauces, why should he now require potions of vinegar, and why is his blood corrupted as if from surfeit? Actually, the Poet is not in the position of the Archbishop; his rebellion is of another order, more comparable with the truancy of Falstaff in Eastcheap. It appears that the Friend's company was not as sweet or as nourishing as it is declared to have been in retrospect. To need potions of eisel now, rather suggests that the Poet had been dining only too well after the thin gruel of the Friend's recent patronage.

But the poorer the Poet's logic, the more urgent is the force of emotion that he seeks to rationalize. In CXIX ('What potions have I drunk of siren tears') he continues his lament at the woes he has suffered in absence. Instead of bitter sauces, they now appear as tears 'distill'd from limbecks foul as hell within'. Some commentators find here a specific reference to the Mistress; but since that particular siren had deserted the Poet for the Friend, it is not clear how the Poet's own desertion returned him to her fatal influence. More likely Shakespeare had a verse from Lodge's *Rosalynde* running in his head:

> In choice of friends, beware of light belief;
> A painted tongue may shroud a subtle heart;
> The Sirens tears do threaten mickle grief.

There were two sirens known to the Elizabethans: one, the classical siren who lured men with her tears; the other, a fabulous medieval serpent whose tongue was deadly poisonous.[1] The association of tears and poison with the mention of drugs in cxviii may have suggested potions distilled from limbecks foul as hell: it is even possible that alchemists of the time (such as Dr Hall's father) had a recipe known as 'siren's tears'. However that may be, the image, at once medical and occult, suggests a drug-induced delirium as a fit description of the Poet's recent state of mind. The sonnet continues with a revealing volubility. The Poet confesses his 'wretched errors' and bemoans 'the distraction of this madding fever'. Significantly he admits that while it raged his heart had 'thought itself so blessed never'. It is evident that the period of truancy was pleasant, however illusory that pleasure may have been. The Poet had, in fact, succumbed to the same temptations of sensuality and flattery as the Friend. And in the latter part of the sonnet another serious admission is made:

O benefit of ill! now I find true

1. The siren of medieval lore was supposed to infest Arabia. It had wings and was extremely venomous. Cf. John of Trevisa: 'In Arabia beth serpentes with winges, that beth icleped Sirene . . . and here venym is so stronge that dethe cometh tofore the biting'. This poisonous serpent has probably been confused with the siren of classical mythology in L. Andrew's *Noble Lyfe* (c. 1520): 'Syrene, the mermayde, is a dedely beste that bringeth a man gladly to dethe'. Sirens' tongues go with crocodiles' tears in J. Dickenson's *Greene in Conceipt* (1598): 'They having sirens tongues and Crocodiles teares, thereby entic'd him to intangle him'. The idea of entangling may come from the old serpent association. (These examples are taken from the Oxford English Dictionary: 'Siren'.)

> That better is by evil still made better;
> And ruin'd love, when it is built anew,
> Grows fairer than at first, more strong, far greater.

Now we know that the 'home of love', located in the Friend's breast, and described so confidently as the Poet's permanent abode, was actually in ruins when he left it. Only through the 'benefit of ill', through a second opportunity of placing the friendship on firm foundations, will love's home be rebuilt, 'more strong, far greater'.

At last in sonnets cxx and cxii the desired reconciliation is brought about. The plea of cxx, 'That you were once unkind befriends me now', is quite different from the Poet's previous attempts to justify himself. It depends on no technical or scientific conceit, no request for sensual faults to be condoned by sense, with a mutual tolerance of moral anarchy. It is instead a simple and direct appeal for human kindness. The recollection of his own suffering at the Friend's hand makes the Poet better understand the wound he has himself inflicted:

> And for that sorrow which I then did feel,
> Needs must I under my transgression bow,
> Unless my nerves were brass or hammered steel.

By sympathetic imagination he experiences the 'hell of time' the Friend underwent in his absence; and his egotistic sorrow at the estrangement is lost in a selfless grief:

> O that our night of woe might have remember'd
> My deepest sense, how hard true sorrow hits,
> And soon to you, as you to me, then tender'd
> The humble salve which wounded bosoms fits!

It is the Friend, not he, who is in need of this salve—ineffably better than all potions and purges—the shedding of heartfelt tears. For he has remembered from a former occasion the tears of the Friend that ransomed all ill deeds. At that time the Poet's reaction had been merely emotional; rationally, he was left with the dilemma of a choice between the relativity of sense and the moral absolutes of a spiritual creed. Now the dilemma is at last overcome as his imagination penetrates to a deeper truth than logic affords. He perceives that the mutual love subsisting between two equally erring, equally culpable

human beings is able to surmount all the antinomies of existence. This love is not Eros but Agape, which *suffereth long and is
kind, . . . envieth not, vaunteth not itself, is not puffed up . . . beareth
all things, believeth all things, hopeth all things, endureth all things*.[1]
Yet the Poet has come to it on purely human grounds,
without any prior inference of Christian salvation, of divine
pardon, or of an after-life of the spirit.

In terms of this human love a reconciliation is effected, not
only of the individual Poet and individual Friend, but on a
universal scale, as between the creative artist and his world.
It is celebrated in CXII, 'Your love and pity doth the impression fill'. The brand on the Poet's brow, the mark of Cain
affixed by scandal, is wiped out, for society and its judgements
have lost all their meaning. His good is allowed for; his bad
'o'ergreened'; restored, like a tract of land after sowing, to
fertile nature:

> You are my all-the-world, and I must strive
> To know my shames and praises from your tongue;
> None else to me, nor I to none alive,
> That my steel'd sense or changes right or wrong.

Poet and Friend together comprise a world independent of
men's laws, ignoring critic and flatterer alike. The Poet will
follow his 'adder's sense'—

> like the deaf adder that stoppeth her ear; Which will not hearken
> to the voice of charmers, charming never so wisely.[2]

Finally he utters his contempt for 'all the world', in comparison with the all-the-world who is his friend.

> You are so strongly in my purpose bred
> That all the world besides methinks yare[3] dead.

Once again, as at the beginning of the sequence, the Poet

1. 1 Corinthians, xiii. 4–7.
2. Psalms, lviii. 4–5. The 'adder' of the Bible represents the wicked, and
would not normally be taken by the Poet to represent himself. But the
'voice of charmers' arouses his antipathy far more, so that he instinctively
identifies himself with the adder.
3. I offer this emendation of the Quarto 'y'are' in the much-disputed
last line of CXII. *Yare* for 'quickly' or 'readily' is good English and good
Shakespeare. The confusion between the crest of '*a*' and an upstroke
apostrophe is easily made in secretary hand: the identical error occurs in
Measure for Measure, IV. ii. 61 (Folio: 'You shall finde me y'are').

is able without reservations to celebrate the Friend as the repository of universal good: not because his beauty or truth are immutable, but because love triumphs over mutability. The evolution of the sonnet relationship is complete. Both Friend and Poet have evinced all frailties that besiege all kinds of blood; both have succumbed to sensuality and vain applause; to faults of the body and the soul, of man and universal nature. And their friendship has survived, through sympathy and mutual forgiveness.

Fortified by this realization, the Poet now rises to the height of his theme, and fulfils his original pledge that he will immortalize the Friend.

(f) *The Immortalization*

The last group of sonnets, from their grave and stately exordium to their triumphant close, are in every sense the culmination of Shakespeare's writing in this medium. Indeed there are no English sonnets to compare with them in imaginative range and intellectual power. Only their extreme disorder in the Quarto arrangement, wedged in irrelevantly between portions of the group on the Poet's Error, or embedded in the middle of the series where their thematic importance is lost, has barred them from more than token recognition down the centuries.

Explored on multiple levels, the underlying theme of these sonnets is the conflict of Love with Time. It is an epic engagement, giving effect to the challenge offered at the end of the Marriage group. Once again Ovidian concepts predominate, in conscious imitation as well as in the unconscious trend of the imagery. Parallel with the re-statement of these concepts, there is a detailed correlation of structural ideas and images which have grown up out of the sequence itself and which here receive their final formulation. The two processes work in close conjunction until they are at last transcended in a new integral vision. I include in this group sonnets c–cviii, cxv–cxvi, and cxxiii–cxxv, together with lv, lix–lx, and lxii–lxv. Here as elsewhere the aim is to trace a continuity of poetic thought, irrespective of the arrangement of individual sonnets in standard editions based on the 1609 Quarto.

An autumn mood pervades the sonnets of this group, as of fulfilment trembling on the verge of decline. Three years, it is said, have passed since the friendship began, and the third high summer has come and gone. The Friend appears still in his pristine beauty, like the sun of noonday in vii, 'resembling strong youth in his middle age'; but the process of decay may already have begun. Hence it is important that the Poet should delay no longer in rescuing him from Time. The group is best appreciated if it is taken to commence with the triple invocation of the Poet's Muse in c, followed by a further invocation of the Muse in ci. This note of epic decorum is rare in Shakespeare: perhaps its closest analogy will be found in the opening lines of the prologue to *Henry V*:

> O for a Muse of fire, that would ascend
> The brightest heaven of invention!

Both the play and the present group of sonnets are culmina-
tions of a long development; both are concerned with pulling
out every stop of Shakespeare's instrument in preparation for
a resounding triumph. The difference is that in the sonnets the
hero is a living individual, not a historical figure; and the
enemy is not a political foe, but Time himself, the archetypal
and universal conqueror.

For long, declares the Poet in c ('Where art thou, Muse'),
the Muse has neglected her primary duty and darkened her
power 'to lend base subjects light'. Now she must again celebrate the Friend; and her first task will be to make a survey of
the beauty menaced by Time:

> Rise, resty Muse, my love's sweet face survey,
> If Time have any wrinkle graven there;
> If any, be a satire to decay,
> And make Time's spoils despised everywhere.

Moreover, the transitory nature of beauty cannot be separated
from truth: both in fact survive only through the immortality
that verse bestows. This is stressed in ci:

> O truant Muse, what shall be thy amends
> For thy neglect of truth in beauty dyed?
> Both truth and beauty on my love depends,
> So dost thou too, and therein dignified.

Truth is the essential fabric of personality, tinged and made
visible by beauty. Such is the final definition replacing those
of earlier groups, where truth had been regarded as an ornament or an insubstantial perfume. And a third category, that
of love, has now been introduced, behind which extends a long
reach of experience. Even the inspiration of verse derives its
power and dignity from love, now revealed as the *primum mobile*
of poetic creation. Hence the authority with which the Poet
commands the Muse to perform her duty:

> Then do thy office, Muse: I teach thee how
> To make him seem long hence as he shows now.

The instruction that the Poet's love provides will not be an
academic training in versecraft, but a strategic planning of the

campaign to be fought against Time. For the emergency requires an unflinching survey of the enemy in all his might, proceeding outward from the threatened position of the Friend and taking into its scope the entire phenomenal world. This will involve a return to the major themes of previous groups, combined with a systematic review of the cosmic battlefield mapped out by Ovid in the last book of his *Metamorphoses*. The relevant passages of the speech attributed to Pythagoras, which furnish material for sonnet after sonnet, must be quoted in full.

> *Et quoniam magno feror aequore plenaque ventis*
> *vela dedi: nihil est toto, quod perstet, in orbe.*
> *Cuncta fluunt, omnisque vagans formatur imago;*
> *ipsa quoque absiduo labuntur tempora motu,*
> *non secus ac flumen; neque enim consistere flumen,*
> *nec levis hora potest: sed ut unda inpellitur unda*
> *urgueturque eadem veniens urguetque priorem,*
> *tempora sic fugiunt pariter pariterque sequuntur*
> *et nova sunt semper; nam quod fuit ante, relictum est*
> *fitque, quod haud fuerat, momentaque cuncta novantur.*
>
> (*Metamorphoses*, xv. 176–85)[1]

> *editus in lucem iacuit sine viribus infans:*
> *mox quadrupes rituque tulit sua membra ferarum,*
> *paulatimque tremens et nondum poplite firmo*
> *constitit adiutis aliquo conamine nervis.*
> *Inde valens veloxque fuit spatiumque iuventae*
> *transit et emeritis medii quoque temporis annis*
> *labitur occiduae per iter declive senectae.*
> *Subruit haec aevi demoliturque prioris*
> *robora: fletque Milon senior cum spectat inanes*
> *illos, qui fuerant solidorum mole tororum*
> *Herculeis similes, fluidos pendere lacertos;*
> *flet quoque ut in speculo rugas adspexit aniles*
> *Tyndaris, et secum, Cur sit bis rapta, requirit.*

1. 'Since I have set sail upon a wide ocean, and spread my canvas to the wind, let me continue further. Nothing is constant in the world. Everything is in a state of flux, and comes into being as a transient appearance. Time itself flows on with constant motion, just like a river: for no more than a river can the fleeting hour stand still. As wave is driven on by wave, and, itself pursued, pursues the one before, so the moments of time at once flee and follow, and are ever new. What was before is left behind, that which was not comes to be, and every minute gives place to another.'

Tempus edax rerum, tuque invidiosa vetustas,
omnia destruitis vitiataque dentibus aevi
paulatim lenta consumitis omnia morte! (221–36)[1]

Nec species sua cuique manet, rerumque novatrix
ex aliis alias reparat natura figuras :
nec perit in toto quicquam, mihi credite, mundo,
sed variat, faciemque novat, nascique vocatur
incipere esse aliud, quam quod fuit ante, morique
desinere illud idem. Cum sint huc forsitan illa,
haec translata illuc, summa tamen omnia constant.
Nil equidem durare diu sub imagine eadem
crediderim: sic ad ferrum venistis ab auro,
saecula, sic totiens versa est fortuna locorum.
Vidi ego quod fuerat quondam solidissima tellus
esse fretum, vidi factas ex aequore terras,
et procul a pelago conchae iacuere marinae,
et vetus inventa est in montibus ancora summis ;
quodque fuit campus, vallem decursus aquarum
fecit, et eluvie mons est deductus in aequor . . . (252–67)[2]

1. 'The baby, first born into the light of day, lies weak and helpless: after that he crawls on all fours, moving his limbs as animals do, and gradually, on legs as yet trembling and unsteady, stands upright, supporting himself by some convenient prop. Then he becomes strong and swift of foot, passing through the stage of youth till, having lived through the years of middle age also, he slips down the incline of old age, towards life's setting. Age undermines and destroys the strength of former years. Milon, grown old, weeps to see those arms hanging limp and thin, whose massive knotted muscles once rivalled those of Hercules. Helen weeps too, when she sees herself in the glass, wrinkled with age, and asks herself why she was twice carried off. Time, the devourer, and the jealous years that pass, destroy all things and, nibbling them away, consume them gradually in a lingering death.'

2. 'Nor does anything retain its own appearance permanently. Ever-inventive nature continually produces one shape from another. Nothing in the entire universe ever perishes, believe me, but things vary, and adopt a new form. The phrase "being born" is used for beginning to be something different from what one was before, while "dying" means ceasing to be the same. Though this thing may pass into that, and that into this, yet the sum of things remains unchanged. For my part, considering how the generations of men have passed from the age of gold to that of iron, how often the fortunes of different places have been reversed, I should believe that nothing lasts long under the same form. I have seen what once was solid earth now changed into sea, and lands created out of what once was ocean. Sea-shells lie far away from ocean's waves, and ancient anchors have been found on mountain tops. What was at one time a level plain has become a valley, thanks to the waters flowing down over it, mountains have been washed away by floods, and levelled into plains.'   (Translations by Mary M. Innes, *Penguin Classics*.)

As a preliminary, and perhaps by way of deflecting the first harsh impact of reality, the Poet in LXII ('Sin of self-love') alludes to his own appearance 'beaten and chopp'd with tann'd antiquity', in contrast to the Friend's still unsullied beauty. But this is followed in LXIII by a frank anticipation of Time's coming attack:

> Against my love shall be, as I am now,
> With Time's injurious hand crush'd and o'erworn;
> When hours have drain'd his blood and fill'd his brow
> With lines and wrinkles; when his youthful morn
> Hath travell'd on to age's steepy night;
> And all those beauties whereof now he's king
> Are vanishing or vanish'd out of sight,
> Stealing away the treasure of his spring . . .

Here the images of the Marriage group are recapitulated: the sun–king correspondence; the hoarded treasure of youth; and in the latter part of the sonnet, by implication, the flower of summer that 'age's cruel knife' threatens to cut from memory. Closely associated with this imagery are borrowings from lines 221–7 of the passage from Ovid, with their description of the course of human life; 'youthful morn' being suggested by the sun metaphor *editus in lucem*, and 'age's steepy night' by the corresponding image of sunset that ends the passage: *labitur occiduae per iter declive senectae*. The sonnet comes to rest on a promise that in the Poet's 'black lines' the Friend's beauty will be preserved 'still green'.

Another theme from the speech of Pythagoras is taken up in LXIV and in LXV, and interwoven with the structural images of the sequence. The opening phrases of each quatrain in LXIV— 'When I have seen by Time's fell hand defac'd . . . When I have seen the hungry ocean gain . . . When I have seen such interchange of state'—echo Ovid's

> *Vidi ego quod fuerat quondam solidissima tellus*
> *esse fretum, vidi factas ex aequore terras*

But the 'lofty towers down-raz'd' belong to Shakespeare's own order of imagination, together with the image of buried treasure, 'the rich-proud cost of outworn buried age', that had first served to illustrate the doctrine of increase. The contest of shore and 'watery main' is suggested by Ovid's lines; while the

political correspondence in the 'kingdom' of the shore and the
economic analogy in 'loss' and 'store' again grow out of the
sequence itself.

   This interweaving of themes is most concisely achieved by
the double use of the word 'state', first in its classical, abstract
sense of circumstance, then in its modern political connotation:

> When I have seen such interchange of state,
> Or state itself confounded to decay . . .

Time is thus invincible in its work of destruction and its perpetual dissolution of existing order, whether this appear in
manifestations of human power and wealth, in the structure of
states, or even in the seeming permanence of land and sea. All
these observations lead to one conclusion, stated in terrible,
quiet-stepping monosyllables:

> That Time will come and take my love away.

   The thought is 'as a death': yet its implications are relent-
lessly scrutinized in LXV. 'Since brass, nor stone, nor earth,
nor boundless sea' can withstand mortality, how can beauty,
whose action is no stronger than a flower, defend itself? What
resistance can 'summer's honey breath' put up against the
'wrackful siege of battering days'? The siege metaphor and
the term 'action', which has both military and legal uses, lead
back to the analogous images in the Marriage group—

> When forty winters shall besiege thy brow (II)

> And summer's lease hath all too short a date . . . (XVIII)

Both images are more closely tied than ever to the flower symbol which as always represents the Friend; while in the sestet
two even more striking images shift attention back to the Poet.
This 'fearful meditation' recalls an earlier anxiety lest the
Friend be stolen by 'some vulgar thief'—the rivals he once had
feared:

> Thee have I not lock'd up in any chest,
> Save where thou art not, though I feel thou art,
> Within the gentle closure of my breast, . . . (XLVIII)

Now instead of mundane robbers, he must fear the hand of
Time itself:

K

> Where, alack,
> Shall Time's best jewel from Time's chest lie hid?
> Or what strong hand can hold his swift foot back?
> Or who his spoil of beauty can forbid?

And the answer to so many questions is inspired likewise by a memory from the past of that sudden nocturnal vision, 'like a jewel hung in ghastly night' (XXVII), which had long ago revealed to him the force of the creative imagination directed by love:

> O none, unless this miracle have might,
> That in black ink my love may still shine bright.

The vision of the Friend as a light shining in darkness is thus perpetuated in the time-defying miracle of Love shining eternally in the black ink of poetry.

Sonnet LX ('Like as the waves') achieves its own poetic miracle by taking an entire chain of images from the speech of Ovid's Pythagoras and fusing them at white heat with the themes of the sonnet sequence. It commences by repeating the description of the waves in lines 181–5 of the Latin.

> Like as the waves make towards the pebbled shore,
> So do our minutes hasten to their end;
> Each changing place with that which goes before,
> In sequent toil all forwards do contend.

Whether Ovid's original, or Golding's rather wooden translation,[1] or some other Elizabethan version was the direct model for this sonnet, it is plain that Shakespeare's own subtle touches have infused new life into the somewhat hackneyed image. Against the background of the 'pebbled shore' the waves become actual and visible, instead of an abstract figure designating motion. As they 'make towards' the land, they cease to be automatically impelled, and now acquire an independent volition; even the minutes 'hasten'; while all 'con-

1. The chyld newborne lyes voyd of strength. Within a season tho
   He wexing fowerfooted lernes like savage beastes too go.
   Then sumwhat foltring, and as yet not firme of foote, he standes
   By getting sumwhat for too helpe his sinewes in his handes.
   From that time growing strong and swift, he passeth foorth the space
   Of youth, and also wearing out his middle age a pace,
   Through drooping ages steepye path he ronneth out his race.
   (1594 edition, p. 299)

tend' energetically in 'sequent toil'. Characteristically Shakespeare viewed the whole universe in terms of human motivation. For this reason the figure of man's growth in lines 221–7
of Ovid was capable of extension on every level of correspondence. The submerged Latin metaphors of sunrise and sunset
had been employed in LXIII in conjunction with the Shakespearean king image. Now, in the second quatrain of LX, the
Ovidian figure *editus in lucem* combined with the English phrase
'the watery main' from LXIV to produce a dynamic new metaphor, 'the main of light'. In the added dimension of space that
this opened out, the sun and king metaphors of LXIII were projected, with their familiar contraries, and associated with
Ovid's figure of the growing child.[1]

> Nativity, once in the main of light,
> Crawls to maturity, wherewith being crown'd,
> Crooked eclipses 'gainst his glory fight,
> And Time that gave doth now his gift confound.

The primary elements of imagery in this amazing verse are so
completely fused in their essence and proper evolutions that it
is impossible to consider any one in isolation from the rest. One
might risk a scientific analogy and say that all three images, of
child, sun, and king, are drawn from their customary orbits to
inhabit a single space-time continuum. Nativity, a sun rising
over the horizon, crawls as an infant up the path of the sky; at
its noontide zenith of maturity it is crowned king; whereupon
the eclipses that stain both moon and sun, 'crooked' by transferred epithet from the shape they impose, also personified
with the infanticidal malice of a Richard Crookback, fight
like usurpers against a glory denoting at once the sun's light
and the king's majesty. Instead of Ovid's description, limited
to an illustration of human life with only incidental comparisons to the sun's course, a compound, universal metaphor has
been created. And instead of the Latin narration of the process
of human growth and decline, here is a drama of cosmic mutability, with catastrophe ironically placed at the zenith of for-

1. The association had been loosely made in VII of the Marriage group—
'Resembling strong youth in his middle age'; 'Like feeble age, he reeleth
from the day'. The development from these similes, obviously influenced
by Golding, to the original telescoped metaphors of LXIII, expresses in
terms of imagery the cumulative tension of the sequence.

254 THE ELIZABETHAN LOVE SONNET

tune: an epitome in three lines of all Shakespearean tragedies,
with the fourth line of the quatrain supplying an epilogue to the
effect that for all phenomena—for all 'sense' as the Poet termed
it—success is a fraud of Time, who presents gifts only to destroy
them.

In the last quatrain Time himself dominates the scene:

> Time doth transfix the flourish set on youth
> And delves the parallels in beauty's brow,
> Feeds on the rarities of nature's truth,
> And nothing stands but for his scythe to mow:

The conceit is taken from lines 228–36 in *Metamorphoses* xv.
Tempus edax, who slowly consumes all things with his teeth, is
the greedy farmer who digs his spade into the flower of youth.
Ovid's description of Milon, the famous athlete, weeping at
his useless limbs that once overcame wild beasts, has probably
suggested the mention here of 'youth', and the juxtaposed
reference to Helen gazing at her wrinkles as she realizes
that Time as well as Paris has seduced her, would prompt the
next phrase, 'beauty's brow'. But here again the Ovidian
images are absorbed into the more complex sonnet structure.
The word 'flourish' for flower brings together mankind and
organic nature as common victims of Time: a more flexible
rendering of the figure in sonnet II of forty winters digging
trenches in beauty's field. Similarly the noun 'rarities', the
verb 'stands', and the 'parallels' that replace the too-definite
word 'trenches', all apply with equal force to both humanity
and nature. With this, the term 'nature's truth' once again
makes it evident that truth belongs to the same world of sense.
Like all else, it too will be chewed by the teeth of Time, distinguished only in that it will be considered a rare tit-bit. The
couplet meets this universal menace with the simple assertion
that the Poet's verse will nevertheless 'stand', after all standing
things have been mowed down:

> And yet to times in hope my verse shall stand,
> Praising thy worth, despite his cruel hand.

In itself the statement may seem an ineffectual anticlimax, as
do many of Shakespeare's couplets when the sonnets they belong to are isolated from their setting. But joined with the anti-

cipation of a 'miracle' in LXV, and with developments about to appear, it is the prelude of a crushing rejoinder to all Time's threats.

For now, when cognizance has been taken of the worst the enemy can do, the counter-attack is about to be launched. The weakness of Time has been detected at one fatal spot: his perpetual quality of flux; his blind unchanging strategy of change. All Time's wonders repeat themselves: *ipsa quoque absiduo labuntur tempora motu . . . et nova sunt semper . . . summa tamen omnia constant.* Thus neither past nor future need dismay the truly creative poet whose love has its constancy above and beyond this flux. In CXXIII the claim that the Poet's verse will stand is reinforced by the beginning of that 'satire to decay' that had been resolved upon in the first sonnets of the group:

> No, Time, thou shalt not boast that I do change:
> Thy pyramids built up with newer might
> To me are nothing novel, nothing strange;
> They are but dressings of a former sight.

Much ink has been spilled in conjectures about this reference to 'pyramids', a word of flexible meaning in Elizabethan English. If the sonnet is properly read, it will be obvious that the pyramids are Time's, and not the work of man: therefore neither the monuments of ancient Egypt nor the Roman remains excavated by Pope Sixtus V have any direct relevance here. The true source of Shakespeare's image lies in that same passage from the *Metamorphoses* which inspired all the sonnets of this group. In lines 252–67 Pythagoras expounds the concept of eternal substance. *Nec perit in toto quicquam, mihi credite, mundo, sed variat, faciemque novat . . .* 'Nothing in the whole world ever perishes, believe me, but things vary, and adopt a new form.' And he proceeds to illustrate his point:

> *Vidi ego, quod fuerat quondam solidissima tellus*
> *esse fretum, vidi factas ex aequore terras,*
> *et procul a pelago conchae iacuere marinae,*
> *et vetus inventa est in montibus anchora summis.*

The too, too solid earth dissolves, and again land is formed from the sea. Far away from the shore lie sea-shells, and old anchors have been found on mountain-tops. These peaks, once submerged, are the veritable pyramids of Time, built up

by Time with newer might; and to point the association between mountain tops and pyramids, the commentary of
Regius found in all good sixteenth-century editions of Ovid
glossed these lines: *tota ægyptus olim mare fuisse narratur.*[1] In
reality, nothing is so deceptive as Time's own works. Men in
their credulity gape at 'new-born' marvels—

> *nascique vocatur*
> *incipere esse aliud, quam quod fuit ante . . .* (255–6)

—or as this sonnet rendered it:

> Our dates are brief, and therefore we admire
> What thou dost foist upon us, that is old;
> And rather make them born to our desire
> Than think that we before have heard them told.

In this way men accept as new the old goods that Time the
mountebank foists upon them. Accordingly the Poet converts
a familiar lament, at the mutability of historical records, into
a further exposure of Time's frauds. *The Rape of Lucrece* had
shown a naïve respect for the old enemy: Time's glory,
Lucrece declared, was 'To blot old books and alter their contents'.[2] But Time's own most impressive records in the Book of
Nature, the mountains and seas Time had written there, were
alterations and deletions; as was proved by the evidence of
sea-shells far from any beach, and anchors on mountain-tops.
All Time's claims were impostures:

> Thy registers and thee I both defy,
> Not wondering at the present nor the past,
> For thy records and what we see doth lie,
> Made more or less by thy continual haste.

Only the Poet remained true, despite the scythe of Time and
the lie in Time's heart.

The train of thought, and Ovidian influence, proceeds without a break in LIX and CVI—two sonnets which are closely
linked in argument. LIX ('If there be nothing new') returns to
the passage in the *Metamorphoses* stating the doctrine of eternal

1. 'It is said that the whole of Egypt once was sea'. If anything more
was needed to set Shakespeare's thoughts on the pyramids, it would be
provided by another gloss of Regius, quoting from Horace in the margin
of the last page of the *Metamorphoses*. See p. 269.
2. *The Rape of Lucrece*, 948.

substance. If men are deceived when they suppose that what
has previously existed is newly 'born', then contemporary
poets 'labouring for invention' merely 'bear amiss The second
burden of a former child'. Accordingly the Poet wishes he
could look back five hundred years into the past and see the
Friend's image in 'some antique book'. The idea is suggested
by the satire on Time's records in CXXIII, carrying with it the
stock Elizabethan figure of the book of nature or fate—

> O God! that one might read the book of fate,
> And see the revolution of the times
> Make mountains level, and the continent—
> Weary of solid firmness—melt itself
> Into the sea! (*2 Henry IV*, III. i. 45 f.)

King Henry IV evidently had in mind the same lines from
Ovid as prompted the present sonnet, 'the revolution of the
times' being perhaps inspired by *rerum novatrix natura*.[1] But the
Poet's concern now is with real, or at least hypothetically real
books and with his own problems as a writer. The estimate of
time is remarkably apt: five hundred years would return him
to the age of the first romances of courtly love. Whether this
was more than a happy guess we cannot tell, but in its context
the description of the period as 'since mind at first in character
was done' can hardly mean (as Knox Pooler believed) 'since
thought was first expressed in writing'.[2] It was obvious that
literature dated back much further than five centuries. The
phrase would have point as a description of the figures of medieval romance, and might be rendered, 'since moral qualities were first represented by outward appearance'.[3] Would an
image of ideal beauty in some lost book be better or worse than
a contemporary portrait of the Friend—'this composed wonder of your frame'? Has there been progress or decline in art?
Nothing, said Ovid, continued for long in the same image—

> *Nil equidem durare diu sub imagine eadem*
> *crediderim . . .* (259)

1. *Res novae* often signified 'revolution'.   2. *Sonnets*, p. 61.
3. Cf. *Twelfth Night*, I. ii. 48–9, where Viola says to the Captain: 'I will
believe thou hast a mind that suits With this thy fair and outward character'. The Oxford Dictionary offers as Definition 10 for *Character*: 'The face
or features as betokening moral qualities'.

But if nature indeed prompted *res novae*, the usual English word for this, 'revolution', might signify not innovation, but only a rotatory motion like the spokes of a wheel. And this might be the answer to the question of progress or decline:

> Whe'r we are mended, or whe'r better they,
> *Or whether revolution be the same.*[1]

The sonnet has strayed away from its first metaphysical conjecture at the pre-existence of the Friend, whose image might be thought to appear in the lost antique book; and the last lines confirm the change of trend:

> O sure I am the wits of former days
> To subjects worse have given admiring praise.

This new approach is closely followed up in CVI, 'When in the chronicle of wasted time', alluding to 'ladies dead and lovely knights' in romances actually read by the Poet. The old writers sought to express such beauty as belongs to the Friend, but failed for lack of a model:

> So all their praises are but prophecies
> Of this our time, all you prefiguring,
> And, for they look'd but with divining eyes,
> They had not skill enough your worth to sing:

whereas contemporary poets have eyes to see this beauty but lack the power to praise it. The difference between the doctrine of pre-existence and this conceit of 'prefiguring' is important, for by implication it distinguishes the Friend's personality from all the works of Time. Although Shakespeare has in these sonnets drawn upon Ovid's Neopythagoreanism—just as in other groups he has borrowed the terms of Renaissance Neoplatonism—his own thought proceeds independently of these influences. The Friend has not lived before, neither will he be reborn. Admittedly he is mortal, but his personality is at least immune to the senseless reiterations of Time, and stands at the unmoved centre of its revolving wheel. Therefore the old writers of romances did not, as was believed, express ideal beauty: they imperfectly foretold the present unique reality.

What then of the Poet, whose verse, as he confesses, is not superior to the writings of the past, and might be thought

1. My emphases.

redundant? This poses much the same question as had been considered in terms of social relationships in the Rival Poets group; and cvIII, 'What's in the brain, that ink may characcter', offers, in a new context, a similar reply. The Poet makes no claim to originality. His verse is distinguished only by the love that calls it forth. Each day he says over the same words; his praises follow an unchanging ritual. Like 'prayers divine', they 'hallow' the Friend's name and give expression to 'eternal love'. Here again, as often in Shakespeare's mature work, the language of religious experience is transposed and secularized to express an essentially human relationship.

> So that eternal love in love's fresh case
> Weighs not the dust and injury of age,
> Nor gives to necessary wrinkles place,
> But makes antiquity for aye his page;
>   Finding the first conceit of love there bred,
>   Where time and outward form would show it dead.

'Love's fresh case', the daily-revived ritual of praise, continues the eulogies of the first romance authors in the chronicles of wasted time. Age may have caused such works to gather dust and suffer injury, but the Poet's love, making them his own page, keeps them alive for ever. For in these antique books the first conceit of love was bred, and might have wasted away together with them but for its constant resuscitation by the Poet.

Sonnet cv ('Let not my love be called idolatry') proceeds to interpret the meaning of this prayer ritual to which the Poet's verse is devoted. Superficially it resembles the facile panegyrics of the minor sonneteers to their 'saints' and 'goddesses': in reality it is of quite another order. Not for a moment is it forgotten that both Poet and Friend are mortals, subject to the dust and injury of age, bearing or liable to bear 'necessary' wrinkles. In the last resort only the strength of human love prevails against Time. Because the Friend's kindness is unchanging, the Poet's verse forms an unalterable liturgy:

> Kind is my love to-day, to-morrow kind,
> Still constant in a wondrous excellence;
> Therefore my verse, to constancy confin'd,
> One thing expressing, leaves out difference.

K*

Thus the immortalization, intended first for beauty, then for truth, is directed at last to kindness, which subsumes the Friend's other attributes and establishes a new, secular trinity of the human spirit—'Fair, kind and true, three themes in one'. These are no mere conventional epithets; they have grown up, sonnet by sonnet, image by image, through the vicissitudes of experience, in consequence of the Poet's obstinate resolution to love on in the face of every moral and rational cause to deter him.

The sonnets taken as a conclusion to the Immortality group celebrate the universal triumph of human love. In the course of this, the great antinomies of life expressed in the structural metaphors of the sequence are resolved, and new symbols of integration replace the former pattern of images. The process is begun in CXV, 'Those lines that I before have writ do lie'. Previously, the Poet declares, he had written that his love could not be surpassed. But this was an untruth prompted by emotional immaturity. The full flame has not changed in essence, but it now burns clearer, since the Poet's early eulogies of the Friend were written before experience had taught him love's true strength.[1] Fearing then 'Time's tyranny', he had sought to 'crown' the present love in haste, lest the accidents of circumstance should later dethrone it: for such 'millioned accidents', creeping in between vows and fulfilment, changing 'decrees of kings', diverting strong minds 'to the course of altering things', had once seemed unavoidable. In these phrases may be descried, with faint outlines as if recalled from a distant past, the tragic procession of images in sonnet LX: nativity crawling to maturity, the newly-crowned king assailed by usurpers, the sun eclipsed at noonday. Now, all such menaces are dissolved into unfounded suppositions. The reasons for the change are not given in the sonnet itself, but the new image in the couplet prepares the way for a coming elaboration:

Love is a babe; then might I not say so,

1. The problem was also considered by Donne in 'I scarce believe my love to be so pure'. But Donne's conceits of circles in a pond or war-taxes retained in peace time, with their analogies from science and politics, could have no relevance to the love of Shakespeare's Poet, which now stands outside the world of phenomena.

To give full growth to that which still doth grow?

Unlike Ovid's infant, or the Poet's personified 'nativity', this babe of Love is no symbol of mortality, but a miraculous creation existing in his own right. CXXIV presents Love's full significance in fourteen lines of telescoped imagery that amount to a categorical denial of all Time's claims:

> If my dear love were but the child of state,
> It might for Fortune's bastard be unfather'd,
> As subject to Time's love or to Time's hate,
> Weeds among weeds or flowers with flowers gather'd.
> No, it was builded far from accident;
> It suffers not in smiling pomp, nor falls
> Under the blow of thralled discontent,
> Whereto the inviting time our fashion calls:
> It fears not policy, that heretic,
> Which works on leases of short number'd hours,
> But all alone stands hugely politic,
> That it nor grows with heat, nor drowns with showers.
>   To this I witness call the fools of time,
>   Which die for goodness, who have liv'd for crime.

The word 'state', as circumstance, provides a generalization for all the images of the sonnet, while as a political term it furnishes the central conceit. Here, as in LX, image fuses with image, resulting in a great compound figure that spans wide reaches of experience. The child Love is not born of 'state', and therefore cannot be disinherited by Fortune: it is not, that is to say, a product of circumstance, and chance cannot cancel its rights. Both State and Fortune are made synonymous with Time in line 3; and the child, on the corresponding plane of nature, becomes a plant immune to Time, which gathers without discrimination both flowers and weeds. In this first quatrain, as throughout the sonnet, the images that signify mutability in the phenomenal world suggest a mystic permanence when associated with Love. The Friend had been shown, in the group on the Friend's fault, as sharing the corruptibility common to all children of nature, whether roses or canker-blooms, chaste lilies or basest weeds. Yet Love as a plant, like Love the child, is timeless and incorruptible. The accumulation of correspondences proceeds in the following lines. Built 'far from accident', despite the 'millioned accidents' the Poet had feared in cxv, the home of Love will stand—though indeed ruin may come to the mansion of the Friend's beauty, unrepaired by progeny and internally decayed by vice. As king, again, Love is exempt from the dangers that threaten contemporary monarchs. It need not fear 'thralled discontent'—the recurring anxieties induced by mobs and traitors; such menaces as Shakespeare dramatized in the Cade revolt and the conspiracies against Henry IV and V. Nor does Love 'suffer in smiling pomp'—the uneasy fate of kings, lamented by both these rulers.[1] At each level of correspondence—the human child, the plant of nature, the house of the body, the king of the state—Love transcends mutability. It does not fear the 'heretic' Policy, who barters away salvation for 'leases of short numbered hours'. Instead, Love itself stands 'hugely politic'; it constitutes its own state independent of the 'state' that is circumstance; and in the natural realm is an autonomous plant, owing no allegiance to the vegetable kingdom, not subject in its growth to heat or showers, and thus differentiated from men and plants alike, which 'increase Cheered and check'd e'en by the self same sky'. Unique, eternal, hugely politic, the vegetable Love will indeed grow vaster than empires and more slow. And the 'fools of Time', who like Hotspur gave their lives to 'state' and cry with their last breath that life's Time's fool, merely bear witness to its power.

In cxxv ('Were't aught to me I bore the canopy') the 'state' conceit takes on a new aspect that has special reference to the Poet's situation. The 'state' was a term for the canopy held over the heads of great public figures on ceremonial occasions. The Poet too has figuratively borne it: he has flattered the successful, honouring in his outer behaviour the outer semblance of honour. Like a time-server he has planned 'great bases for eternity', to find them speedily overtaken by waste and ruin. Now he knows that all this was vanity. For he has seen 'dwellers on form and favour' overreach themselves by paying too high a price for doubtful gain—'for compound sweet foregoing simple savour'—and thereby losing the benefits of true

---

1. Cf. *Henry IV*, III. i. 4–31; *Henry V*, IV. i. 250–304. The verbal echoes in the latter passage should especially be noted—'What kind of god art thou that *suffer'st* more Of mortal griefs than do thy worshippers . . . the tide of *pomp* That beats upon the high shore of this world'. Ovid's shore and sea image, suggesting mutability, has recurred in this last line.

loyalty. Seeking 'form and favour', these men are vain suitors
who court advantage, 'pitiful thrivers in their gazing spent':
for their love is fancy, a child engendered in the eyes, with
gazing fed, that dies in his cradle. But the Poet's suit, being the
simple and sincere one of true friendship, is addressed to the
heart, and cannot be rejected:

> No, let me be obsequious in thy heart,
> And take thou my oblation, poor but free,
> Which is not mix'd with seconds, knows no art,
> But mutual render, only me for thee.
> Hence, thou suborn'd informer! a true soul
> When most impeach'd, stands least in thy control.

It is sometimes helpful to bear in mind contemporary events
that may have prompted a metaphor or conceit; but there is
no gain in treating Shakespeare's sonnets as if they were historical cryptograms. The 'suborn'd informer' in the couplet of
cxxv did not take his pay from Burleigh's secret service. The
conceit implied in the latter part of this sonnet, growing from
the mention of pitiful thrivers in their gazing spent, is of a
figurative wooing. The Poet, unlike his rivals, is 'obsequious'
in the heart, 'poor but free', and his oblation, not 'mixed with
seconds', is the traditional bride-cake of pure flour:[1] 'seconds'
or poorer grades signifying the admixture in the lover's
thoughts of ulterior motives, the fallacious hope for 'compound sweet', and by a further word-play on 'seconds' carrying the implication of time-serving. It is a love that 'knows no
art But mutual render, only me for thee': best expressed in the
traditional handfasting of two persons who give themselves to
one another. This honest country wooing that follows the

1. Something like the old Roman marriage ritual of *confarreatio*, with its
consecration by cakes made of spelt, survived in England until the
seventeenth century. Bride-cake was the husband's symbolical offering or
oblation. Brand's *Popular Antiquities* has some relevant remarks on this
custom, under 'Nuptial Usages': 'The ceremony used at the solemnization
of a marriage was called *confarreation*, in token of a most firm conjunction
between the man and the wife, with a cake of wheat or barley... Aubrey,
writing about 1670, relates that when he was a boy, it was usual for the
bride and bridegroom to kiss over the cakes at the table. He adds that the
cakes were laid, at the end of the dinner, one on another, like the shew-
bread in the old Bible prints. The bridegroom was expected to wait at
table on this occasion.' (*Popular Antiquities of Great Britain*, ed. W. C.
Hazlitt (1870), II, p. 58.)

defeat of Time has its dramatic parallel in Henry V's courtship of Katharine after the conquest of France:

> . . . thou wouldst find me such a plain king that thou wouldst
> think I had sold my farm to buy my crown. I know no ways to
> mince it in love, but directly to say 'I love you' . . . Give me your
> answer; i' faith do: and so clap hands and a bargain . . .
>
> (*Henry V*, v. ii. 127 ff.)

—As for the mysterious 'suborned informer', it is evident that
he merely typifies any mischief-maker who has been bribed to
contest the banns when true lovers come to be wedded.

It is, of course, a figurative match: a marriage of true minds,
whose progeny will be immortal verse instead of the physical
union the Poet had urged at the beginning of the sequence.
cxvi celebrates this with a leap of imagination that signifies the
ultimate surmounting of all conflicts:

> Let me not to the marriage of true minds
> Admit impediments. Love is not love
> Which alters when it alteration finds,
> Or bends with the remover to remove:
> O, no! it is an ever-fixed mark,
> That looks on tempests and is never shaken;
> It is the star to every wandering bark,
> Whose worth's unknown, although his height be taken.
> Love's not Time's fool, though rosy lips and cheeks
> Within his bending sickle's compass come;
> Love alters not with his brief hours and weeks,
> But bears it out even to the edge of doom.
>   If this be error, and upon me prov'd,
>   I never writ, nor no man ever lov'd.

In the first lines of this sonnet the words of the marriage service
are solemnly recalled:

> If any of you know cause or just impediment why these persons
> should not be joined together . . .

At this point the 'informer' must speak, or for ever hold his
peace. But his objections in the present case would not be upheld. Just impediments would be change of circumstance or
inconstancy. But the Poet's love has not changed: it has only
grown the greater, transcending all circumstance and remaining for ever constant. This consideration guides the train of

thought in the following lines of the sonnet, where two new images are projected to override the structural metaphors of the sequence. The genesis of these images may well lie in Peter de Medina's exposition of the Ptolemaic universe, as translated by John Frampton in the first book of *The Arte of Navigation* (1595). Here the planets, or movable stars, are described as follows:

> ... these seauen planets are called starres, which are moueable not because they erre, but because their mouings be not vniforme nor agreeable, these doe moue the elements, and doe corrupt the things that are corruptible, they bring cloudy weather, and raiseth vp the waues of the sea, they moue tempests and causeth flowers to growe ... and in men, they incline more to one then to other: but although they doe so incline and moue, they do not constraine nor binde by force, but rather as *Ptholomie* saith: the wiseman is Lord ouer the starres, he is wise that followeth not sensualitie, but reason...[1]

The lover in the marriage of true minds is in the position of the wise man. No earthly power can invalidate his love, whether human or elemental; nor indeed the supernal influences which move these powers, corrupting 'the things that are corruptible'.

Love is not love
Which alters when it alteration finds,
Or bends with the remover to remove.

Love accordingly towers over the waves of the sea and the tempests raised up and moved by the planets, an 'ever-fixed mark' or lighthouse, that shines serenely upon the Ovidian contest of waves and shore. Moreover, since the wise man is lord of the planets, his love is exalted above their spheres, becoming itself a fixed star, beyond sun and moon that are stained by clouds and eclipses. Yet love is not abstracted from the life it transcends. The fixed stars have their empirical value for mankind; this is in fact the main theme of *The Arte of Navigation* as set forth in the introduction:

> And who is able to speake of so great a secret, that with a round instrument no greater than the palme of a mans hand called *Astrolabio*, the roundnesse of the heauen is measured, being so

1. Sig. B₆.

great that the vnderstanding of man cannot attaine therunto
... and in like maner the height of the Starres are taken, and by
this we are so certainlie guided, that so much as one pointe
faileth not.[1]

And in the fifth book the practical means of taking the height
of the north star for the purposes of navigation are set forth—
as in Chapter VIII, 'How the height of the North starre may be
taken, although the guards be not seene', and Chapter IX,
'How the altitude of the North starre may be taken, although
the Horizon be not seene'. Love, whose symbol is the north
star, is in essence a mystery, its intrinsic virtue unknown. But
it sets the course of all 'wandering barks', battered by the
waves of circumstance and unable to see the horizon—the
traditional figure for lovers and poets, as in Petrarch's *nave
colma d'obblio*, and Spenser's bark 'in dread of death and daungerous dismay'. After this great positive sublimation, the third
quatrain of the sonnet briefly sums up the rebuttal of Time's
claims that had been made in CXXIV–CXXV. Love is not 'Time's
fool', like the heretic Policy, and the vain dwellers on form and
favour. It survives, though the 'rosy lips and cheeks' of human
beauty be gathered—weeds among weeds, or flowers with
flowers—by Time's 'bending sickle'—synonymous for the
'crooked knife' of sonnet C. And although Policy works on
'leases of short number'd hours', Love is not modified by
Time's 'brief hours and weeks', but endures 'even to the edge
of doom'. Lastly, the couplet asserts that all this makes up a
declaration of faith. Whatever Ptolemy may have said concerning the wise man, its application to human love has no
philosophical authority, only the weight of poetic conviction.
Nothing has been proved, all is believed. Reason may argue
thus and thus against what the heart has taught; but if this
affirmation be proved in error, neither poetry nor love could
ever exist. Speculation can go no further: it is the *ultima ratio*
of faith.

> If the Sun and Moon should doubt
> They'd immediately go out.

From the infinite reaches of extended love the Poet returns
in CVII to his own day and the present situation.

1. Sig. A₄ʳ⁻ᵛ

Not mine own fears, nor the prophetic soul
Of the wide world dreaming on things to come,
Can yet the lease of my true love control,
Suppos'd as forfeit to a confin'd doom.
The mortal moon hath her eclipse endur'd,
And the sad augurs mock their own presage;
Incertainties now crown themselves assur'd,
And peace proclaims olives of endless age.
Now with the drops of this most balmy time
My love looks fresh, and Death to me subscribes,
Since, spite of him, I'll live in this poor rime,
While he insults o'er dull and speechless tribes:
    And thou in this shalt find thy monument,
    When tyrants' crests and tombs of brass are spent.

This poem has been trailed with a drag-net for allusions that might supply a date, with no better results, alas, than a steady accumulation of well-argued claims for any year between 1588 and 1603. One thing is clear, that the sonnet is not a Commentary on the News, whether the news be the defeat of the Armada, the Queen's survival of her grand climacteric, or the accession of King James. In the context of the group, it commemorates a moment of stillness when all the contradictions of life are suspended in the autumn glow of Love's victory over Time. And since in the final couplet the Friend is explicitly addressed in the second person, it is equally clear that the word 'love' through the rest of the sonnet is used as an abstract noun; so that the 'confined doom' in line four need have nothing to do with a spell of imprisonment for the Friend, whether actual or figurative.

The Poet has cast off all fears as to the impermanence of love, such as he had known in the course of his 'fearful meditation' on cosmic mutability in LXV, or when, as he wrote in CXV, 'fearing of Time's tyranny', he had doubted all but the present. The Babe of Love has grown up and will never be unfathered. Nor does the 'prophetic soul of the wide world' cause any anxiety. It is Love the King whose death has been falsely prophesied, and the appropriate analogies are to be found in the history plays: the portents when it was mistakenly believed that Richard II was dead—

The bay-trees in our country are all wither'd,

> And meteors fright the fixed stars of heaven,
> The pale-fac'd moon looks bloody on the earth
> And lean-look'd prophets whisper fearful change;
> > (*Richard II*, ii. iv. 8–11)

—the prophecy of the Bishop of Carlisle at Henry IV's usurpation—

> Peace shall go sleep with Turks and infidels,
> And in this seat of peace tumultuous wars
> Shall kin with kin and kind with kind confound;
> > (iv. i. 139–41)

and the suspension of its dire effects—the triumphant accession of Henry V:

> I survive,
> To mock the expectation of the world,
> To frustrate prophecies, and to raze out
> Rotten opinion . . . (*2 Henry IV*, v. ii. 125–8)

To understand these last sonnets we must learn to read the shorthand of Shakespearean imagery. In the first quatrain of cvii Love as the Miraculous Babe and the Conqueror King survives the menace of Time; and Love the Eternal Summer wins its action against the intended forfeiture of its lease, so that the anxiously-awaited 'doom', or sentence of court, has not confined its tenure. In the second quatrain Love as the mortal moon (it could have been the fixed star of cxvi, or the sun, as in the main structural metaphors, but the most vulnerable of astral bodies is chosen for vigour of contrast) 'endures' or survives its eclipse; while instead of the 'tumultuous wars' and 'fearful change' that have been foretold, an endless peace ensues, the olives ripening where the bay-trees withered. In this 'most balmy time' the transient autumn of nature which was the setting of civ is changed to a season of fruition for the poetic imagination, and that sonnet's mention of the still-fresh appearance of the Friend is transferred to Love itself, now radiant with perpetual youth.

In the last lines of cvii a powerful new image has come into being. The tyrant Death, like a Caesar of antiquity, may 'insult' over the bodies of inarticulate barbarians: but the Poet, a citizen of the free state of Love, has built an impregnable monument in 'this poor rime'. The tyrants' crests and tombs of brass will perish, but in the monument of poetry the Friend will

remain secure. The source of this image takes us back to the
contemporary editions of Ovid, where at the conclusion to the
last book of the *Metamorphoses* Regius quoted Horace's ending
to his own last book of Odes:

> *Exegi monumentum aere perennius* . . .

To this day the majority of editors take the poem of six
couplets numbered CXXVI, with its warning to the Friend to
fear Nature as a 'minion of her pleasure', as the end of the
sequence. Perhaps at one time Shakespeare intended it as the
envoi to a group of sonnets; perhaps it was an occasional piece
with no direct relation to any group. After the immortalization
of the Friend in these last sonnets such an ending is quite inconceivable. Nor indeed can LXXXVII, 'Farewell, thou art too
dear for my possessing', be thought of in this place. There is in
fact one unmistakable conclusion, and sonnet LV supplies it.

The monument image, and the inspiration that prompts its
use, originated in Ovid and Horace. Both these Latin poets
had chosen to end their major works with the proud claim that
their verse would outlast fire and sword. Horace's boast dared
Time to do its worst—

> *Exegi monumentum aere perennius*
> *Regalique situ pyramidum altius,*
> *Quod non imber edax, non Aquilo impotens*
> *Possit diruere, aut innumerabilis*
> *Annorum series et fuga temporum.*[1]

And Ovid, whose great discourse on mutability reverberates
through all these sonnets like a beating of drums, concluded
with a similar blast of defiance:

> *Iamque opus exegi, quod nec Iovis ira nec ignis,*
> *Nec poterit ferrum nec edax abolere vetustas.*
> *Cum volet, illa dies, quae nil nisi corporis huius*
> *Ius habet, incerti spatium mihi finiat aevi:*
> *Parte tamen meliore mei super alta perennis*
> *Astra ferar, nomenque erit indelebile nostrum,*
> *Quaque patet domitis Romana potentia terris,*

---

1. *Odes*, III. xxx: 'My work is done, the memorial more enduring than
brass and loftier than the kingly building of the pyramids—something that
neither the corroding rain nor the wild rage of Aquilo can ever destroy,
nor the numberless succession of years and flight of ages.' (Translation by
E. C. Wickham, Oxford, 1903.)

Ore legar populi, perque omnia saecula fama,
Siquid habent veri vatum praesagia, vivam.[1]

Ovidius Naso was the man: always Shakespeare turned to him
for guidance; and never so fittingly as now, when the finale of
his sequence called for an English sonnet that would ring out a
Roman boast with equal assurance:

> Not marble, nor the gilded monuments
> Of princes, shall outlive this powerful rime;
> But you shall shine more bright in these contents
> Than unswept stone, besmear'd with sluttish time.
> When wasteful war shall statues overturn,
> And broils root out the work of masonry,
> Nor Mars his sword nor war's quick fire shall burn
> The living record of your memory.
> 'Gainst death and all-oblivious enmity
> Shall you pace forth; your praise shall still find room
> Even in the eyes of all posterity
> That wear this world out to the ending doom.
>   So, till the judgment that yourself arise,
>   You live in this, and dwell in lovers' eyes.

Here the hostile forces of existence are assembled and total
victory over their massed forces is proclaimed. Time and
Death which tyrannize over the phenomenal world; war that
destroys civilizations and their monuments; all-oblivious enmity that breeds murder and rebellion: these are vanquished
as the Friend 'paces forth' a conqueror in Love's name. No
other sonnet of Shakespeare's breathes such magnificent assurance. The 'poor rime' of cvii is transformed into 'this powerful
rime'; the 'tyrants' crests and tombs of brass' give place, under
the guidance of Horace's *regalique situ*, to 'marble and the
gilded monuments of princes' as foils to the Friend's glory. The
English words themselves take on the weight and sonorousness
of their Latin derivation. Yet the sonnet is no mere paraphrase:

1. *Metam.*, xv. 871 *et seq.*: 'My work is complete; a work which neither
Jove's anger, nor fire nor sword shall destroy, nor yet the gnawing tooth
of time. That day which has power over nothing but my body may,
when it pleases, put an end to my uncertain span of years. Yet with my
better part I shall soar, undying, far above the stars, and my name will
be imperishable. Wherever Roman power extends over the lands Rome
has subdued, people will read my verse. If there be any truth in poets'
prophecies, I shall live to all eternity, immortalized by fame.'
(Translation by Mary M. Innes, *Penguin Classics.*)

the pagan allusion to Jove is omitted, and the 'broils' and 'enmity' of sixteenth-century politics add a contemporary significance. More noteworthy still is the assertion that the Friend will 'shine more bright in these contents', completing an image that has persisted right through the sequence: the portrait in 'perspective' on the heart; the vision of the Friend seen in darkness; the jewel in its chest; the miracle of love shining in black ink. As the sonnet sweeps to its conclusion, the great name of Rome is coupled to the Friend's eternalization. Wherever Roman power extends over the conquered lands, Ovid proclaimed, *quaque patet domitis Romana potentia terris*, there he would live on throughout all the ages. A famous English homonym supplied the translation of both *patet* and *Romana potentia*: it was *room* or *Rome*:

> Now is it Rome indeed and room enough, . . .
> > *(Julius Caesar*, i. ii. 155)

Or as Spenser declared,

> *Rome* was th' whole world, and al the world was *Rome*,
> And if things nam'd their names doo equalize,
> When land and sea ye name, then name ye *Rome*;
> And naming *Rome* ye land and sea comprize:
> > *(Ruines of Rome*, 359–62)

Thus the conquest of Time is also a conquest of space; and the Friend's praise will still 'find room'—and Rome, which is all the world—until the last judgement of the quick and dead, when he himself shall rise.

Unlike the Latin poets, Shakespeare proclaimed to the last sonnet of his sequence that immortality was conferred on the creation, not on its creator; that his monument celebrated not the poet but his theme. Eternity in verse—

> So long as men can breathe, or eyes can see

—stood in place of such faith in an after-life of the spirit as even the pagan Ovid had affirmed. His phrase, *parte tamen meliore mei super alta perennis / astra ferar*, significantly found no rendering in Shakespeare's sonnet; and the substituted reference to a physical resurrection at the last judgement would suggest that, until time and the whole cosmos reached its end, only the works of man could preserve man's image. The operative faith in these sonnets has been centred upon a love growing out of sense-perception and personal experience, subject to 'all frailties that besiege all kinds of blood', yet transcending the world of sense through the power of the human spirit. In so far as the Friend is a microcosm of the universe, the Poet's love for him effects a universal redemption: yet in the last reckoning it is only through individual human beings and personal relationships that the creative spirit can perform its task. Such a faith may be illogical, unphilosophical, even un-Christian; yet it supplies the forces which animate a Lear and a Cleopatra in Shakespeare's tragedies and which prevent these plays from becoming an insufferable holocaust. Here, it may be said, this faith underlies the complex genius of Shakespeare's sonnets, immortalizing—even in the eyes of all posterity—a certain unidentified Friend whom he declared to have been his all-the-world.

CONCLUSION

ON New Year's Day 1610, a few months after the first publication of Shakespeare's sonnets, a boy of sixteen enclosed two recent poems of his own in a letter to his mother, with the comment:

> my meaning (*dear Mother*) is in these Sonnets, to declare my resolution to be, that my poor Abilities in *Poetry*, shall be all and ever consecrated to Gods glory.[1]

This resolve was poetically formulated in the first sonnet, addressed, significantly, to God:

> Doth Poetry
> Wear *Venus* Livery? only serve her turn?
> Why are not *Sonnets* made of thee? and layes
> Upon thine Altar burnt? Cannot thy love
> Heighten a spirit to sound out thy praise
> As well as any she?[2]

Such sentiments have often been indulged in by pious adolescents; but George Herbert kept his pledge in manhood by writing religious lyrics that rank with the finest verse of the metaphysical school, and there is some reason for treating his views as typical of the changing spirit of seventeenth-century poetry. However, the transposition of romance ardour to the service of religion meant a more serious break with literary tradition than Herbert as a youth could have foreseen. It resulted in a kind of lyric which escaped from the mould of the sonnet form, and a kind of religious poetry which, in its acutely subjective vision, turned inwards from the customary range of Christian experience as a total interpretation of life. Much the same tendency may be noted in other verse of this school. Donne's *Holy Sonnets* were indeed closer to the Elizabethan model, using Sidney's form to present a more terrible conflict of the soul than Astrophel had undergone; but they too sacrificed range for intensity,[3] and depicted only a single, lurid phase

1. *The Works of George Herbert*, ed. F. E. Hutchinson (Oxford, 1941), p. 363.
2. Ibid., p. 206.
3. [This may be said, too, of the sonnets of William Alabaster (ed. Story and Gardner, 1959).]

of experience. Even in Donne's earlier, secular verse—brilliant, flexible, and thought-provoking as it was—the shift to a world of private ideas and sensations had already taken place. The macrocosm, the body politic, and the humours and elements that made up the human frame, no longer constituted an integral whole. The chain of being was broken into numerous shining links, to serve in the shaping of individual patterns of thought. Donne could appropriate the sun as his *valet-de-chambre* ('This bed thy center is, these walls, thy spheare'), and transform his mistress's tears, not into coaches, but into newly-created worlds, to be drowned in new floods. In minor metaphysical verse this style was to degenerate into what has been well described as 'a mental habit or technique cut loose from philosophic totality and applied to heterogeneous and tendential objects and sensations'.[1] But even at its best, metaphysical poetry may be said to mark the first stage in that separation of individuality from tradition which spelt the end of Renaissance culture and the kind of writing with which this book has been concerned.

In Shakespeare's sonnets the Renaissance poetic tradition found its true English consummation, and with it the central impulse of the Elizabethan lyric. Without doubt, the unprecedented scope, diversity, and power of these poems can only be apprehended in terms of Shakespeare's own genius, and whoever hopes to interpret them must plunge, at his own peril, into that sea. Yet they derive historically from the great order of European love poetry which originates in the sonnets of Petrarch; and, transformed by a different national heritage, spiritual allegiance, and personal outlook, they complete a development which Petrarch began.

We have seen how, from the very start, the Petrarchan sonnet underwent a process of radical modification in English. The deep-seated national distrust for a class of poetry which, in Herbert's words, 'wore Venus' livery', interacted with the need of the age for a means of personal expression. This fruitful tension was manifested, not only in the independent treatment of traditional themes, but also, and concurrently, in the original approach to verse-form and imagery. In contrast to

1. Douglas Bush, *English Literature in the Earlier Seventeenth Century* (Oxford, 1945), p. 127.

the Italian sonnet as a vehicle of intuition and revelation, the sonnet form of Wyatt and Surrey was especially designed for progressive exposition and inferential reasoning; while Sidney's adaptation of it added a paradoxical turn reflecting the sharp conflicts precipitated by courtly love in the psyche of a sixteenth-century Englishman. At the same time these poets largely replaced the Petrarchan metaphor, expressing a conviction of the essential unity of all being, by similes drawn from common observation and direct perception, or, as in Sidney's most characteristic sonnets, by personifications and conceits whose function was primarily to forward self-analysis.

During this first period, the Elizabethan sonnet mainly expressed an effort to apprehend disparate modes of experience rather than to affirm new values. But in the poetry and poetic drama of the last decade of the century there appeared a greatly heightened curiosity and sensibility, combined with a tendency to envisage all reality with primary reference to the individual human being. Spirit and nature were reintegrated; not, as in Petrarch's verse, through the immanent magic of sexual love, but through the transcendent dynamic of personality. The poets of the fifteen nineties, attracted by the possibilities of the love sonnet, tried hard to accommodate their outlook to this medium. In the attempt they considerably expanded its range. Their conceits touched upon a wide field of contemporary interests, and their metaphors and similes often revealed a finely sympathetic insight into the common fortunes of man and impersonal nature. In their best work the verse-form of Wyatt and Surrey revealed itself as a highly suitable instrument for the critical, experiential approach to life of the younger generation of writers. But what vitiated the late Elizabethan sonnet was its failure to evolve a new and arresting central theme which could replace the obsolete conventions of courtly love and serve to clarify the vision of the age. Hence the apparently pointless repetition of trite sentiments and the superfluous ingenuities which brought the sonnet into ill repute.

Two important attempts at a new synthesis were made. Spenser's way, the result of a complex, highly individual development, was to substitute for the romance theme of *amour courtois* the Protestant-Platonist ideal of virtuous courtship, leading through betrothal to sacramental union. The English sonnet tradition, however, with its roots in experience, was to militate against the philosophical and religious preconceptions of *Amoretti*; so that, despite much incidental beauty and even sublimity, Spenser's sequence could provide no solution. The true answer to the problem was found by Shakespeare, who shared in essentials the vision of his contemporaries and gave it supreme expression in the drama.

In all likelihood we shall never know to what factors of experience Shakespeare owed his choice of theme. Even if the identity of the Friend were to be proved beyond reasonable doubt, we should not be any nearer to understanding the poetic transmutation effected in the Sonnets—just as we are no nearer to understanding Petrarch's vision through those shreds of half-legendary information which have come down to us concerning Laura. What may be said with certainty is that, in taking the noble friend as his theme, Shakespeare freed himself from all the encumbrances which hampered the sonnet poets of his time. Without impropriety or strain, this theme admitted a consideration, at once intellectual and impassioned, of the wide vistas of politics and society, cosmic destiny and the human predicament, which exercised the imagination of the age; while all these concerns were centred upon, and subordinated to, the supreme reality of a unique individual in his weakness and power. Thus the co-existence of beauty and corruption, of truth and mutability, and the universal tyranny of Time, which were the tissue of Shakespearean drama, became in these sonnets the touchstone of personal integrity; and through the prepotency of human love, on a plane customarily reserved for divine grace, a poetic resolution was affirmed for the antinomies of life.

One last consideration may be added. In the greatest works of literature, the writer does not create for himself alone; nor even for his own society and times. He becomes the *vates* of a whole people, past, present, and future. This is no less true of personal poetry than of the epic or novel, and the English genius speaks through Shakespeare's sonnets as surely as the Italian genius speaks through the sonnets of Petrarch. The English imagination operates in Shakespeare's great compound metaphors, reaching down to a dark core of elemental conflict, while Petrarch's metaphors diffuse an Italian vision of the radiant integrity of spirit and nature. The English intellect works through the dialectic of the sonnet form Shakespeare perfected, whose terse appositions and antitheses find only a precarious balance in the last couplet, preparing the way to fresh encounters with a dilemma that is perpetually reasserting itself: while the Italian form, in contrast, functions as the instrument of an act of intuition, complete in itself, seeking through a variety of circumstances to crystallize and apprehend a timeless state of being. Finally, the English spirit is triumphantly ascendant in the figure of the Friend, the doomed yet immortal victim and conqueror of Time, who stands in place of Petrarch's Lady, the mistress of spring and universal rebirth. In Madonna Laura it is possible to discern, through the spiritualizations of Christianity and individualizations of humanism, the still uneffaced features of that primeval Mediterranean goddess, Venus or Aphrodite orAstarte, whom all men must at some time serve. But in the Friend—whichever Elizabethan nobleman provided his living counterpart, whatever Renaissance or Christian virtues he embodied—we may recognize the archetypal, all too human *monndryhten* of northern epic and lay, such a fated hero as was Beowulf or Sigemund or the lost lord of *The Wanderer*, in whose patronage the poet found his sole source of joy upon earth and whose love surpassed the love of women—

> þinceð him in mode þæt he his monndryhten
> clyppe and cysse, and on cneo lecge
> honda and heafod, swa he hwilum ær
> in geardagum giefstoles breac . . .

The unknown poet of *The Wanderer*, alone and exiled amidst the ravages of winter and war, solacing himself with memories of the Golden Friend to whom his allegiance was vowed, would have understood the experience of Shakespeare's 'When in disgrace with fortune and men's eyes':

> For thy sweet love remember'd such wealth brings
> That then I scorn to change my state with kings.

And even the Englishman of the twentieth century may find that Wyrd and the world have not so greatly changed that he is unable to respond to the same perennial theme.

INDEX

Allegory
  Allegorical Romance, 2, 4, 5, 7, 11–12, 65, 72, 103, 113, 131, 190
  Allegory of Dante, 2, 7, 9
  English Allegorical Tradition, 11–12, 84–5, 133, 139, 209
  Allegorical elements in Petrarch's sonnets, 26, 46
  Allegorical conceits in Sidney's sonnets, 84–5, 205
  Allegory of Spenser, 75, 94–5, 100, 102–3, 119–20, 129–30, 131 n., 133, 134
Anacreontic verse, 65, 130, 144, 147
Anne of Cleves, 32
Ariosto, *Orlando Furioso*, 47 n.
Armada, 267
Armstrong, Edward A., 228 n.
Ascham, Roger, 58, 77–8

Bacon, Francis, *Essays*, 139
Baldwin, T. W., 170 n., 172 n.
Barnes, Barnabe, 55, 144, 156, 175; *Parthenophil and Parthenophe*, 145, 148
Barnfield, Richard, *The Affectionate Shepherd*, 165 n.
Bateson, F. W., 27 n.
Bellay, Du, 92
Bembo, 164, 165, 181; *Gli Asolani*, 79; (for Discourse of Bembo in The Courtier, *see* Castiglione)
Benson, John, 171
Berni, 52 n., 175
Blake, William, 9, 215, 266
Boccaccio, 11, 179 n.
Boleyn, Anne, 32
Brand, *Popular Antiquities*, 263 n.
Bray, Sir Denys, 172 n.
Bright, Timothy, *A Treatise of Melancholie*, 177 n.
Burleigh, Lord, 263
Burns, Robert, 4
Bush, Douglas, 274 n.

Caloria, T. di, 3
Caine, T. Hall, vi
Canticles, *see* Song of Solomon
Castiglione, 124, 164, 181; *The Cour-*

tier (transl. Hoby), 103–4, 116–17, 122–3, 127
Catullus, 151
Chambers, E. K., 164, 172 n.; and Sidgwick, F., 10
Chapman, George, 164, 208
Chariteo, 66–7
Chaucer, Geoffrey, 11, 12, 18–19 n., 23, 26, 30, 133; *Troilus and Criseyde*, 11, 30, 141
Chaytor, H. J., 10 n., 207 n.
Colonna, 33
Confarreation, ritual of, 263 n.
Constable, Henry, 55, 144, 145, 156, 175; *Diana*, 144, 145, 147–8, 148–9, 175, 200, 202
Corinthians, Epistle to, 244 n.
Cour d'Amour, Le, 8, 11
Coward, Noël, 57
Cromwell, Thomas, 31, 32, 33
Custance, John, 234 n.

Daniel, Samuel, 50, 55, 150, 160, 161, 167, 189; *Delia*, 151–4, 155, 168–9
Dante, 2, 4, 6, 7, 8, 22; *Paradiso*, 9; *Vita Nuova*, 9
Della Casa, 79, 165
Desportes, 104–7, 119, 143, 150–1, 157 n.
Devereux, Penelope, *see* Rich
Donne, John, 31, 127 n., 139, 260 n., 273, 274
Drayton, Michael, 50, 55, 150, 161; *Idea*, 154–60; *Ideas Mirrour*, 157, 158; *Mortimeriados*, 203 n.
Dunstable, John, 12

Edward III, 220–1 n.
Elizabeth I, 81, 126, 267
Empson, William, 219 n.
Epigram
  Epigrammatic qualities in Wyatt's sonnets, 20, 28, 31–2
  Italian *strambotti*, 31 n., 85, 105
  Influence of epigram on Surrey's sonnets, 42, 45
  Epigrams in Sidney's *Arcadia*, 51, 52

As model for Sidney's sonnets, 62–4, 66–7, 85.

Epigrams published with *Amoretti*, 96, 101

Erasmus, *De Conscribendis* (transl. in Wilson's *Art of Rhetorike*), 190–1, 192, 194, 195 n., 196 n., 219

Ferrara, Duke of (patron of Tasso), 165

Filosseno, 31 n.

Fletcher, Giles, 144, 156; *Licia*, 144, 146, 147, 149, 203

Foxwell, Agnes K., 16 n.

Francis I, 37

Frampton, John, *see* Medina

Fuller, T., *Worthies of England*, 230 n.

Gascoigne, G., *Sundrie Flowers*, 51

Gawain and the Grene Kinght, Sir, 11, 29

Golding, Arthur, 252 n., 253 n.

Gorgious Gallery of Gallant Inventions, A, 50

Greene, Robert, *Alcida*, 220; *Friar Bacon and Friar Bungay*, 120 n.

Greek Anthology, 66

Grey, Lord (patron of Spenser), 165

Grocyn, William, 78

Grosart, A. B., 82

Guinicelli, 2

Hall, Joseph, 163

Harding, D. W., 16 n.

Harvey, Gabriel, 230 n.

Henry VIII, 37, 48, 49

Herbert, George, 273, 274

Hoby, Sir Thomas, *see* Castiglione

Hopkins, Gerard Manley, 16

Horace, 151, 256 n., 269, 270; (transl. E. C. Wickham), 269 n.

Imagist poets, 15

Inge, W. R., 115, 127

James I, 267

Jamyn, 63 n.

Jodelle, 165 n.

John, L. C., 55

Jonson, Benjamin, 134, 230

Kastner, L. E., 97, 104 n., 105 n.

Keats, John, 186–7

Ker, W. P., 12 n.

Klein, David, 202 n.

Knights, L. C., 219 n.

Koeppel, Emil, 54

Langland, *Piers Plowman*, 11–12

Lawrence, D. H., 9

Lee, Sidney, v, 54–5, 97, 104 n., 165 n.

Legouis, 100 n.

Lewis, C. S., 8 n., 12 n., 19 n., 131 n.

Linacre, Thomas, 78

Lodge, Thomas, 55, 175; *A Fig for Momus*, 150; *Phillis*, 145, 149–50, 200; *Rosalynde*, 149, 220 n., 242

Long, Percy W., 97

Lorris, De, 4, 11, 12

Lydgate, John, 18

Lyly, John, *Endimion*, 175 n.; *Euphues*, 164, 216 n.

Lyric, v, vii, 3, 4, 6, 7, 35
   Provençal, 1–2, 3, 7, 8, 10, 143, 207 n.
   Tuscan, 2, 3, 4, 7, 8
   Traditional English, 9–11, 13, 32
   Fifteenth Century and Tudor, 12–13, 15, 38
   Elizabethan, 13, 35, 139, 141–2, 148, 274
   Lyrics in Sidney's *Arcadia*, 51
   Lyrics in *Astrophel and Stella*, 53, 82
   Metaphysical, v, 273–4

Malone, Edmund, 206

Marlowe, Christopher, *Doctor Faustus*, 139; *Edward II*, 156; *Hero and Leander*, 146, 162, 191–2, 193, 196

Marot, 92

Marston, John, 163

Matthew, Gospel of, 216 n.

Medina, P. de (transl. John Frampton, *The Arte of Navigation*), 197 n., 265–6

Miller, F. J., *see* Ovid

Montemayor, 50

Muir, Kenneth, 15 n., 90, 221 n.

Nashe, Thomas, 139, 230 n.

Neoplatonism, 79, 103, 104, 105, 111, 113, 115, 127, 135, 143, 181, 183, 258

Neopythagoreanism, *see* Ovid

Noodt, Van der, *Theatre for Worldlings*, 92–3

Norden, John, *A Christian Familiar Comfort*, 217 n.

Ovid, 162, 163, 166, 192, 193, 246, 258; *Metamorphoses*, 166, 201 n., 248–72 *passim*; (transl. by F. J. Miller), 248–9 n.; *Tristia*, 201 n.

Ovidian Romance, 139, 142, 162, 192, 227

Owl and The Nightingale, The, 11 n.

Padelford, F. M., 38, 42

Passionate Pilgrim, The, 163

Pericles, 164

Petrarch, vii, 3, 4–5, 8, 9, 72, 143; Sonnets, vi, 5–7, 9 n., 16, 19, 56, 92, 98, 102, 108, 111, 157, 165, 185; as model for Wyatt, 20–35 *passim*, 124, 186 n., 275; as model for Surrey, 38–44 *passim*, 46–7, 49, 50, 151, 275; as model for Sidney, 58–62, 65, 88–90, 275; as model for Spenser, 121, 122, 275–6; compared with Shakespeare's Sonnets, vii, 186, 266, 276–7; in relation to the Elizabethan Sonnet generally, vi–vii, 274–7

Petrarchan School, 74, 85, 97, 105, 121, 143, 146, 151, 175, 182

Plato, 27, 60–1, 74, 109, 117; *Symposium*, 74, 116

Platonism, 78, 79, 80, 84–5, 104, 105, 108, 109, 164, 176, 182, 184, 198, 226, 275

Pléiade school of poets, 56, 71, 143, 165

Plotinus, 113, 115

Ponsonby, William, 96, 101

Pontano, 62–4, 67

Pooler, C. Knox, 170 n., 228 n., 257

Post-Chaucerians, 18

Protestantism, 9, 77, 78, 95, 104, 109, 111, 136, 141, 185, 275

Provençal lyric, *see* Lyric, Provençal

Psalms, Book of, 244 n.

Ptolemaic system, 60

Ptolemy, 266

Puttenham, George, *The Arte of English Poesie*, 145

Pythagoras, Discourse of, *see* Ovid, *Metamorphoses*

Quattrocento school of poetry, 16, 52, 56, 63, 85

Raimon-Jordan, 2 n.

Regius, 256 n., 269

Rich, Lady Penelope, 54, 57

Rich, Lord, 73

Rogier, Peire, 1

Romans, Folquet de (transl. H. J. Chaytor), 207 n.

Romei, Annibale, *The Courtier's Academy*, 112 n.

Ronsard, 56, 143, 151–2, 153, 167, 202 n.

Saintsbury, George, 12 n., 35

Sannazaro, 50

Scève, 63 n.

Scott, Janet G., 52 n., 55, 63 n., 66, 97, 104 n., 165 n.

Seafarer, The, 11

Selincourt, E. De, 133

Seneca, 27

Serafino (dell' Aquila), 31 n., 54, 58, 66–8, 143, 165

Seymour, Jane, 32

Shakespeare, William, v, vi, vii, 1, 46, 50, 55, 88, 114, 139, 142, 162–272, 274, 276–7; *Sonnets*, 157, 160, 163–272, 274, 276–7; *2 Henry IV*, 236–7, 238, 239 n.; 257, 262n., 268; *Henry V*, 246–7, 262 n., 264; *1 Henry VI*, 221; *Julius Caesar*, 271; *King John*, 221–2; *Love's Labour's Lost*, 162–3, 176–7, 197; *Measure for Measure*, 219, 244 n.; *Merchant of Venice*, 180, 209, 210–12, 227, 231; *Midsummer Night's Dream*, 237 n.; *Othello*, 179 n., 214 n.; *Rape of Lucrece*, 171, 256; *Richard II*, 222, 227, 231, 267–8; *Romeo and Juliet*, 206, 237 n.; *Twelfth Night*, 257 n.; *Venus and Adonis*, 142, 171, 192.

Shaw, G. B., 70

Shelley, Percy B., 9

Sidney, Sir Philip, vi, 1, 31, 50, 51–91, 93, 94, 95, 96, 129–30, 133, 134, 144, 145, 147, 155, 156, 157, 160, 168, 179, 185, 186, 205, 273, 275; *Arcadia*, 51–3, 91, 149, 164, 169, 175, 191 n., 192, 193, 194, 195, 197, 207, 217–18; *Defence of Poetry*, 57; *Astrophel and Stella*, 53–91, 92, 97, 109, 115, 128, 130, 135, 143, 148, 150, 155, 156, 167, 168, 169, 172, 174, 175–6, 177, 186, 200 n., 203–4, 204–5, 206–7 n., 229; Sonnets *Thou blind mans marke, Leaue me ô Loue*, 82, 91, 153, 181

Sixtus V, 255
Skeltonic verse, 28
Smith, Hallett, 14 n.
Smith, J. C., 97
Socrates, 8
Song of Solomon, 44, 123-4, 132 n.
Spencer, Theodore, 55-6, 112 n.
Spens, Janet, 83
Spenser, Edmund, vi, 50, 55, 75, 77, 92-137, 141, 153, 161, 165, 166, 181, 185, 189, 271, 275-6; *Amoretti*, 96-137, 157, 166, 169, 172, 181, 184, 207, 266, 276; *Colin Clouts Come Home Againe*, 100 n., 114, 129 n.; *Epithalamion*, 96, 97, 101, 126, 129, 132 n.; *Faerie Queene*, 94-5, 100, 102-3, 107, 119-20, 129, 130, 133, 169; *Hymnes*, 96, 112, 114 n., 118; *Ruines of Rome*, 93 n., 271; *Shepheardes Calender*, 93-4, 95; *Theatre for Worldlings* (verse in), 92-3; *Visions of Bellay*, 92-3 n.; *Visions of Petrarch*, 92-3; *Visions of the Worlds Vanitie*, 93
Stendhal, 57
Surrey, Henry Howard, Earl of, vii, 34, 35, 37-50, 51, 52, 61, 88, 89, 90, 91, 92, 93, 119 n., 134, 135, 145, 151, 153-4, 160, 189, 275

Tasso, Torquato, 56, 79, 93, 104-5, 107-9, 109-13, 125, 131, 152-3, 165
Thomas, Edward, 162
Thorpe, Thomas, 163, 171, 189, 240
Tilley, M. P., 216 n., 237 n.
Tillotson, Kathleen, 203 n.
Tillyard, E. M. W., 14, 40 n.
Tolkein, J. R. R., 9
Tottel, Richard (publisher), *Songes and Sonnettes* (or *Miscellany*), 31 n., 37, 44, 51, 90
Troubadour poets, *see* Lyric, Provençal
Tuscan poets, Tuscan *Stornelli*, *see* Lyric, Tuscan

Ventadorn, Bernart de, 1

Wanderer, The, 11, 277
Wickham, E. C., *see* Horace
Wilson, Mona, 53 n., 87 n.
Wilson, Thomas, *Art of Rhetorike*, *see* Erasmus
Wolff, M. J., 165 n.
Wyatt, Sir Thomas, v, vii, viii, 14-36, 37, 38, 42, 44, 45, 46, 48, 50, 51, 52, 86, 87, 90, 91, 92, 124, 133, 134, 143, 145, 157, 160, 186 n., 275
Wyndham, George, 183-4

University Paperbacks

A COMPLETE LIST OF TITLES

Titles marked thus: * are to be published during 1966

ARCHAEOLOGY AND ANTHROPOLOGY

UP   94   Antiquities of the Irish Countryside, *Seán P. O'Ríordáin*
UP   1   Archaeology and Society, *Grahame Clark*
UP 118   Archaeology in the Holy Land, *Kathleen Kenyon*
UP 164   The Greek Stones Speak, *Paul MacKendrick*
UP   58   Habitat, Economy and Society, *C. Daryll Forde*
UP 150   Industrial Archaeology, *K. Hudson*

ART AND ARCHITECTURE

UP   33   The Architecture of Humanism, *Geoffrey Scott*
UP 101   The Classical Language of Architecture, *John Summerson*

BIOGRAPHY

UP 102   An Autobiography, *Edwin Muir*
UP 130   Elizabeth the Great, *Elizabeth Jenkins*
UP   50   The Great Mathematicians, *H. W. Turnbull*
UP   90   Horace Walpole, *R. W. Ketton-Cremer*
UP 100   Mozart: The Man and His Works, *W. J. Turner*
UP   9   Plato: The Man and His Work, *A. E. Taylor*
UP   76   Thackeray the Novelist, *Geoffrey Tillotson*
UP   13   William the Silent, *C. V. Wedgewood*
*UP 178   Max Weber: An Intellectual Portrait, *Reinhard Bendix*

ECONOMICS

UP 134   Beyond the Welfare State, *Gunnar Myrdal*
UP   21   An Economic History of the British Isles, *Arthur Birnie*
UP   52   An Economic History of Europe, *Arthur Birnie*

UP 66 Economic Theory and Underdeveloped Regions, *Gunnar Myrdal*

UP 104 Economics, *H. Speight*

UP 58 Habitat, Economy and Society (See under Archaelogy and Anthropology)

UP 44 Introduction to Money, *H. Croome*

UP 145 The Rise of Modern Industry, *J. L. and Barbara Hammond*

UP 14 The Wealth of Nations, Vol. I, *Adam Smith,* ed. *Edwin Cannan*

UP 15 The Wealth of Nations, Vol. II, *Adam Smith,* ed. *Edwin Cannan*

EDUCATION

UP 57 The Art of Teaching, *Gilbert Highet*

UP 106 Culture and General Education, *Kenneth Richmond*

UP 87 Teaching: A Psychological Analysis, *C. M. Fleming*

*UP 172 An Introduction to Educational Psychology, *E. Stones*

GEOGRAPHY

UP 58 Habitat, Economy and Society (See under Archaeology and Anthropology)

UP 169 An Historical Geography of Europe, *W. G. East*

UP 147 A Hundred Years of Geography, *T. W. Freeman*

UP 75 Maps and Diagrams, *F. J. Monkhouse and H. R. Wilkinson*

UP 117 The Skin of the Earth, *A. Austin Miller*

GREECE AND ROME

UP 65 Aristotle, *Sir David Ross*

UP 56 From the Gracchi to Nero, *H. H. Scullard*

UP 3 Greek Political Theory, *Ernest Barker*

*UP 140 Greek Tragedy, *H. D. F. Kitto*

UP 49 The Greek View of Life, *G. Lowes Dickinson*

UP 69 A Handbook of Greek Literature, *H. J. Rose*

UP 70 A Handbook of Greek Mythology, *H. J. Rose*

UP 160 A Handbook of Latin Literature, *H. J. Rose*

UP 170 Hellenistic Civilization, *Sir William Tarn and G. T. Griffith*

UP 27 Life and Thought in the Greek and Roman World, *M. Cary and T. J. Haarhoff*

UP 9 Plato: The Man and His Work (See under Biography)

HISTORY

UP 35 Byzantine Civilization, *Steven Runciman*

UP 22 The Common People, *G. D. H. Cole and Raymond Postgate*

UP 30 The Congress of Vienna, *Harold Nicolson*

UP 37 The Course of German History, *A. J. P. Taylor*

UP 40 Cromwell's Army, *C. Firth*

UP 88 The Decline of Imperial Russia, *Hugh Seton-Watson*

UP 158 A Diplomatic History of Europe, *René Albrecht-Carrié*

UP 21 An Economic History of the British Isles (See under Economics)

UP 52 An Economic History of Europe (See under Economics)

UP 154 England under the Stuarts, *G. M. Trevelyan*

UP 31 English Wayfaring Life in the Middle Ages, *J. J. Jusserand*

UP 130 Elizabeth the Great (See under Biography)

UP 29 Elizabethan Life in Town and Country, *M. St Clare Byrne*

UP 51 The Fifth French Republic, *Dorothy Pickles*

UP 56 From the Gracchi to Nero (See under Greece and Rome)

UP 83 From Vienna to Versailles, *L. C. B. Seaman*

UP 39 A History of England, *E. L. Woodward*

UP 73 A History of France, *André Maurois*

UP 23 A History of Ireland, *Edmund Curtis*

UP   4 A History of Political Thought in the 16th Century, *J. W. Allen*

UP 46 A History of Russia, *Bernard Pares*

UP 90 Horace Walpole (See under Biography)

UP 74 The Industrial Revolution in the Eighteenth Century, *Paul Mantoux*

UP 116 The Influence of Sea Power upon History, *A. T. Mahan*

UP 27 Life and Thought in the Greek and Roman World (See under Greece and Rome)

UP 162 The Making of Victorian England, *G. Kitson Clark*

UP 77 The Medieval Centuries, *Denys Hay*

UP 149 The Medieval Foundations of England, *G. O. Sayles*

UP 63 Medieval People, *Eileen Power*

UP 122 Peacemaking 1919, *Sir Harold Nicolson*

UP 61 A Short History of the Middle East, *George E. Kirk*

UP 17 A Survey of Russian History, *B. H. Sumner*

UP 13 William the Silent (See under Biography)

UP 167 The World we have lost, *Peter Laslett*

LAW

UP 79 The Law of International Institutions, *D. W. Bowett*
*UP 144 Trial by Jury, *Patrick Devlin*

LITERATURE

UP   68 Art and Artifice in Shakespeare, *E. E. Stoll*
UP 157 The Art of Rudyard Kipling, *J. M. S. Tompkins*
UP 112 The Augustan World, *A. R. Humphreys*
*UP 180 The Bloomsday Book, *Harry Blamires*
*UP 182 A Century of George Eliot Criticism, *Gordon S. Haight*
UP   47 Chaucer and His England, *G. G. Coulton*
UP 137 The Contexts of Poetry, *Hazard Adams*
UP 127 The Crown of Life, *G. Wilson Knight*
UP 171 The Development of Shakespeare's Imagery,
         Wolfgang H. Clemens
UP 105 Edmund Spenser, *W. L. Renwick*
UP 136 T. S. Eliot, the Invisible Poet, *Hugh Kennet*
*UP 176 The Elizabethan Love Sonnet, *J. W. Lever*
UP   67 The English Bible, *F. F. Bruce*
UP 175 English Literary Criticism in the 17th and 18th
         Centuries, *J. W. H. Atkins*
UP   54 English Literature and Society in the 18th Century,
         Leslie Stephen
UP 166 The English Moralists, *Basil Willey*
UP 138 English Poetry, *Douglas Bush*
UP 110 Etymology, *A. S. C. Ross*
UP 159 The Fire and the Fountain, *John Press*
UP   2 Form and Meaning in Drama, *H. D. F. Kitto*
UP   92 The Frontiers of Drama, *Una Ellis-Fermor*
UP 111 The German Novel, *Roy Pascal*
UP 125 The Golden Labyrinth, *G. Wilson Knight*
UP   28 The Growth of the English Novel, *Richard Church*
UP   96 A Guide to the Plays of Bernard Shaw, *C. B. Purdom*
*UP 177 The Harvest of Tragedy, *T. R. Henn*
UP 153 The Imagination of Charles Dickens, *A. O. J. Cockshut*
UP 124 The Imperial Theme, *G. Wilson Knight*
UP   5 Introduction to the French Poets, *Geoffrey Brereton*
UP 143 Jacobean Drama, *Una Ellis-Fermor*
UP   60 Keats' Craftmanship, *M. R. Ridley*

UP   7 Landmarks in Russian Literature, *Maurice Baring*

UP 113 The Language of Shakespeare's Plays, *Ifor Evans*

UP 18 The Last Romantics, *Graham Hough*

UP 172 The Lion and the Fox, *Wyndham Lewis*

UP 126 The Lonely Tower, *T. R. Henn*

UP 103 Modern German Drama, *H. F. Garten*

UP 64 Outlines of Tudor and Stuart Plays, *K. J. Holzknecht*

UP 163 The Poems of Alexander Pope, *edited by John Butt*

UP 89 The Poetry of France: 1400–1600, *Alan Boase*

UP 11 The Sacred Wood, *T. S. Eliot*

UP 142 The Secret Places, *David Holbrook*

UP 156 Shakespearian Comedy, *H. B. Charlton*

UP 93 Shakespeare's Histories, *Lily B. Campbell*

UP 43 Shakespeare's Tragic Heroes, *Lily B. Campbell*

UP 141 The Struggle of the Modern, *Stephen Spender*

UP 76 Thackeray the Novelist (See under Biography)

*UP 184 The Theatre of Bertolt Brecht, *John Willett*

UP 95 Twentieth-Century English Literature: 1901–1960, *A. C. Ward*

*UP 186 Volpone, *Ben Jonson*

*UP 151 The Well-Wrought Urn, *C. Brooks*

UP 12 The Wheel of Fire, *G. Wilson Knight*

UP 36 The Wound and the Bow, *Edmund Wilson*

MATHEMATICS

UP 71 The Fascination of Numbers, *W. J. Reichmann*

UP 50 The Great Mathematicians, *H. W. Turnbull*

UP 26 The Mathematics of Engineering Systems, *Derek F. Lawden*

MUSIC

UP 85 A Hundred Years of Music, *G. Abraham*

UP 42 The Instruments of Music, *R. Donington*

UP 100 Mozart: The Man and His Works (See under Biography)

UP 45 The Physics of Music, *A. Wood*

ORGANIZATION AND ADMINISTRATION

UP 120 A Guide to Operational Research, *Eric Duckworth*

UP 133 Human Relations in Industry, *R. F. Tredgold*

PHILOSOPHY

UP   32 Comparative Religion, *E. O. James*
UP 155 Elements of Formal Logic, *G. E. Hughes and D. G. Landey*
UP   25 Elements of Metaphysics, *A. E. Taylor*
UP   49 The Greek View of Life (See under Greece and Rome)
UP   81 Individuals, *P. F. Strawson*
UP 161 An Introduction to Ancient Philosophy, *A. H. Armstrong*
UP   24 An Introduction to Ethics, *William Lillie*
UP   72 Introduction to Logical Theory, *P. F. Strawson*
UP   16 Modern Elementary Logic, *L. Susan Stebbing*
UP 128 Moral Theory, *G. C. Field*
UP   9 Plato: The Man and His Work (See under Biography)
UP 107 The Spirit of Islam, *Ameer Ali*
UP   41 The Theory of Beauty, *E. F. Carritt*

POLITICS

UP 129 The American System of Government, *Ernest S. Griffith*
UP 148 An Atlas of African Affairs, *A. Boyd and P. Van Rensburg*
*UP 179 An Atlas of Middle Eastern Affairs, *R. Kingsbury and N. J. G. Pounds*
UP   91 An Atlas of World Affairs, *Andrew Boyd*
UP 139 Britain's Moment in the Middle East, *Elizabeth Monroe*
UP   55 The Communist Party of the Soviet Union, *Leonard Schapiro*
UP   51 The Fifth French Republic (See under History)
UP 121 The Government of Germany, *Arnold J. Heidenheimer*
UP 108 The Government of Great Britain, *Graeme C. Moodie*
UP 168 The Government of Japan, *Ardath W. Burks*
UP   3 Greek Political Theory (See under Greece and Rome)
UP   4 A History of Political Thought in the 16th Century (See under History)
UP   53 Ideas in Conflict, *E. M. Burns*
*UP 173 The Idea of Politics, *Maurice Duverger*
UP 119 Introduction to Politics, *Dorothy Pickles*
UP   82 Political Parties, *M. Duverger*
UP   62 Political Theory, *G. C. Field*
*UP 181 The Study of Africa, edited by *P. J. M. McEwen and R. B. Sutcliffe*
UP   19 Western Political Thought, *John Bowle*

PSYCHOLOGY

UP 99 Behaviour, *D. W. Broadbent*

UP 135 Freud: The Mind of the Moralist, *Philip Rieff*

UP 86 A Hundred Years of Psychology, *J. C. Flugel* revised by *D. J. West*

*UP 172 An Introduction to Educational Psychology, *E. Stones*

UP 6 Introduction to Social Psychology, *W. McDougall*

UP 97 Learning, *Winifred Hill*

UP 59 Psychology, *R. S. Woodworth and D. G. Marquis*

UP 84 Psychology and Morals, *J. A. Hadfield*

UP 78 The Psychology of Society, *Morris Ginsberg*

UP 109 Small Social Groups in England, *Margaret Phillips*

UP 87 Teaching: A Psychological Analysis (See under Education)

UP 41 The Theory of Beauty, *E. F. Carritt*

SCIENCE

UP 146 The Biology of Art, *D. Morris*

UP 34 A Direct Entry to Organic Chemistry, *John Read*

UP 115 A Hundred Years of Chemistry, *Alexander Findlay*

UP 132 The Ideas of Biology, *John Tyle Bonner*

UP 20 Introduction to Astronomy, *C. Payne-Gaposchkin*

UP 80 An Introduction to Cybernetics, *W. Ross Ashby*

UP 38 King Solomon's Ring, *Konrad Lorenz*

UP 26 The Mathematics of Engineering Systems (See under Mathematics)

UP 123 Patterns of Sexual Behaviour, *Clellan S. Ford and Frank A. Beach*

UP 45 The Physics of Music (See under Music)

UP 10 Relativity, *Albert Einstein*

UP 98 The Release and Use of Atomic Energy, *T. E. Allibone*

*UP 152 Stars in the Making, *C. Payne-Gaposchkin*

UP 114 Statistical Analysis in Biology, *K. Mather*